Continuing Professional Development for Clinical Psychologists

This is dedicated to Pam Gray and Adrian Turner for patiently tolerating this book's intrusion into their lives, for their support and understanding.

Continuing Professional Development

for Clinical Psychologists

A PRACTICAL HANDBOOK

Edited by
LAURA GOLDING AND IAN GRAY

The British Psychological Society

BPS Blackwell

© 2006 by The British Psychological Society and Blackwell Publishing Ltd
except for editorial material and organization © 2006 by Laura Golding and
Ian Gray

BLACKWELL PUBLISHING
350 Main Street, Malden, MA 02148-5020, USA
9600 Garsington Road, Oxford OX4 2DQ, UK
550 Swanston Street, Carlton, Victoria 3053, Australia

First published 2006 by The British Psychological Society and Blackwell
Publishing Ltd

1   2006

Library of Congress Cataloging-in-Publication Data

Continuing professional development for clinical psychologists : a practical
handbook/edited by Laura Golding and Ian Gray.
    p.   cm.
    Includes bibliographical references and index.
    ISBN-13: 978-1-4051-2397-6 (pbk. : alk. paper)
    ISBN-10: 1-4051-2397-4 (pbk. : alk. paper)   1. Clinical psychology—Study
and teaching (Continuing education)   2. Clinical psychologists—In-service
training.   I. Golding, Laura.   II. Gray, Ian.   III. Title.
    RC467.7.C66 2006
    616.89'0071—dc22

2005029046

A catalogue record for this title is available from the British Library.

Set in 10/12.5 Palatino
by SNP Best-set Typesetter Ltd, Hong Kong
Printed and bound in India
by Replika Press

The publisher's policy is to use permanent paper from mills that operate a
sustainable forestry policy, and which has been manufactured from pulp
processed using acid-free and elementary chlorine-free practices.
Furthermore, the publisher ensures that the text paper and cover board used
have met acceptable environmental accreditation standards.

For further information on
BPS Blackwell, visit our website:
www.bpsblackwell.co.uk

Contents

Foreword

The importance of continuous professional development (CPD) cannot be understated. There are clear moral obligations, and emerging regulatory requirements, that make CPD an integral and everyday part of daily activity for professionals in health and social care. Easy words, difficult to do! Help is here, however, and can be found in this thoughtful and very interesting book. The book is a first in many ways. It takes and describes what should be commonplace activity but surrounds it with essential and helpful information, some research-based evidence and very helpful advice.

In reflecting on 'a career for life' it struck me that there are important milestones and 'aha' moments as one makes progress as a professional. The first probably appears following qualification as a professional. For a brief moment you are filled with confidence and a mission to succeed. This is very quickly followed by anxiety and doubt when faced with clinical encounters never previously experienced. Confidence and knowledge is challenged and uncertainty sets in. This is when CPD can make its first impact and no better than through well-constructed clinical supervision and a programme for new staff, subjects well dealt with in this book.

The second comes when trying to make sense of complex clinical situations. The temptation is to take the best evidenced-based assessment and intervention, surround it by well-constructed case notes and make sure that everyone in the team is properly informed and engaged. This is all good practice and to be applauded, but there are other skills that should be sharpened and honed to equal measure and they belong to more subtle processes. Hills (2004) takes some of the foundations of modern education and offers a succinct view of the relationship between implicit knowledge – that which grows from personal experience and explicit knowledge – that which grows from the acquisition of knowledge. He argues that 'the value of explicit knowledge lies not in its ownership but in its application. If explicit knowledge is the basis of the human intellect, then the implicit kind is surely the basis of human intelligence.' In other words, it is important to consciously use your implicit knowledge, do not let it be overwhelmed by explicit knowledge or clever science.

It is arguable that when clinicians are at their best it is because they have responded to the implicit understanding of what good interventions can offer in the practice setting and can locate this within explicit knowledge. They will have gained implicit understanding from various life experiences and their properly supervised clinical practice. Through this, good clinicians gain capability. Explicit knowledge asks for different but nonetheless essential detail. However, where implicit understanding becomes drowned out by explicit knowledge, poor practice will surely follow. The best CPD is sensitive to this and it is dealt with sensibly here. Authors in this book offer well-balanced solutions to this complex conundrum.

Finally, those with well-found experience have a duty to continue to be immersed in CPD (showing by example)! I have always taken the view that you are never too old to learn. I have an example from my own experience. Despite a number of years of clinical experience, my assessment and questioning techniques, as well as my capacity to listen, had not been assessed 'in vivo' by other expert practitioners for some time. I took the opportunity to observe and then participate in some systemic family work in a local mental health service. Their model was theoretically rigorous and demanded that clinical work was properly supervised and recorded on video and audiotape. When asking questions of people or families a small earpiece allowed observers in a separate room to encourage me to re-phrase or ask questions differently. While somewhat disconcerting, this was a tremendous opportunity to hear others comment on my performance and say (live and in my ear!) such things as 'they cannot understand that question' or 'it's clear that you were not listening to that answer.' It was disconcerting to be exposed to this but very informative. I am convinced that it helped me to listen better and frame questions more purposefully than I had done for some time.

It is plain from this that I believe that any clinical psychologist's skills can be constantly improved and developed no matter how long in the tooth! I have little doubt that this book will be immensely helpful in the debate on CPD. I welcome its thoughtful approach and have little doubt that it will offer considerable support to those in practice and those who will craft continuous professional development programmes.

Tony Butterworth
March 2005

REFERENCE

Hills, G. (2004). In from the cold – the rise of vocational education. *RSA Journal*, November.

Notes on Contributors

Tony Butterworth has had an extensive career in the NHS and Higher Education sector. He was most recently Dean of School and then Pro Vice Chancellor at the University of Manchester and then moved to be the Chief Executive of the Trent NHS Workforce Development Confederation. He chairs several national committees relating to research and to workforce development, and has just become Director of the Centre for Clinical and Academic Workforce Innovation at the University of Lincoln.

Amanda Caine is Clinical Psychology Services Manager for Rochdale Borough, Pennine Care NHS Trust. Her previous clinical specialty was in learning disabilities and she now works in adult primary care. She is co-editor of *Clinical Psychology and People with Intellectual Disabilities* (1998 – eds Eric Emerson, Chris Hatton, Jo Bromley and Amanda Caine). She is a member of the North West (England) Clinical Psychology CPD Scheme's Strategy Group.

Carol Collins is the Administrative Coordinator for the North West (England) Clinical Psychology CPD Scheme and previously for the North West (England) Clinical Psychology CPD Project.

Anna Daiches is currently Senior Clinical Tutor/Research Tutor for the Lancaster University Doctorate in Clinical Psychology. Her clinical work is within the child and family specialty. Her current research and clinical interests lie within the community psychology field. Her publications include a special issue of the British Psychological Society's publication *Clinical Psychology* on *Racism, Diversity and Responsibility* (2005 – eds Anna Daiches and Laura Golding).

David Green is Clinical Director of the Doctorate in Clinical Psychology programme at the University of Leeds. He has been the convenor of the Yorkshire Psychologists' Post-Qualification Training consortium for 17 years and is also a past Chair of the CPD subcommittee of the Division of Clinical Psychology. His doctoral research topic was clinical supervision and he has published articles on various aspects of professional training. His clinical work is currently in the field of paediatric oncology.

Claire Grout is Project Manager for Modernising Medical Careers at the North Western Postgraduate Medical Deanery. She trained and worked as a pharmacist in hospital and academic environments before moving into medical workforce issues. She has presented and published a number of papers on pharmacy practice, multiprofessional recruitment and retention, and education, particularly CPD.

Polly Kaiser is a Consultant Clinical Psychologist for Older People's Services in Oldham, Pennine Care NHS Trust. She was a CPD Tutor for the North West (England) Clinical Psychology CPD Scheme. Polly has worked with older people since 1984. Her research and clinical interest has focused mainly on carers, families and systemic work.

Gundi Kiemle is a Tutor on the North West (England) Clinical Psychology CPD Scheme, Consultant Clinical Psychologist in Sexual Health (Royal Bolton Hospital), and Honorary Senior Lecturer at the University of Central Lancashire. For the past 20 years she has worked and variously published in the areas of adult mental health, psychotherapy, drug misuse, HIV/AIDS, physical health and sexual dysfunction.

Ian James is a Consultant Clinical Psychologist in Older Adult Services, Newcastle, North Tyneside and Northumberland Mental Health NHS Trust and part-time Research Tutor, University of Newcastle. He heads the challenging behaviour service, and is a supervisor on the Newcastle Cognitive Behaviour Therapy course. He has published in a number of areas including older adult, dementia, cognitive behaviour therapy, and supervision and training.

Angela Latham is a Clinical Psychologist working in the child specialty at Booth Hall Children's Hospital, Manchester. She has a specialist interest in early intervention and community working. Angela was vice-chair and speaker co-ordinator of the CONTACT scheme from

2002 to 2003 and is a member of the North West (England) Clinical Psychology CPD Scheme's Strategy Group. Her research interests lie in the field of cognitive behaviour therapy with a particular interest in family working and parental mental health.

Annie Mercer is Head of Clinical Psychology and Clinical Director of Children and Adolescent Mental Health Services (CAMHS), Royal Liverpool Children's NHS Trust. She manages a wide range of services from those drawing on community psychology models through to intensive multi-systemic interventions. Her clinical work is in paediatric oncology. Her publications include the Clinical Psychologist's contribution to children's pain, and the development psychological services in paediatrics.

Derek Milne is Director of the Newcastle University Doctorate in Clinical Psychology, where his input includes teaching and supervising the 'evaluation' aspect of the course and preparing the trainees for CPD. He has had a career-long interest in staff development and its evaluation and has published books on *Training Behaviour Therapists* (1986: based on his PhD) and on *Evaluating Mental Health Practice* (1987). Subsequently there has been a steady stream of related books and scientific and professional papers, some 100 in total. His current specialism is staff development.

Zenobia Nadirshaw is Head of Psychology with Kensington and Chelsea NHS PCT and Professor with the Thames Valley University Faculty of Health and Human Science. She is a clinical psychologist with 30 years' NHS experience and is committed to equal opportunities issues, double discrimination relating to 'race' and culture issues in clinical psychology training, mental health and learning disabilities services. She has lectured and published widely at local, national and international levels. She was the BPS Award Winner (1996–7) for challenging inequality of opportunity and is the current Chair of the British Psychological Society's Division of Clinical Psychology's CPD sub-committee.

Alia Sheikh is Academic Tutor for the Doctorate in Clinical Psychology at the University of Newcastle and practices as a Counselling Psychologist within a local NHS Trust. Her research interests include trauma, stress and coping. Her tutor work includes developing frameworks relating to personal professional development and she has an ongoing interest in evaluation and assessment.

Richard Toogood is District Psychologist for Dudley South PCT. Richard is the BPS's Professional Practice Board's representative on the Society's Standing Committee on CPD. He is also the Division of Clinical Psychology's lead on the Amicus/Family of Psychology Working Group on the NHS Knowledge and Skills Framework (KSF). He is the principal author of the Amicus/BPS Family of Psychology joint KSF guidance which the BPS published in June 2005.

Karla Toye completed her clinical training at the University of Manchester in 2001 and has worked since then as a clinical psychologist at the Manchester and Salford Pain Centre, Hope Hospital NHS Trust. She is a past Chair (2002–3) of CONTACT, the North West post-qualification training scheme, and is currently a member of the North West (England) Clinical Psychology CPD Scheme's Strategy Group. Her clinical and research interests are in the application of cognitive behavioural models to the management of chronic pain.

Chrissie Verduyn is Director of Clinical Psychology/Joint Clinical Director for the CAMHS Directorate, Central Manchester and Manchester Children's University Hospital NHS Trust. Her clinical speciality is with children and young people. Her publications include work on service development, cognitive behaviour therapy for depression and other service-related issues. She has had a longstanding involvement in pre- and post-qualification training in clinical psychology.

Acknowledgements

Many people have assisted us with the content and production of this book. Our thanks go to all of our contributors for the quality of their work and for allowing us to pester them regularly during the production of the manuscript. Much of the content of the book has come about as a direct result of the North West Clinical Psychology CPD Scheme and its predecessor, the North West Clinical Psychology CPD Project. The scheme, and the project, would not have been possible without funding from the former Greater Manchester NHS Workforce Development Confederation (GMWDC, now part of the Greater Manchester Strategic Health Authority, GMSHA) and without the support, advice and encouragement of Su Fowler-Johnson, Kirstie Baxter and a number of other GMWDC/SHA employees.

For enabling us to produce this book, we must also thank Sarah Bird and Will Maddox, and others at BPS Blackwell for sharing their expertise, advice and encouragement, our anonymous reviewers for their constructive suggestions and positive comments, and Carol Collins, Administrative Coordinator for the North West (England) Clinical Psychology CPD Scheme, for her administrative support and much more.

Laura Golding and Ian Gray

Chapter 1

What a Difference a Day Makes

Laura Golding and Ian Gray

The majority of applied psychologists, indeed NHS professionals in general, know that their continuing professional development is important. They take it seriously. But for some, when they hear the phrase 'continuing professional development' this is met by a yawn and then a groan. They think 'log books'. They tot up the number of hours they have spent on activities that could 'count' as CPD and then they worry about whether these are the right 'type' of activities. They worry about where they will find the time, and the resources, to pursue CPD activities.

Having completed a first degree in psychology, and then a three-year doctorate in clinical psychology, most clinical psychologists feel as if they have learned enough on qualifying and want to be allowed to get into practice. However, many do want to attend conferences, read about new developments in their area of specialty and keep up to date. But, how many of us construe these activities as being the means to maintaining and improving our professional competence – about CPD? For many members of the profession, until very recently, CPD was just that. It was the pursuit of such activities, driven largely by a self-motivation to keep up to date and pursue areas of personal and professional interest. We cherry-picked courses and conferences according to individual preference inspired, perhaps, by a spate of referrals of a particular type or by the latest trend for a particular therapy or intervention. This was not about looking coherently at our service needs balanced against our own development needs as professionals. This was not about engaging in CPD activity as part of a coherent whole, as part of a multiprofessional NHS-wide commitment to maintaining and improving competence. It was a largely piecemeal, haphazard and uneconomical process.

Now though, the context has changed. Over the past few years, the need for all NHS professionals to undertake CPD activities regularly, based on needs identified through a systematic appraisal process, has become mandatory (Department of Health, 1998, 1999b). For applied psychologists, this was reinforced by the British Psychological Society's members' vote to make CPD activity mandatory for all chartered psychologists holding practising certificates in 2000 (BPS, 2003). This will become a legal requirement when the statutory regulation of all applied psychologists comes into place. With the Society's rejection (BPS, June 2005a), of the current proposals for statutory regulation by the HPC, the when and the how of statutory regulation remains uncertain. The context has changed from one of voluntary cherry picking to mandatory, systematic selection of CPD activity. The day after we qualify as clinical psychologists, just when we thought we had done with formal learning, our life long learning begins – what a difference a day makes . . .

What is CPD?

Within the NHS, the terms 'continuing professional development' and 'life long learning' often seem to be used interchangeably. The Department of Health's consultation paper, 'Clinical Governance in the New NHS' clarifies this by defining CPD as 'a process of lifelong learning for all individuals and teams which meets the needs of patients and delivers the health outcomes and healthcare priorities of the NHS and which enables professionals to expand and fulfil their potential' (DoH, 1999a). For the purposes of this book, the term continuing professional development is used to describe the activities we undertake that maintain and improve our professional competence (Miller, 1990).

This notion is developed further by the Professional Associations Research Network which highlights the wide applicability of this notion of CPD to any professional group: CPD is 'any process or activity that provides added value to the capability of the professional through the increase in knowledge, skills and personal qualities necessary for the appropriate execution of professional and technical duties, often termed competence' (Professional Associations Research Network, www.parn.org.uk).

The Health Professions Council's literature on CPD makes the link between this process of CPD and registration: 'CPD is learning that develops your knowledge and skills beyond the minimum' required to achieve registration (HPC, 2003). The HPC is 'developing a system to link re-registration to continuous professional development' (HPC, 2003). The HPC estimates that a system linking CPD to re-registration is likely to be in place in 2006.

CPD for All

Within the NHS, we are familiar with the notion of individuals completing their pre-qualification training fit for award, fit for practice and fit for purpose (QAA, 2003). The trick then, throughout our careers, is to ensure that we remain fit for purpose as our clinical training becomes a distant memory and the context in which most of us work, the public sector, constantly changes. This is achieved through our CPD activity. Regularly undertaking CPD activity of an appropriate type and quality should keep us safe to practice and fit for purpose throughout our careers.

Whether you have just qualified or have been qualified for 30 years and are the manager of a large psychology service, CPD is for you. CPD is, in fact, a great leveller. No matter where you are in the hierarchy, it is just as important – no one is immune from having to maintain and improve their competence. So, although the type of CPD activities that a newly qualified clinical psychologist may undertake will differ greatly to those undertaken by an experienced psychology manager and clinician, the importance to both is the same. We all need to ensure that we are fit for purpose, safe to practice and up to date throughout our careers. This book aims to set out the context for this need and provide readers with the research and relevant literature in the area as well as practical information about how to go about meeting our CPD needs throughout our careers.

Continuing Professional Development for Clinical Psychologists: A Practical Handbook

The changing context and hugely increased emphasis and importance placed on CPD within the NHS in recent years have meant that we have much to do in this area. We need to know about the best ways to go about meeting our individual CPD needs, and the needs of our services. We also need to know if what we are doing is effective. We need to link in with our colleagues in other professions and do some of our CPD activities with them. It seemed to us, that there is much to say on this subject and that this is about the right time to say it.

So, this book is a collection of edited chapters written by clinical psychologists, and others, who have expertise in professional issues and continuing professional development. It is aimed, primarily, at clinical psychologists working in the UK but is relevant reading for all applied psychologists working in healthcare as well as other health professionals, especially those who work in mental health. Here we aim to provide readers with an accessible, practical self-help guide to all you need to know about your own continuing professional development and that of the services and organizations you work in. The book has a clear practical focus throughout and aims to be a practical 'how to do it' handbook at a time when statutory regulation and other healthcare developments mean that undertaking CPD activity has renewed importance.

Chapter 2 asks 'CPD, Why Bother?'. It takes us through a thorough look at what CPD is, its context in wider society and why it is important. It sets the context for why we do, indeed, need to bother about meeting our CPD needs in the most effective and systematic way possible. This is then followed, in Chapter 3, by a comprehensive overview of the policy context to the need for CPD in the NHS and the profession. This includes an overview of the relevant NHS legislation, the implications of statutory regulation, the role of the Health Professions Council and the impact of *Agenda for Change* and the NHS Knowledge and Skills Framework.

Chapter 4 explores the many practical issues involved in meeting CPD needs. This includes everything you need to know about undertaking CPD activities in local services including suggestions of funding sources for CPD activity, ways of doing CPD for free, finding out what CPD activities or materials are available through a comprehensive checklist to use when organizing conferences and courses. The next three chapters explore the CPD needs of members of the profession at different stages of their careers – newly qualified, transition to management and service manager level. These chapters discuss the literature and issues relevant to each career stage and describe examples of good practice within the UK where CPD initiatives are meeting identified needs.

Chapter 8 looks at evaluating CPD activity. In recent years, so much emphasis has been placed, within the NHS, on the need to undertake CPD activity but much less on the effectiveness of these activities and the overall process. Chapter 8 addresses the rarely discussed issue of outcome, drawing on examples from the research on supervision. This is followed by Chapter 9 which looks at the work of the British Psychological Society in relation to CPD for applied psychologists. The

Society has been engaged in a great deal of activity in this area for several years as the moves towards statutory regulation become mandatory for all. This chapter looks at the Society's work and the additional role of the Division of Clinical Psychology and the Division's guidance to members regarding CPD. Chapter 10 addresses the multiprofessional context in relation to CPD. As a profession, we are often seen as being parochial when it comes to education and training within the NHS. In fact, the evidence suggests that we are engaged daily in work with members of a range of other health professions, including in our CPD activity (e.g., Golding, 2003). It is essential that our thinking and work around CPD is set within a wider multiprofessional context and that we join our colleagues from other professions, as appropriate, in meeting some of our CPD needs jointly. This chapter looks at the work of some of the other major professional groups in this area and discusses the implications for us as a profession. Chapter 11 discusses in some detail the Knowledge and Skills Framework (KSF) and the joint work of the Society and Amicus (BPS June 2005b) to facilitate its implementation within the family of applied psychology. It links the KSF to the wider NHS CPD context and discusses the far-reaching implications of this new framework. The book ends with a chapter looking at the way forward in CPD for clinical psychologists and a guess at what is ahead in terms of the policy context. We provide lists of useful addresses and websites to enable readers to pursue the ideas and issues raised in this book further.

REFERENCES

British Psychological Society (2003). Statutory regulation: Your questions answered. *The Psychologist*, 16(5), 264–5.

British Psychological Society (2005a, June). *Response of the British Psychological Society to 'Applied Psychology: Enhancing Public Protection: Proposals for the Statutory Regulation of Applied Psychologists'*. BPS, Leicester.

British Psychological Society (2005b, June). *Lifelong learning and the Knowledge and Skills Framework for Applied Psychology*. BPS Leicester.

Department of Health (1998). *A First Class Service: Quality in the New NHS*. HSC 1998/113. Department of Health, London.

Department of Health (1999a). *Clinical Governance in the New NHS*. HSC 1999/065. Department of Health, London.

Department of Health (1999b). *Continuing Professional Development: Quality in the New NHS*. HSC 1999/154. Department of Health, London.

Golding, L. (2003). The continuing professional development needs of clinical psychologists in the North West of England. *Clinical Psychology*, 26, 23–7.

Health Professions Council (2003). *Continuing Professional Development*. HPC, London.

Miller, R. (1990). The role of the DCP in continuing professional development. *Clinical Psychology Forum*, 28, 36–7.

Quality Assurance Agency for Higher Education (2003). *Handbook for Major Review of Healthcare Programmes*. QAA.

Chapter 2

CPD: Why Bother?

David Green

Introduction

Continued professional development. The very phrase has a reassuring ring to it. It sounds like just the sort of activity that ought to be being undertaken in our universities and hospitals, where committed and competent healthcare professionals demonstrate their enduring commitment to become even more competent at their jobs. If ever there was an uncomplicated 'good thing' that deserves widespread public support, helping qualified doctors, nurses, clinical psychologists and their ilk keep up to date in current good practice is surely it! So why would the introductory chapter of a fine volume such as this start by sounding a loud and deliberately cautionary note? Because there is a lot more to the case for, and against CPD, than immediately meets the eye.

Definition

If investment in the continued development of clinical psychologists is to be justified certain essential components of the educational process must work and be seen to work. First the individual psychologist must find a way to recognize specific skills deficits that need to be remedied or identify developmental opportunities to expand their professional competence. Then she needs to seek out an appropriate training experience that will result in demonstrable changes in her capacity to perform her duties. Now she has to generate enough energy and enthusiasm to complete her chosen course of study. However staying the educational course is not an end in itself. The *raison d'être* of CPD is improving the quality of patient care by incorporating lessons learned on Fancy Dan residential training events in the everyday good practice of health professionals. Finally, of course, there are economic realities to be considered. The cost/benefit sums must add up. We would be unwise to assume that achieving any of these elements is a straightforward business.

Self-Appraisal

Clinical psychologists undergo an extensive, and expensive, basic training during which they receive a constant flow of feedback designed to shape up their evolving skills. Surely we are entitled to assume that once qualified these characters will be equipped with the self-knowledge and theoretical awareness to allow them to critically appraise their own professional performance? They are psychologists after all. There is not much in the way of empirical evidence expressly concerned with the self-assessment skills of clinical psychologists, but research conducted with members of other health disciplines strongly suggests that we should take professionals' claims to know their own training needs with a substantial pinch of salt.

When medical students enter training we would perhaps anticipate that, lacking prior experience on which to anchor their judgements, the novice doctors might make judgements of their competence that vary somewhat from the appraisals made by their course tutors. (Gordon, 1991). However we would expect the degree of this divergence to diminish over the course of medical training. In fact the opposite seems to be the case (Wooliscroft et al., 1993). On average self-appraisals of students' performance moved away from, not closer to, the opinions of their educational mentors. This was not a result of staff and students using different criteria for judging professional competence. When medical students appraised their classmates, their views tended to converge with those of the tutors over time. The mismatch only came when students held a mirror up to themselves. Furthermore other studies suggest that neither the introduction of self-directed learning into the medical curriculum (Tousignant and DesMarchais, 2002) nor the accumulation of post-qualification experience (Tracey et al., 1997) do much to improve doctors' capacity to appraise their own competence.

This makes psychological sense. Actors and observers have importantly different perspectives on the way they interpret their world (Jones and Nisbet, 1972). We are all prone to the 'above average' effect and tend to view our own achievements through somewhat rose-coloured glasses (Alicke et al., 1995). Under most circumstances this is a highly adaptive stance to adopt and looking on the bright side can bestow significant health benefits (Snyder, 2000; Taylor et al., 2000). However the self-same systematic positive bias that protects patients can turn into a dangerous liability when employed by those charged with their care.

Marteau and colleagues (1989) reported an intriguing study investigating nurses' assessment of their ability to resuscitate patients after cardiac arrest. The researchers asked nurses of varying levels of seniority and experience to gauge their own competence and provide a measure of their confidence in their own ability. Actual performance in life-support skills was then assessed against operationalized procedural standards. The nurses used a manikin to demonstrate how they would respond to a real patient who had lost consciousness following a heart attack. The results of this study are not reassuring. All nurses overestimated their competence. None got the procedure entirely right. Furthermore the mismatch between confidence and competence was most marked in the more experienced staff group. How could this happen? Apparently most nurses in this setting would only infrequently be called upon to administer life-support. As sadly these emergency interventions may not have resulted in the patient's survival even when conducted properly, there was limited opportunity for collecting feedback on ineffective performance. We shall return to the pivotal role of feedback shortly.

Added to this suggestion that the more we progress in our careers the less capable we are of making a clear-eyed assessment of our abilities, is the repeated finding that it is the least capable members of any training cohort that are likely to have the most positively distorted view of their own capabilities (Kruger and Dunning, 1999) This has been described as a dual-handicap in that the learner is not only performing relatively poorly but does not appreciate that his work is substandard. As a consequence he lacks any motivation to improve. This persistent pattern has proved highly resistant to change probably because it is highly adaptive in terms of enhancing self-esteem under conditions of threat.

Another psychological trick we tend to employ to maintain our professional self-esteem involves favourably comparing our current capability with the way we formerly practised. So an experienced child clinical psychologist might shake her head in disbelief at how insensitive to picking up clues of potential sexual abuse she was earlier in her career. Nowadays of course she is on top of her game. This apparently reassuring developmental trajectory ('from chump to champ' as described by Wilson and Ross, 2000) may boost practitioner morale but relying on the wisdom of hindsight has its costs. Do we have to wait until tomorrow to recognize what we could be doing better today?

The trouble is that it seems to take a lot for us to shift our established views of our own abilities (Ehrlinger and Dunning, 2003). We have our cherished theories of what we are (and are not) good at, and make generalized assumptions about how well we perform that seem to rely surprisingly little on the actual results of our efforts. These 'chronic' self-views may lead to unwise CPD decisions. The complacent will fail to take remedial action to correct their professional failings. The pessimistic may never take up the training opportunities that could help them achieve their full occupational potential. Women's attitudes to a career in science are arguably a case in point (DeBacker and Nelson, 2000).

So the headline message from this brief and selective literature review is clear enough. Self-appraisal of our professional competence is neither easy nor straightforward. Those who most need to improve their skills are probably those who are least equipped to recognize their training needs. Furthermore the Great and Good of our trade are likely to be at least as prone to self-delusion as the rest of us!

Has clinical psychology therefore fallen at the first fence in the CPD steeplechase? Not necessarily. First let us not overstate our fallibility. The correlations between self-appraisals and objective measures of performance across a range of domains are consistently positive albeit weakly (Mabe and West, 1982). Second it behoves psychologists of all professions to pay heed to research findings suggesting ways to develop self-assessment skills (Gordon, 1992). We need to take the time and care needed to examine systematically the evidence that should inform our judgements (Parboosingh, 1998). Crucially this means being prepared to seek out the opinions of all those who can offer a legitimate and credible commentary on our working lives. It is not only (or indeed necessarily) a psychologist's supervisor or line manager who is in a position to pass judgement on her professional competence. Several other important voices need to be heard – the defining principle of 360 degree feedback (Goodge and Burr, 1999). If it makes sense for trainee doctors undertaking placements in obstetrics to be evaluated by their patients and colleagues not only in medicine but also nursing and allied health professions (Joshi et al., 2004), it is not hard to envisage a comparable process that could be initiated by a clinical psychologist working in say a community mental health team. If, or as research findings would suggest, when these opinions differ significantly from the practitioner's own appraisal of his or her performance, the reasons for the mismatch need to be investigated and understood. It is the respectful resolution of these disparities that will most probably lead to the soundest CPD planning.

Motivation

It was formerly considered characteristic of a member of a profession, be they architect, doctor or lawyer, that they would be committed to continually updating their skills so as to provide an optimum service to their clients (Cheshire and Pilgrim, 2004). So continued professional development was not expressed as an option, it was sold as a fundamental condition of club membership. Unfortunately it has become increasingly evident that not everyone has been abiding by the club rules. High profile cases of professional misconduct in medicine, law and indeed clinical psychology itself have drawn adverse publicity towards the notion of self-policing professions. It is difficult to refute the charge that a professional body that has been formed to represent the interests of its members may be inherently compromised when it comes to investigating malpractice by one of its own. A common response to this challenge by professional authorities such as the British Psychological Society has been to take a more muscular stance regarding expectations of CPD activity (BPS 2002). Where formerly continued professional development was considered an obligation on the individual, it has now become a mandatory requirement to be overseen by the accrediting professional organization. 'You've got to do it – and we'll check that you've done it' is the unambiguous contemporary message to the practising psychologist. It is interesting to pose the reflexive psychological question: What difference will 'having to' engage in CPD have on psychologists' motivation to participate in that activity?

Consider what might happen if a zealous infant school teacher decided to encourage her young charges to learn to read by rewarding them with their favourite sweets whenever they opened a book. Would this inducement lure them into discovering the joys of a good story (as no doubt intended) or would the provision of external reinforcement undermine the intrinsic satisfactions that pupils gain as their literacy skills develop? The latter prediction has been dubbed the 'overjustification' hypothesis and has received substantial empirical support (Deci et al., 1999). If as benign a strategy as offering prizes for good performance can have a deleterious impact on our sense of self-determination, what do we imagine the effects of the current panoply of rules and regulations and scarcely veiled threats will be on a clinical psychologist who is already committed to CPD for its own sake? In theoretical terms the clear prediction is that the more extrinsic factors feature in an individual's decision to pursue an activity the less likely they are to get the 'buzz' of intrinsic satisfaction that has been termed the 'flow experience' (Carr, 2004). Certainly there is evidence from other health professions that mandatory CPD has not been shown to produce positive changes in practitioners' motivation to pursue extra educational activities (Tassone and Heck, 1997) and some commentators have voiced their anxieties about the organizational consequences of the stance that has been adopted by the British Psychological Society (Raven, 2003).

However it would, in my opinion, be wrong to convey the impression that the BPS is in the process of imposing a Draconian new CPD policy on an unwilling membership. There are economic as well as psychological considerations to be borne in mind here. The National Health Service employs the vast majority of UK clinical psychologists. Their collective expectation could be summarized as 'if I've GOT to do it; then someone else has GOT to pay for it.' Mandatory CPD appears to offer an opportunity for clinical psychologists to get their fair share of the post-qualification training budget. This is an understandable if somewhat ignoble motivation for supporting the new policy – and tough luck if you work in independent private practice. But it is undeniable that CPD is an expensive business – or a lucrative one depending on whether you are purchaser or provider – and easy money and dodgy dealings tend to go hand in glove. The CPD industry in counselling has been lampooned as having more than its share of charlatans (Sivyer, 2003). Trainee GPs reputedly signed each other into training seminars that most didn't attend. A UK governmental scheme to co-fund individual CPD learner accounts to encourage all workers to invest in developing their skills was hurriedly withdrawn, when a scam paying large sums of cash to bogus education providers was uncovered. In Australia the regulations governing mandatory CPD in industry ended up providing unwitting tax breaks for tired Sydney executives to take wintertime 'stress management' courses in northern Queensland (Green, 1995). It all makes the small matter of drug company sponsorship of conferences seem quite innocuous by comparison! Whichever way we look at it, it seems there is a very hefty price to pay for making people engage in continuing professional development for which they might well have volunteered in the first place.

However there are sound reasons for thinking that a healthy degree of external influence on professionals' CPD decision taking may not be incompatible with principled and motivated personal development. Rather than construe the issue external versus internal control as a simplistic dichotomy, we can position ourselves on a continuum of self-determination (Ryan and Deci, 2000). At one extreme we might consider ourselves to have been cornered into participating in activities that have no inherent appeal whatsoever to us. At the other extreme we feel we are going our own sweet way unhindered by any external influences whatsoever. But even our most personal and idiosyncratic preferences have probably been socially shaped by important figures and experiences in our lives. In the adult life of a qualified clinical psychologist those formative influences are likely to include the socialization of professional training and the role models provided by respected colleagues. It seems credible therefore that the value system that has informed the emergent BPS policy on CPD (that entailed widespread consultation with its membership) is congruent with what matters to most working clinicians in the UK. As these commonly held professional values become internalized the distinction between extrinsic and intrinsic motivation becomes increasingly blurred. Ryan and Deci (2000) propose a sequential movement from external regulation through introjection and internalization to integration. Ultimately when we have integrated someone else's values into our own scheme of things, undertaking a 'set task' becomes an enjoyable, personal and involving experience that has all the hallmarks of an intrinsically satisfying pastime.

This makes developmental sense. As adults we enjoy many pleasurable activities that would have held no appeal to us at all in our distant youth (jazz concerts, watching the news on TV, eating olives etc). Children's discovery of the world around them is both self-directed and externally managed. The developmental psychologist Valsiner (Valsiner, 1987) has extended Vigotsky's notion of the 'zone of proximal development' to incorporate these cultural influences on the directions taken by young people's learning. He proposed two other overlapping zones – the 'zone of free movement' and the 'zone of promoted action'. The zone of free movement represents the boundaries of safe exploration imposed by parents on their child's experimentation. So a toddler would not be given free access to play in every area of the home environment that they might be tempted to investigate. The zone of promoted activity represents those routes of discovery that parents actively encourage their offspring to follow, like learning to swim for example. Valsiner argues that development proceeds most quickly where these three zones (of proximal development, free movement and promoted action) all point in the same direction. Crucially his model predicts that the external cultural influences represented by the zones of free movement and promoted action will not undermine the child's motivational drive to discover what she nearly knows (the essential principle behind the zone of proximal development). If these ideas are transferable to the world of adult professional development we would expect that when a qualified clinical psychologist takes care to ensure that their personal CPD ambitions coincide judiciously with their employer's business plans and their profession's extant guidelines, this will not necessarily diminish their motivational sense of being just ready for a particular learning experience. Indeed the increased probability of getting financial support for their proposed venture might further fuel their enthusiasm!

Another reason for not being pessimistic about the malign influence of compulsory CPD on individual motivation comes, fittingly enough, from the field of positive psychology. Seligman and his colleagues (Seligman, 2002; Peterson and Seligman, 2001) have identified six universal virtues (wisdom, courage, humanity, justice, temperance and transcendence) that have been valued by humans across different times and cultures. People who achieve these various virtues are considered (by themselves and others) to possess enduring character strengths that are fundamental to their personalities. When an individual has the opportunity to display or even enhance one of these key 'signature strengths' they are reckoned to experience a level of personal gratification that transcends mere sensual enjoyment. There are certain enabling conditions that increase the probability that persons will experience this deep sense of fulfilment such as our close relationships with our romantic partners or our children. However Seligman also identifies the work setting as a place where some people are able to taste the feeling of authentic happiness that comes from exercising an important signature strength. I have long considered it an immense privilege to be allowed to earn a decent living as a clinical psychologist. The work has always felt worthwhile. There is little to match the satisfactions to be derived from helping a client recover from crisis or contributing to a trainee's evolving competence. Perhaps that is why I still find myself enthusiastic about my job more than 25 years after qualifying as a clinical psychologist. Perhaps also I have been lucky enough to have had access to educational opportunities that enabled me to feel I could not only use abilities that I like in myself but that I could develop those talents further. I trust I am not alone in holding this view. If I am correct in this assumption then the intrinsic satisfaction that clinical psychologists can get from doing their job well and aspiring to do it even better, will be likely to outweigh the potentially dispiriting impact of mandatory CPD in the profession.

Does CPD Work?

Having somewhat laboured the point that CPD is an expensive business, it is now timely to consider its cost-effectiveness. Major investments in CPD at both an individual and organizational level could be simply justified if it delivered the goods. Without pre-empting the more detailed discussion of the research evidence in the field reviewed in a later chapter (see Milne), a few headline findings will set the scene sufficiently for the current discussion.

Contemporary CPD practice, in clinical psychology as in all other healthcare professions, cannot be presented as an empirically based endeavour. Large-scale studies using randomly controlled trials to test carefully selected educational and clinical outcomes over significant periods of time are few and far between (Davis et al., 1992). Those studies that have been conducted (primarily in medicine) have had mixed results (e.g., Tu and Davis, 2002). Within clinical psychology the research base is even more limited (Bourg, 1998) especially in the UK context. Crucially the assumption that when a qualified health professional engages in a programme of CPD activity this will result in predictable changes in the care she provides for her clients that are reliably identifiable in improved treatment outcomes, has not been established.

While this regrettable position may simply reflect the familiar way in which research lags behind practice and we can therefore just smugly wait until the evidence rolls in to support our established practice, there are sound reasons to doubt the wisdom of adopting that complacent position. Do we know whether practitioners actually learn much at all from the current CPD curriculum? Can we simply assume that skills learned in educational settings such as training courses are likely to get incorporated in everyday professional practice?

The 'adult learner' model has been highly influential in CPD circles. Adult education tends to be self-directed, problem-based, and experiential in nature. Compared to traditional teaching methods programmes designed with this framework in mind are less structured and rely on the learners' ability to assess their own training needs, set their own educational goals, and make their own connections with both their past experience and their future working practice. As we have already noted in the review of self-assessment these assumptions about the capacities of adult learners may not be well founded and hence result in ineffective educational provision (Norman, 1999). A particularly seductive fallacy is the expectation that once health professionals have acquired a new competence through participation in a formal CPD programme, they will automatically transfer that skill or understanding into their regular clinical practice. Unfortunately when researchers have taken the care to check on the 'real world' practical consequences of CPD activity the results have often been disappointing. Police officers who could demonstrate their competence in child-sensitive interviewing skills while on a specialist training programme showed no evidence of change in their subsequent practice once the course was completed (Aldridge and Cameron, 1999). While counsellors who attended a clinical workshop on motivational interviewing reported that they were putting its principles into practice four months later, the evidence from direct observation of therapy and assessment of client outcomes painted a much less convincing picture (Miller and Mount, 2001). Coming closer to home, clinical psychologists who attended a three-day series of Introduction to Supervision workshops reported on the final day that they had achieved or exceeded all the educational goals that they had set for themselves. Participants then set themselves a revised set of goals concerned with applying the lessons they had learned about good supervisory practice in their subsequent working lives. When these goal-attainment scales were reviewed three months later the novice supervisors reported that they had most frequently failed to meet their expected targets. (Gaston et al., 2004). One reason for this reported lack of impact on everyday practice may well be that much CPD is delivered in the form of brief 'one-off' events. No doubt this format appeals to busy time-starved clinicians but it may prove a false economy as the available evidence suggests that these short educational experiences are unlikely to have any discernable impact on their work (Davis et al., 1995).

All in all, it is perhaps not surprising that the belief that 'continuing education improves the effectiveness of clinicians' has been described as one of the most prevalent professional myths about mental health services (Bickman, 1999). However . . .

There are several comments to be made in defence of the current evidence base for continued professional development in clinical psychology. The first plaintive plea might be 'Why pick on CPD?' The format of basic professional training in clinical psychology and psychotherapy has been around much longer and remains, by and large, gloriously untainted by empirical investigation (Binder, 1993). In contrast to the immense effort that has been put into demonstrating the value of our collective product (psychological therapy), relatively few resources have been invested in researching the means of production (professional training programmes). The credibility of CPD courses has suffered as a consequence – but they are not alone in that regard. Indeed it is arguable, particularly in medicine, that the evidence on which those designing and attending CPD courses in the health professions can draw has expanded encouragingly in recent years. Not only have enough quantitative outcome studies been conducted to warrant focused systematic reviews in the field (e.g., Greenhalgh et al., 2003; O'Brien et al., 2004) but a broader array of research methodologies, such as theoretically driven qualitative investigations, have been employed to extend our understandings of the learner's experience (Prideaux, 2002). The net result is that tentative evidence-based recommendations of good practice in discrete areas are beginning to emerge in the scientific literature (e.g., Davis, 2001).

Of course in clinical psychology we are very far from possessing a comprehensive empirical foundation to inform our CPD ambitions. There is, however, a wider-disciplinary knowledge base on which we can draw that supplements the evolving research evidence with relevant conceptual understandings and experientially proven practice-based recommendations (Cape and Barkham, 2002; Fox, 2000). A good example of a creative theoretically driven response to empirical research findings is the development of 'commitment to change' strategies to promote transfer of learning into professional practice (Dolcourt, 2000). Furthermore it's not such an unusual experience for qualified clinical psychologists to find themselves delving into areas where there are no obvious research findings to light the way! The recommended response is to collect your own evidence carefully as you go using the small-scale research skills that are fostered during basic professional training (see for example Green and Sherrard (1999) on evaluating the outcomes of post-qualification clinical supervision). Rather than sit on our hands bemoaning the absence of research findings to inform our CPD decisions clinical psychologists need to make good use of the evidence that is available and contribute to expanding that knowledge base by conducting their own applied research.

Preventing Malpractice

A final important consideration regarding the outcome of committed CPD activity concerns the protection of the public. Part of the rhetoric of the CPD movement is an attempt to persuade the consumers of a profession's services that the substantial investment of resources in

CPD will guarantee the quality of the product it provides. As we have seen, the assertion that more CPD equals better treatment outcomes is unproven at best. What about the claim that a directed programme of continued professional education can reassure the public about the future competence of a health professional who has been found guilty of malpractice? The relationship between training and competence in psychological therapies is far from straightforward (Parry and Richardson, 1996). Not everyone who undergoes a training experience learns from it. Not everyone who acquires skills in an educational setting manages to apply them in their daily practice. Sadly even those capable of excellent work can also on occasions be guilty of improper professional conduct. Even mandatory CPD is unlikely to rid any profession of the risk of malpractice. There are however grounds for hoping that a commitment to CPD makes any clinical psychologist a safer bet from a consumer's viewpoint than they might otherwise have been.

Ours is a fast-moving and oddly fashion-conscious profession. Ideas and methods that may have been 'state of the art' during a psychologist's initial training can fall out of favour remarkably quickly (and not always on scientific grounds). New therapeutic approaches are developed and practised enthusiastically. CPD offers the experienced practitioner an opportunity both to appraise carefully the evidence supporting different psychotherapeutic approaches and to undertake some disciplined preparation for the novel tack he intends to take. In one sense any professional development forces a clinician to practise beyond their existing level of competence, but there are degrees of safe and unsafe experimentation. Structured CPD lies on the safe end of that spectrum.

Part of the public protection that a CPD programme can legitimately offer lies in the social demands it places on participants. One of the most virulent feeding grounds in which malpractice flourishes is professional isolation (Napier, 1993). Clinicians who work in a closed system do not have access to the feedback loops that could correct their errors and prompt more critical reflection on their own working methods. Maybe some miscreants organize their schedules with just that outcome in mind, but I suspect that many 'fall' into misconduct because they are denied access to the self-righting social influences that are part and parcel of operating within a 'learning organization' (Birleson, 1999). If mandatory CPD results in reducing the professional isolation of clinical psychologists in the UK it will, I suspect, have done a service not only to the practitioners themselves but also to the clients they serve.

Conclusions

So continued professional development is not the simple 'good thing' it first appears. Certainly it has a persuasive sales pitch and offers the promise of an increasingly motivated and skilled workforce in the healthcare sector. However, the siren call of CPD could also result in the diversion of significant resources from other clinical priorities with no assurance that appreciable benefits will follow. Caveat emptor. For CPD to deliver its potential to all stakeholders in the venture (clients, professional bodies, employers as well as individual practitioners) a complex series of steps have to be negotiated successfully. These include self-appraisal, identification of training needs, discovery of optimal educational opportunities, disciplined learning, and incorporating new skills into established working routines. This is a serious undertaking that needs to be undertaken seriously. For clinical psychologists the challenge is to use their psychology reflexively so as to understand the processes of evaluation, motivation and transfer of learning that drive successful post-qualification development. The remainder of this book represents a significant move in that direction.

REFERENCES

Aldridge, J. and Cameron, S. (1999). Interviewing child witnesses: Questioning strategies and the effectiveness of training. *Applied Developmental Science*, 3, 136–47.

Alicke, M., Klotz, M., Breitenbecher, D., Yurak, T. and Vredenburg, D. (1995). Personal contact, individuation, and the better-than-average effect. *Journal of Personality and Social Psychology*, 68, 804–25.

Bickman, L. (1999). Practice makes perfect and other myths about mental health services. *American Psychologist*, 54, 963–78.

Binder, J. (1993). Is it time to improve psychotherapy training? *Clinical Psychology Review*, 13, 301–18.

Birleson, P. (1999). Turning child and adolescent mental health services into learning organizations. *Clinical Child Psychology and Psychiatry*, 4, 265–74.

Bourg, E. (1998). Continuing education: Updating of knowledge and skills. In A. Bellack, and M. Hersen, (eds), *Comprehensive Clinical Psychology*, vol. 2, *Professional Issues*. Elsevier, New York.

British Psychological Society (2002). *Society CPD Guidelines: Revised Draft*. British Psychological Society, Leicester.

Cape, J. and Barkham, M. (2002). Practice improvement methods: Conceptual base, evidence-based research, and practice-based recommendations. *British Journal of Clinical Psychology*, 41, 285–307.

Carr, A. (2004). *Positive Psychology. The Science of Happiness and Human Strengths.* Brunner-Routledge, Hove.

Chesire, K. and Pilgrim, D. (2004). *A Short Introduction to Clinical Psychology.* Sage, London.

Davis, D., Thompson, M., Oxman, A. and Haynes, R. (1992). Evidence for the effectiveness of CME: A review of 50 randomized controlled trials. *JAMA,* 268, 1111–17.

Davis, D., Thompson, M., Oxman, A. and Haynes, R. (1995). Changing physician performance: A systematic review of the effect of continuing education strategies. *JAMA,* 274, 700–5.

Davis, N. (2001). Enhancing the effectiveness of meetings and workshops through research. *Journal of Continuing Education in the Health Professions,* 21, 3, 188–90.

DeBacker, T. and Nelson, R. (2000). Motivation to learn science: Differences related to gender, class type and ability. *The Journal of Educational Research,* 93, 245–54.

Deci, R., Koestner, R. and Ryan, R. (1999). A meta-analytic review of experiments examining the effects of extrinsic rewards on intrinsic motivation. *Psychological Bulletin,* 125, 627–68.

Dolcourt, J. (2000). Commitment to change: A strategy for promoting educational effectiveness. *Journal of Continuing Education in the Health Professions,* 20, 3, 156–63.

Ehrlinger, J. and Dunning, D. (2003). How chronic self-views influence (and potentially mislead) estimates of performance. *Journal of Personality and Social Psychology,* 84, 1, 5–17.

Fox, R. (2000). Using theory and research to shape the practice of continuing professional development. *Journal of Continuing Education in the Health Professions,* 20, 4, 238–46.

Gaston, A., Hughes, J. and Green, D. (2004). What difference does supervisor training make? Poster presented at the PLAT 2004 conference in Glasgow.

Goodge, P. and Burr, J. (1999). 360-degree feedback – for once the research is useful. *Selection and Development Review,* 15, 2, 3–7.

Gordon, M. (1991). A review of the validity and accuracy of self-assessments in health professions training. *Academic Medicine,* 66, 12, 762–9.

Gordon, M. (1992). Self-assessment programs and their implications for health professions training. *Academic Medicine,* 67, 10, 672–9.

Green, D. (1995). Carry on learning. *Clinical Psychology Forum,* 76, 37–40.

Green, D. and Sherrard, C. (1999). Developing an evidence base for postqualification clinical supervision. *Clinical Psychology Forum,* 134, 17–20.

Greenhalgh, T., Toon, P., Russell, J., Wong, G., Plumb, L. and Macfarlane, F. (2003). Transferability of principles of evidence based medicine to improve educational quality: Systematic review and case study of an online course in primary healthcare. *British Medical Journal,* 326, 142–5.

Jones, E. and Nisbett, R. (1972). The actor and the observer: Divergent perceptions of the causes of behaviour. In E. Jones (ed.), *Attribution: Perceiving the Causes of Behaviour.* General Learning Press, Morristown NJ.

Joshi, R., Ling, F. and Jaeger, J. (2004). Assessment of a 360-degree instrument to evaluate residents' competency in interpersonal and communication skills. *Academic Medicine*, 79, 5, 458–63.

Kruger, J. and Dunning, D. (1999). Unskilled and unaware of it: How difficulties in recognizing one's own incompetence lead to inflated self-assessments. *Journal of Personality and Social Psychology*, 77, 6, 1121–34.

Mabe, P. and West, S. (1982). Validity of self-evaluation of ability: A review and meta-analysis. *Journal of Applied Psychology*, 67, 280–96.

Marteau, T., Johnston, M., Wynne, G. and Evans, T. (1989). Cognitive factors in the explanation of the mismatch between confidence and competence in performing basic life support. *Psychology and Health*, 3, 173–82.

Miller, W. and Mount, K. (2001). A small study of training in motivational interviewing: Does one workshop change clinician and client behaviour? *Behavioural and Cognitive Psychotherapy*, 29, 457–71.

Napier, B. (1993). Striving towards the ethical practice of clinical psychology. *Clinical Psychology Forum*, 54, 20–2.

Norman, G. (1999). The adult learner: A mythical species. *Academic Medicine*, 74, 886–9.

O'Brien, T., Freemantle, N., Oxman, A., Wolf, F., Davis, D. and Herrin, J. (2004). Continuing education meetings and workshops. *Cochrane Database of Systematic Reviews 1.*

Parboosingh, J. (1998). Role of self-assessment in identification of learning needs. *Journal of Continuing Education in the Health Professions*, 18, 4, 213–20.

Parry, G. and Richardson, A. (1996). *NHS Psychotherapy Services in England. Review of Strategic Policy.* NHS Executive, London.

Peterson, C. and Seligman, M. (2001). *Values in Action (VIA) Classification of Strengths.* www.positivepsychology.org/taxonomy.htm

Prideaux, D. (2002). Researching the outcomes of educational interventions: A matter of design. RCTs have important limitations in evaluating educational interventions. *British Medical Journal*, 324, 126–7.

Raven, J. (2003). CPD – What should we be developing? *The Psychologist*, 16, 7, 160–2.

Ryan, R. and Deci, R. (2000). Self-determination theory and the facilitation of intrinsic motivation, social development and well being. *American Psychologist*, 55, 68–78.

Seligman, M. (2002). *Authentic Happiness: Using the New Positive Psychology to Realize your Potential for Lasting Fulfilment.* Free Press, New York.

Sivyer, J. (2003). CPD – A Fool's Gold? *Self and Society*, 31, 2, 37–8.

Snyder, C. (2000). *Handbook of Hope.* Academic Press, Orlando Fl.

Tassone, M. and Heck, C. (1997). Motivational orientations of allied healthcare professionals participating in continuing education. *The Journal of Continuing Education in the Health Professions*, 17, 97–105.

Taylor, S., kemeny, N., Bower, J. and Gruenewald, T. (2000). Psychological resources, positive illusions and health. *American Psychologist*, 55, 99–109.

Tousignant, M. and DesMarchais, J. (2002). Accuracy of student self-assessment ability compared to their own performance in a problem-based learning medical program: A correlation study. *Advances in Health Sciences Education*, 7, 19–27.

Tracey, J., Arrol, B., Richmond, D. and Barham, P. (1997). The validity of general practitioners' self-assessment of knowledge. *British Medical Journal*, 315, 1426–8.

Tu, K. and Davis, D. (2002). Can we alter physician behaviour by educational methods? Lessons learned from studies of the management and follow-up of hypertension. *The Journal of Continuing Education in the Health Professions*, 22, 1, 11–22.

Valsiner, J. (1987). *Culture and the Development of Children's Action*. Wiley, Chichester.

Wilson, A. and Ross, M. (2000). From chump to champ: People's appraisals of their earlier and present selves. *Journal of Personality and Social Psychology*, 80, 4, 572–84.

Wooliscroft, J., Tenhaken, J., Smith, J. and Calhoun J (1993). Medical students' clinical self-assessments: Comparisons with external measures of performance and the students' self-assessments of overall performance and effort. *Academic Medicine*, 68, 4, 285–94.

Chapter 3

The NHS Policy Context
Ian Gray

Introduction

Since taking office in 1997, the Labour government has made a firm commitment to reform of the NHS. With substantial increases in funding, the Department of Health (DoH) has implemented a series of policy initiatives with the explicit aim of modernizing the National Health Service (NHS). In particular there has been a drive to modernize the workforce. As early as 1998, in its consultation document, *A First Class Service* (DoH, July 1998), development of the workforce has been emphasized. Continuing professional development (CPD) was seen as a key component in contributing to lifelong learning across all professions in the NHS, with a clear statement that it should be designed to meet service as well as individual needs. It is within this broad policy context that we need to examine the detailed guidance with a specific focus on applied psychology and the allied health professions. Chapter 9 discusses the specific response of the clinical psychology profession.

Chapter Plan

This chapter has four main sections focusing on four broad areas of policy development; first the early policy development phase 1996/2000; then, *The NHS Plan* and its implementation; followed by, specific policies focusing on lifelong learning, CPD and the role of Workforce Development Confederations (WDC) and Strategic Health Authorities

(SHA); and finally, *Agenda for Change*; Health Professions Council (HPC) and mandatory CPD.

Early Policy Development Phase

The New NHS: Modern, Dependable (DoH, October 1997)

This government white paper set out a ten-year vision for the modernization of a healthcare system moving away from the previous government's emphasis on competition to one of cooperation. One of its main aims was to focus on quality in the NHS and it set out three broad areas for action as follows:

1. National standards and guidelines through:
   - evidence based National Service frameworks; and
   - a new National Institute for Clinical Excellence.
2. A local drive for quality through:
   - establishing local Primary Care Groups;
   - explicit quality standards in long-term service agreements; and
   - a new system of clinical governance.
3. A new organization to tackle shortcomings:
   - a new Commission for Health Improvement.

Specific references to CPD are few in this White Paper but commitment to this is evident. In setting out a broad agenda for developing high quality services, paragraph 6.9 of the White Paper states, 'It [the Government] will strengthen continuing professional development. It will introduce a system of clinical governance in NHS Trusts to guarantee quality.' Likewise, paragraph 6.10 states, 'The Government will work with the professions to reach a shared understanding of the principles that should underpin effective continuing professional development and the respective roles of the state, the professions and individual practitioners in supporting this activity.'

The White Paper (DoH, October 1997) made explicit the links between the provision of high quality services and the need for CPD: 'A quality organisation will ensure that (amongst other things), all professional development programmes will reflect the principles of clinical governance' (paragraph 6.12). Later still in paragraph 6.29 a commitment is given that, 'The Government will work with the NHS to give a higher priority to human resource development. . . . It will emphasise the need to bring equality and development issues into the mainstream work of the NHS.'

A First Class Service: Quality in the New NHS (DoH, July 1998)

The theme of quality of care, a key aspect of the government's strategy outlined above is developed in more detail in this consultation document. The document introduced three major initiatives to ensure delivery of high quality services namely:

1. Setting Quality Standards through:
   - the National Institute for Clinical Excellence: to provide a single focus for clear, consistent guidance for clinicians about which treatments work best for which patients.
   - National Service Frameworks which will set out what patients can expect to receive from the NHS in major care areas or disease groups.
2. Delivering Quality Standards through:
   - Clinical Governance, a process by which each part of the NHS quality assures its clinical decisions.
   - Lifelong Learning to provide NHS staff with the opportunity to continuously update their skills and knowledge.
   - Professional Self-Regulation providing clinicians with the opportunity to help set standards and contribute to early identification of possible lapses in clinical quality.
3. Monitoring Quality Standards through:
   - The Commission for Health Improvement, a new statutory body providing an independent assessment of local action to improve quality.
   - The National Framework for Assessing Performance focusing on six key areas: health improvement; fair access to service; effective delivery of healthcare; efficiency; patient and carer experience; and health outcome of NHS care.
   - The National Survey of Patient and User Experience providing annual feedback on the things that matter most to patients.

Of particular relevance to this chapter are the developments described in *A First Class Service* (DoH, July 1998) around clinical governance and lifelong learning. Clinical governance is defined in the consultation paper, as 'A framework through which NHS organisations are accountable for continuously improving the quality of their services and safeguarding high standards of care by creating an environment in which excellence will flourish'. Clinical governance makes Chief Executives of NHS Trusts accountable for assuring the quality of NHS Trust services. Paragraph 3.12 of the consultation document sets out the key components of clinical governance which must be in place, one of which is, 'continuing professional development programmes aimed at meeting the development needs of individual health professionals and the service needs of the organisation are in place and supported locally'.

Structural and accountability issues of clinical governance are set out in more detail in *Clinical Governance in the New NHS* (DoH, March 1999). This consultation paper defines CPD as 'a process of lifelong learning for all individuals and teams which meets the needs of patients and delivers the health outcomes and healthcare priorities of the NHS and which enables professionals to expand and fulfil their potential' (DoH, March 1999). It stresses the importance of the need to create, partly through clinical governance, a culture that values lifelong learning and recognizes the key part it plays in improving quality. It is acknowledged that it is vital to develop an integrated approach whereby individual practitioner needs, client needs, service and professional needs are carefully and effectively balanced.

A model of a CPD cycle is presented whereby *Assessment* of individual and service needs leads to the production of a *Personal Development Plan* (PDP). This, in turn requires an *Implementation Plan* which will be required to be *Evaluated* for effectiveness which leads on to a further cycle of *Assessment*. There is acknowledgment that individual PDPs need to be complemented by effective organizational development plans. Although suggesting that the financial resource allocated to CPD is substantial, this is not spelt out other than making a plea for effective use of resources and establishing that the level of resourcing is a matter for local health service employers to decide within the clinical governance framework.

The consultation paper established an aim that, by April 2000, all NHS employers would have training and development plans in place for the majority of health professionals. It also outlined a number of tasks for action including:

- the role of peer review and appraisal;
- the role of new technology and distance learning in maximizing learning opportunities and customizing the process;
- how the expertise of professional and statutory bodies can best support local CPD, within the context of clinical governance; and

- the educational infrastructure required to identify and meet CPD needs.

Continuing Professional Development: Quality in the New NHS (DoH, July 1999)

This is a guidance document, the product of the consultation exercise set out in *A First Class Service* (DoH, July 1998). It draws on the principles and criteria published in the Chief Medical Officer's Report on CPD in General Practice (DoH, March 1998).

It states that CPD should be:

- purposeful and patient-centred;
- participative, i.e. fully involving the individual and other relevant stakeholders; targeted at identified educational need; educationally effective;
- part of a wider organizational developmental plan in support of local and national service objectives;
- focused on development needs of clinical teams, across traditional professional and service boundaries;
- designed to build on previous knowledge, skills and experience; and
- designed to enhance the skills of interpreting and applying knowledge-based research and development.

The document emphasizes that CPD is an integral part of the quality improvement process set out in *A First Class Service* (DoH, July 1998) and reinforced by the clinical governance agenda (DoH, March 1999). In addition, it repeats the point that the exact level of resource investment in CPD is for local determination but it links this with pay reform. A key element of *Agenda for Change* (DoH, October 1999) is greater flexibility of roles underpinned by lifelong learning.

The guidance for local implementation within this document outlines some of the practical issues which are included in the delivery of CPD, e.g.:

- coaching on the job;
- mentoring;
- job rotation and job shadowing;
- learning sets; and
- work-based projects.

It also outlines ways of delivering CPD including:

- work-based learning;
- information technology; and
- learning in multidisciplinary teams.

Deciding what is needed for each individual can be achieved through the four-part cycle outlined above, namely; *Assessment, PDP, Implementation* and *Evaluation*. This guidance document also sets out criteria for local health authorities to assist establishment of a systematic approach to CPD and to allocate roles and responsibilities to the various stakeholders at a range of levels.

Developing the NHS Workforce (House of Commons Health Select Committee, February 1999)

In July 1998, The House of Commons Health Select Committee sent out a request for written evidence for a proposed Report on Future NHS Staffing Requirements. The report, above, was finally published in February 1999. Paragraph 138 of the Report recommended 'that the NHS finances in full the relevant professional educational needs of its staff. We also believe that current study arrangements are inadequate and need to be extended.' In its response (DoH, June 1999) there was a clear recognition by the government of the importance of lifelong learning. The need for all staff to have PDPs was reiterated with a target date for implementation by April 2000. There was guidance to local health authorities to align investment in CPD with clinical governance plans. The government response draws attention to the breadth of means for delivering CPD beyond the traditional attendance at courses.

The British Psychological Society's submission of evidence (July 1998) focused more on narrower workforce planning matters and did not raise the issues of lifelong learning and CPD.

Another publication in this early phase was the consultation document, *A Health Service of all the Talents: Developing the NHS Workforce* (DoH, April 2000). This was aimed at ensuring that the NHS had a workforce, 'which has the skills and flexibility to deliver the right care at the right time to those who need it – a workforce which has the right number of staff deployed in the right places and working to the maximum of their ability'. It makes few references to CPD. However, in paragraph 5.21 there is a recommendation for the establishment of local Workforce Development Confederations (WDC) with a remit among others, 'to plan post-basic professional training and other staff training requirements . . .'. Later, in the same paragraph, there is a steer to NHS Trusts, 'we believe that NHS Trusts, in developing strategies for continuing professional development and lifelong learning, should gear their thinking and resourcing to supporting greater flexibility and the development of additional skill for staff.'

In their responses to this consultation document both the British Psychological Society (BPS, June 2000) and the trade union Manufacturing, Science, Finance (MSF, June 2000), highlighted the rather minimal proposals regarding CPD, in general, and specifically with regard to professions other than doctors and nurses.

In summarizing the results of the consultation exercise, the Department of Health (February, 2001b) makes no mention of CPD.

Summary

We can see these early policy documents coming together to develop and articulate government policy on lifelong learning and CPD. This is emphasized in the government's intention that by April 2000 employers should have had in place training and development plans for the majority of health professionals.

The NHS Plan (DoH, July 2000)

In introducing *The NHS Plan* (DoH, July 2000) the Prime Minister indicated that, with substantially increased funding, significant modernization and reform of the NHS would be needed. This would include increased inspection and accountability, expansion in the role of nurses and other health professionals, proposals for closer integration of health and social services, closer working between public and private sectors and patient advocacy. There was also a strong commitment to NHS staff development.

In Chapter 5 of the Plan, 'Investing in NHS Staff', the 'Improving Working Lives Standard' is introduced. Paragraph 5.16 states, 'The Improving Working Lives Standard means that every member of staff in the NHS is entitled to belong to an organisation which can prove that it is investing in their training and development . . .'

This is supported by the promise of increased resources. Paragraph 5.17 states 'We will ensure more help with personal development and training: by investing an extra £140 million by 2003/04 to ensure that all professional staff are supported in keeping their skills up to date and to provide access to learning for all NHS staff without a professional qualification . . .'

These points are reiterated and emphasized in Chapter 9 of *The NHS Plan* (DoH, July 2000). Paragraph 9.12 states, 'For professional staff there will be investment to support their continuing development. All members of staff should receive support from their employers to fulfil the requirements of clinical governance and revalidation. Better use will be made of the investment in continuing professional development with greater emphasis on accredited workplace based systems of learning.'

In its comments on *The NHS Plan*, the BPS (BPS, June 2000) drew attention to, among other issues, 'a need for structured approaches to CPD and lifelong learning for staff involved in delivering psychological services'. The point was made that, in the past, funded CPD had been concentrated on medical and nursing staff and that there was a need to ensure a more balanced approach in future. The trade union MSF, in its response (August 2000), warmly welcomed the Improving Working Lives measures outlined in Chapter 5 of the Plan and the promise of an additional £140 million for delivering CPD. It too cautioned the need to ensure that the additional funding should be distributed equitably across the NHS professions.

A number of guidance and strategic documents followed as part of the implementation of *The NHS Plan*. Of particular importance for this chapter was, *Meeting the Challenge: A Strategy for the Allied Health Professions* (DoH, November 2000). This document again stresses that CPD is a process of lifelong learning for all individuals and teams, essential for good quality patient care and reinforces the assertion that CPD is an integral part of the government's strategy for clinical governance.

Meeting the Challenge encourages Trusts to be creative in the delivery of CPD with suggestions:

- for work between as well as within Trusts;
- to establish multiprofessional networks;
- for more use of team learning, distance learning and project work;
- to think beyond menu-driven Higher Education programmes; and

- to pick up priorities such as leadership development.

This last point in the above list is given emphasis with specific mention of funding for a programme of leadership development in the allied health professions. There is also an indication that there will be increased government investment in CPD and a strengthened link between CPD and professional regulation via the Health Professions Council. This issue will be developed later in this chapter.

This guidance document makes reference to modernizing the pay system through *Agenda for Change* which will, says the government, make it easier to reward staff for what they do and their skills and ability, in essence ensuring that there are rewards for developing, through CPD, new and enhanced competence. This issue will also be developed later in this chapter.

In its review of progress in implementing *The NHS Plan, Investment and Reform for NHS Staff* (DoH, February 2001a), Chapter 6 reiterates the government's commitment to developing the workforce. A strategic framework for lifelong learning is promised. There is also a promise that by April 2001 funding will be provided to ensure that all trusts have the capacity to deliver effectively CPD for professional staff. The point made by the BPS in its response (BPS, June 2000) that CPD funding is largely directed to doctors and nurses, is acknowledged with a commitment to help: 'those professionals – for example in the Allied Health Professions – who receive little CPD support at present'. Paragraph 6.4 states 'We will continue to ensure that NHS staff have personal development plans. Already the majority of NHS professional staff have PDPs'. However, no evidence for this claim is offered.

Summary

The government's strategic direction for the NHS is articulated in *The NHS Plan* and its subsequent implementation policies and guidance. Broad aims for raising the importance of CPD and lifelong learning are set out.

Lifelong Learning and CPD – Specific Policies

From the general aims and objectives outlined in previous sections, the government developed more specific guidance and policy. The

DoH has published a number of documents in the past few years specifically addressing the need for lifelong learning and CPD in the NHS.

Most significantly, in terms of CPD, the DoH published, *Working Together, Learning Together: A Framework for Lifelong Learning in the NHS* (DoH, November 2001). It was seen as fundamental to delivery of *The NHS Plan* (DoH, July 2001) and set out what staff could expect from employers who really embraced the concept of lifelong learning. It is intended to address the learning needs of all NHS staff, not just the 'traditional professions' and covers both pre- and post-registration training needs. It introduces flexible ways of learning for staff including NHS learning accounts and National Vocational Qualifications (NVQs). The paper also signals the establishment of the NHS University (NHSU) from 2003, an important resource to make learning more accessible and flexible for people at work and in their homes.

In the foreword, to this document Andrew Foster identifies three key supporting elements of Human Resources which contribute to the wider policy context, namely:

- effective workforce planning previously referred to in the *A Health Service of all the Talents* (DoH, April 2000) proposals;
- modernizing pay and contracts via *Agenda for Change* (DoH, October 1999); and
- developing a modern regulatory framework, e.g. Health Professions Council (DoH, April 2001).

Chapter 1 of *Working Together, Learning Together* (DoH, November 2001), sets out a vision for lifelong learning which includes:

- NHS staff are entitled to work in an environment which equips them with the skills to perform their current jobs to the best of their ability, developing their roles and career potential, working individually and in teams in more creative and fulfilling ways;
- access to education, training and development should be as open and flexible as possible – with no discrimination in terms of age, gender, ethnicity, availability to part-time/full-time staff, geographical location;
- wherever practical, learning should be shared by different staff groups and professions; and
- planning and evaluation of lifelong learning should be central to organizational development and service improvements, backed by robust information about skill gaps and needs.

It goes on to emphasize the need for 'the basic building blocks of induction, appraisal, personal development plans and the learning culture' to be in place.

In Chapter 2, of this document, on 'Effective Learning Organisations', the report draws on the work of the Audit Commission Report, *Hidden Talents* (Audit Commission, 2001), which highlighted a number of shortcomings in the way NHS organizations lead, manage, invest in, evaluate and ensure all staff have access to education and training. In particular it 'shows that training needs are not always well identified at either the organisational or individual level. Significant numbers of staff providing services to patients and clients do not have their training needs identified or recorded and where this does occur the process can be of poor quality.' It goes on to describe, 'how access to education, training and development opportunities depends on where you work, or who you are and what you do, as much as on individual or service needs'. Barriers for staff and services in meeting training needs include lack of funding and time, availability of convenient training opportunities and in some cases availability of mentors/assessors. Even where there are well organized systems, 'Trusts need to have a culture where everyone's role in training and development is clear.'

Pre-registration is the main focus of Chapter 4 with the previously identified need for reform given impetus by such high profile publications as the DoH's enquiry into children's heart surgery at the Bristol Royal Infirmary (DoH, July 2001a). A major aspect of this report was the focus on professional competence, 'Professional competence requires firm educational grounding . . . it depends on the professional standards individuals are required to meet and on the wider systems for ensuring these standards are adhered to.' A second major emphasis was a need to increase and expand inter-professional education based on key areas of competence.

Of particular relevance to this book chapter is Chapter 5, 'Maintaining and Extending Skills and Careers'. 'Continually updating and extending knowledge and skill is essential to professional life – post-registration education and CPD frameworks must constantly evolve to take account of developments in health and social care, primarily for protection of the public.' The importance of the Bristol Royal Infirmary Enquiry is further acknowledged, no doubt because of both its relevance and public impact, 'Continuing Professional Development must be part of the process of lifelong learning for all healthcare professionals – its purpose is to help professionals care for patients. It must be supported by the NHS and by the professions' (DoH, July 2001a).

In *Working Together, Learning Together* (DoH, November, 2001), broader issues such as a move to mandatory re-registration and a shift towards a competency framework in pre-registration training emphasize the need for CPD. There is acknowledgment of the overlap and blurring of the concepts of post-registration training and CPD. This chapter goes on to set out a number of principles. Post-registration training/CPD:

- will be patient-centred;
- should meet local service needs as well as the personal and professional development needs of individuals;
- should be increasingly focused on the development needs of clinical teams across traditional professional and service boundaries;
- will increasingly be work-based. The acid test must be 'competence in doing';
- will involve users and carers wherever practicable in designing and evaluating the outcomes and in the delivery of learning programmes;
- will make use of the full range of development approaches and methods, rather than rely solely or largely on formal courses; and
- will be grounded in clinical governance and draw on clinical audit, clinical effectiveness and enable the development of a research aware workforce.

This document places a particular emphasis on quality assurance of CPD via regulatory bodies and revalidation through employers' clinical governance responsibility and through the individual's own sense of what constitutes an effective learning experience.

Further chapters in the same document focus on leadership and management training and development to create a learning culture within Trusts and the infrastructure necessary to deliver lifelong learning. There is little detail although the future establishment of the NHS University is seen as a central resource along with enhanced library, e-learning support and competence in computer skills e.g., the European Computer Driving Licence (ECDL).

Further policy guidance on lifelong learning/CPD has followed. Interim guidance on implementation was provided to Workforce Development Confederations, Post Graduate Deans, The Health Professional and Regulatory Bodies and UK Universities (Pearson, July 2002). This was followed by the consultation document on *Funding Learning and Development for the Healthcare Workforce* (DoH, July 2002b). This proposed that funding should be reorganized on an interdisciplinary basis, ending the present rigid demarcations in the support given to different professions and occupational groups and should be under-pinned by key values including:

- transparency;
- equity – the main driver being the need to deliver particular health-care skills to patients rather than the delivery of particular types of professional;
- comprehensiveness – support should be available to all health service staff;
- responsiveness;
- integration – healthcare staff should learn together;
- partnership – the health and education sectors, social care, and private and voluntary sectors should work together to deliver train-ing; and
- flexibility.

Drawing on previous reports, e.g., *A Health Service of all the Talents* (DoH, April 2000) and the National Audit Office (February 2001), it was recommended that there be a merging of a range of distinct and often profession-specific budgets including; the Non Medical Educa-tion and Training Budget (NMET), the Medical and Dental Levy (MADEL) and the Service Increment for Teaching (SIFT). The consulta-tion document states 'these arrangements reflected long established divisions in workforce planning, learning and development for the different healthcare professions. The lack of commonality made it dif-ficult to develop integrated approaches to learning and development across professional staff groups and the professional focus of the major budgets excluded other staff groups from access to these funds.' It also recommended a looser designation of the budget into different ele-ments supporting innovation, placements, pre-registration tuition, bursaries, continuing professional development, development of staff without professional qualifications and capital in support of education in the NHS.

Specifically it recommends that the learning and development budget should contribute consistently and significantly to 'Educational innovation and developments linked to the NHS Plan, service mod-ernisation and the NHS lifelong learning agenda'. Additionally, in part-nership with the individual and their employing organization, the learning and development funds must support, 'Tuition costs for people working in NHS organisations undertaking continuing personal and professional development'.

Workforce Development Confederations (DoH, April 2002) were established in 2001 after consultation on *A Health Service of all the Talents* (DoH, February 2001b). They were partnership organizations comprising both NHS and non-NHS member organizations. Until recent reorganization when they were fully incorporated into Strategic Health Authorities (SHAs) from April 2004, they were required to work closely with SHAs and postgraduate Deaneries. They were allocated a key role in driving forward work to increase staff numbers and change the way in which staff are trained and educated.

From April 2002 there were 27 Workforce Development Confederations (WDCs), later to be increased to 28, with boundaries aligned to SHAs from October 2002. Functions of WDCs included:

- The WDC will take a leading role in visioning the future healthcare workforce.
- The WDC will have overall responsibility for developing the existing and future healthcare workforce to underpin delivery of the NHS Plan. Importantly this would include taking forward the NHS Lifelong Learning framework principles and priorities set out in *Working Together, Learning Together* (DoH, November 2001) for appraisal and personal development.
- The WDC will co-ordinate the strategic management of local learning and education facilities.

A specific innovative example of taking forward the Lifelong Learning framework is the North West Clinical Psychology Continuing Professional Development Scheme begun in October 2003 and funded by Greater Manchester WDC, now incorporated into Greater Manchester Strategic Health Authority (Golding, 2003).

Another policy document addressing lifelong learning/CPD for healthcare professionals, as well as other issues, was *Improving Working Lives for the Allied Health Professions and Healthcare Scientists*, (DoH, November 2002a). In his introduction to this document, Andrew Foster Director of HR at the Department of Health, makes the point, among others, that being a good employer includes treating staff fairly, providing job security and lifelong learning. This document is another element in the delivery of *The NHS Plan* (DoH, July 2000). It expands on the Improving Working Lives (IWL) standard to be implemented by April 2003 whereby employers committed to Improving Working Lives:

- recognize that modern health services require modern employment services;

- understand that staff work best for patients when they can strike a healthy balance between work and other aspects of their life outside work;
- accept joint responsibility with staff to develop a range of working arrangements that balance the needs of patients and service with the needs of staff; and
- provide personal and professional development and training opportunities that are accessible and open to all staff irrespective of their working patterns.

More recently, the Department of Health in its publication, *Organising and Delivering Psychological Therapies* (DoH, July 2004), has the stated aim of improving psychological services to patients. A key element is the emphasis on a 'capable workforce' and the need for providing training opportunities as part of a CPD strategy, (paragraph 2.14). In particular paragraph 5.17 identifies the need for an effective CPD programme to support quality and interestingly, safety of clinical staff. The guidance recommends linking CPD with appraisal and clinical supervision.

Within the specific area of mental health the 'capable workforce' concept is fleshed out in the recent Department of Health Publication, *The Ten Essential Shared Capabilities – A Framework for the Whole of the Mental Health Workforce* (DoH August 2004). This is a response to a perceived need to ensure that all mental health staff have appropriate pre- and post-qualification training in key areas of competence. Of specific relevance to this chapter are the implications for training at the post-qualification stage. It is suggested that the implementation strategy for CPD should:

- support the development of web-based a Training Needs Analysis (TNA) tool consistent with the Essential Shared Capabilities (ESC);
- provide examples of TNA that are consistent with ESC;
- support the development of an appraisal tool that is consistent with the ESC; and
- support the development of a framework for practice supervision based on the ESC.

Summary

The above policy and guidance documents develop the CPD and life-long learning agenda, set in place infrastructure, in the shape of WDCs, establish accountability and indicate resource responsibilities. In addition there is clear acknowledgement of the CPD needs of the wider NHS rather than a narrow range of professional groups. Identifying and meeting the CPD needs of applied psychologists within the NHS, therefore, must be seen within this much wider NHS context.

Agenda for Change

Part of the wider human resource framework, *Working Together: Securing a Quality Workforce for the NHS* (DoH, September 1998) to improve the quality of working life for all NHS staff, *Agenda for Change* (DoH, October 1999) had the aim 'to ensure fair reward for work done, encourage staff to develop their competencies and improve the quality of patient care and enable staff to give their best for patients'.

A number of principles are set out and include:

- Proposals should assist ways of working which best deliver the range and quality of services required in as efficient and effective a way as possible and organised to best meet the needs of patients.
- Proposals should assist the goal of achieving a quality workforce in the right numbers with the right skills and diversity, organized in the right way.
- Proposals should improve the recruitment and retention and morale of the NHS workforce.
- Proposals should seek to improve all aspects of equal opportunity and diversity – especially in the areas of career and training opportunities and working practices that are not easily flexible to family commitments.

After four years of development, *Agenda for Change* (DoH, March 2003a) set out the proposed agreement. Of particular relevance here is Chapter 6 on Career and Pay Progression where a development review process is described and summarized as follows:

- All staff will have annual developmental reviews which will include appraisal, assessment against the *NHS Knowledge and Skills Framework*, (DoH, March 2003b, October 2004) and production of a personal development plan using the Knowledge and Skills Framework (KSF).
- The main purpose of the developmental review will be to look at the way a member of staff is developing with reference to current

delivery of their job, application of knowledge and skills in the workplace and their consequent development needs.

- The primary output of a developmental review will be a personal development plan which links to the need of the job and defines future objectives and learning needs.
- Development will primarily focus on helping staff carry out their job to the highest standard although personal interests and opportunities for career progression will be taken into account.
- Where appropriate, employers should be expected to ensure that all staff have appropriate time to fulfil training and/or development needs related to their current job and to provide appropriate financial and other support. Wherever possible employers will also provide similar encouragement and support for elements of the Personal Development Plan which reflects personal interests or career development.

The above development review will be integral to pay progression through the Gateway System. However this is only feasible if and when the employer has put in place reasonable arrangements to ensure that staff have access to developmental reviews, personal development plans and appropriate support for training and development to meet the applied knowledge and skills required at the gateway concerned. A deadline of October 2006 has been set for implementation.

The NHS Knowledge and Skills Framework (NHS KSF) on which the developmental review is based, is designed to:

- identify the knowledge and skills that individuals need to apply in their post;
- help guide the development of individuals;
- provide a fair and objective framework on which to base review and development for all staff; and
- provide the basis for pay progression in the service.

The NHS KSF has been developed through a partnership approach between management and staff. It is essentially a developmental approach which will also contribute to decisions about pay progression. It is made up of a number of dimensions, 6 core and 24 specific. For example, the 6 core are:

- communication;
- personal and people development;
- health, safety and security;
- service development;

- quality; and
- equality, diversity and rights.

All the 30 dimensions are further elaborated by a series of descriptors indicating levels of knowledge and complexity. The key process is the *developmental review*, defined as an ongoing cycle of review, planning, development and evaluation for staff in the NHS linked to organizational and individual developmental needs. The main purpose of the developmental review is to:

- Review how individuals are applying knowledge and skills to meet the demands of their current post – this would take place between the individual and their line manager.
- Review the developmental needs of the individual members of staff and ensure the production of a PDP which identifies the individual's learning needs, short- and long-term goals and join planning as to how these goals will be met.
- Evaluation of the learning and development that has taken place and the application of this learning and development.

The BPS's joint Amicus/Family of Psychology KSF working group produced detailed guidance on the implementation of the KSF for applied psychology in June 2005, including recommendations for post outlines. The working group's guidance, along with a detailed description of the KSF and its implications for applied psychologists is provided in Chapter 11.

Summary

Agenda for Change contributes to the further development of the process and procedures of CPD and lifelong learning. Crucially it adds the incentive of linking CPD to career and pay progression. Of particular importance it reflects a commitment from both staff and management sides to the earlier principles outlined above.

The Health Professions Council

The Health Professions Council (HPC) replaces previous regulatory bodies established by the Professions Supplementary to Medicine Act 1960.

This new body was introduced in *The NHS Plan* (DoH, July 2000) as part of the government's modernization of professional regulation. It aims to reform structure and function by:

- giving wider powers to deal effectively with individuals who pose unacceptable risks to patients;
- creating a smaller Council comprising directly elected practitioners and a strong lay input with strategic responsibility for setting and monitoring standards of professional training, performance and conduct;
- linking registration with evidence of continuing professional development;
- providing stronger protection of professional titles; and
- enabling the registration to new groups.

The Health Professions Order 2001 (DoH, April 2001) established four committees of the HPC namely; the Investigating Committee, the Conduct and Competence Committee, the Education and Training Committee and the Health Committee. The Education Committee has the role of ensuring that registrants have the education and training needed to do their job safely. Among other things they advise the HPC Council on Standards of Proficiency (HPC, July 2003) and admissions requirements.

In the HPC Annual Report of 2003 (HPC, 2003), the chief executive and registrar describe some of the work of the past year including development of Standards of Proficiency for the current 12 registered professions. The chief executive states that 'these are a set of standards which health professionals in the UK must prove that they are keeping to so that they can use a protected title.' He goes on to say 'We have recommended to the Secretary of State that we should regulate operating department practitioners and applied psychologists.'

Of particular relevance is the plan to link re-registration with CPD. Currently once a professional is on the HPC register she/he does not have to do any further post-registration education or training, as long as she/he continues to meet the Council's Standards of Proficiency (HPC, July 2003).

The HPC defines CPD as learning that develops knowledge and skills beyond the minimum required to have in order to register. Its focus is on the *outcome* of registrants' CPD activity. During the public consultation in 2000 there was strong support for linking CPD to re-registration with some reservations regarding the practicalities. The HPC in consultation with, among others, the Allied Health Professions

Forum, is developing proposals for linking CPD to re-registration with a possible implementation date of 2006 (HPC, April 2003b). In September 2004 The HPC published a consultation paper (HPC September 2004) seeking views on proposals for statutory rules and standards for CPD with the aim of submitting them to the Privy Council for parliamentary approval in 2005.

The Council has already decided some key requirements for its plans for CPD:

- no monitoring of registrants' compliance based simply on the number of hours undertaken each year;
- links to national standards of proficiency;
- taking account of the work of others, such as the Allied Health Professions Forum which is currently undertaking a project on demonstrating competence through CPD;
- taking account of the needs of part-time and self-employed registrants; and
- requiring individual registrants to commit themselves to CPD.

The basis of the HPC's proposed CPD scheme will be that registrants will make a self-declaration of their compliance when they renew their registration. The HPC additionally proposes to audit a random sample of 2.5 per cent of registrants' CPD records from each registered group.

With the commitment of the British Psychological Society (BPS, March 2002) to seek statutory regulation and the support of the Health Professions Council confirmed in the HPC Annual Report outlined above, the developments with regard to CPD are particularly relevant. It was expected that registration of applied psychologists within the HPC would occur within 2005 or early 2006. However the Society in its response (BPS, June 2005) to the HPC consultation exercise DoH (2005) has rejected the current proposal for statutory regulation by the HPC.

Developing a Shared Framework for CPD

The language and terminology of CPD and lifelong learning has often been unclear and capable of misinterpretation. The Department of Health has awarded a contract to a partnership headed by the University of Salford: *Developing a Shared Framework for all Health Professional*

Learning Beyond Registration (DoH, July 2003). Due to report towards the end of 2004, key outcomes are:

- common definitions, terminology and understanding of the application of CPD and post-registration learning, across all professions;
- the identification of a shared credit framework that will enable all relevant learning to be valued, recognized and transferable;
- a shared approach, including agreed standards and processes, for quality assurance and evaluation of new and existing education and development; and
- recommendations about the structures and systems needed for implementing, evaluating and developing the framework.

Conclusions

This chapter has traced the development of government interest and policy over the past seven years in relation to CPD within the NHS. This has developed from broad statements of intent and principle to much more detailed specification of the nature, content and process of continuing professional development. This has included the responsibilities of individuals and employers to address CPD needs to ensure safe and high quality services to patients and enable staff to develop their careers both in the individual and service interest.

Starting with the early vision set out in *The New NHS: Modern Dependable* (DoH, October 1997) and *A First Class Service: Quality in the New NHS* (DoH, July 1998), the chapter reviewed the early development of policy and guidance, for example, *Continuing Professional Development: Quality in the New NHS* (DoH, July 1999). The cornerstone of government policy *The NHS Plan* (DoH, July 2000) and its relevance to CPD was then reviewed along with consequent implementation guidance, for example, *Meeting the Challenge: A Strategy for the Allied Health Professions* (DoH, November 2000) and *Working Together, Learning Together: A Framework for Lifelong Learning in the NHS* (DoH, November 2001). The relevance of and influence on CPD of major DoH initiatives such as the Workforce Development Confederations, *Agenda for Change*, Knowledge and Skills Framework and the Health Professions Council were addressed in some detail, the chapter concluding with reference to work in progress, namely developing a shared framework for CPD.

Subsequent chapters will address in detail the implications for and impact of the above policy and guidance initiatives on NHS staff in general and the clinical psychology profession in particular.

REFERENCES

Audit Commission (2001). *Hidden Talents: Education, Training and Development for Healthcare Staff in NHS Trusts*. 2002-07-17, London.

British Psychological Society (July 1998). *Future NHS Staffing Requirements: Request for Written Evidence*. Evidence of the British Psychological Society.

British Psychological Society (June 2000). *A Health Service of all the Talents: Developing the NHS Workforce*. Response of the British Psychological Society.

British Psychological Society (March 2002). *Minutes of the Annual General Meeting of the British Psychological Society*. BPS, Leicester.

British Psychological Society (June 2005). *Response of the British Psychological Society to 'Applied Psychology: Enhancing Public Protection: Proposals for the Statutory Regulation of Applied Psychologists'*. BPS, Leicester.

Department for Education (1998). *The Learning Age; A Renaissance for a New Britain*.

Department of Health (October 1997). *The New NHS: Modern, Dependable*. HSC 1998/167. Department of Health, London.

Department of Health (March 1998). *A Review of Continuing Professional Development in General Practice*. A Report of the Chief Medical Officer. Department of Health, London.

Department of Health (July 1998). *A First Class Service: Quality in the New NHS*. HSC 1998/113. Department of Health, London.

Department of Health. (September 1998). *Working Together: Securing a Quality Workforce for the NHS*. HSC 1998/162. Department of Health, London.

Department of Health (March 1999). *Clinical Governance in the New NHS*. HSC 1999/065. Department of Health, London.

Department of Health (May 1999). *Modernising Health and Social Services: Developing the Workforce*. Department of Health, London.

Department of Health (June 1999). *Department of Health Future Staffing Requirements*: The Government's Response to the Health Committee's Report on Future Staffing Requirements. Department of Health, London.

Department of Health (July 1999). *Continuing Professional Development: Quality in the New NHS*. Department of Health, London.

Department of Health (October 1999). *Agenda for Change: Joint Framework of Principles and Agreed Statement on the Way Forward*. (HSC 1999/035), (HSC 1999/227). Department of Health, London.

Department of Health (April 2000). *A Health Service of all the Talents: Developing the NHS Workforce*. Consultation Document on the Review of Workforce Planning. Department of Health, London.

Department of Health (July 2000). *The NHS Plan: A Plan for Investment; A Plan for Reform*. Department of Health, London.

Department of Health (November 2000). *Meeting the Challenge: A Strategy for the Allied Health Professions*. Department of Health, London.

Department of Health (January 2001). *The NHS Plan: Implementing the Performance Improvement Agenda. A Policy Statement and Consultation Document*. Department of Health, London.

Department of Health (February 2001a). *Investment and Reform for NHS Staff: Taking Forward the NHS Plan*. Department of Health, London.

Department of Health (February 2001b). *A Health Service of all the Talents: Developing the NHS Workforce. Results of Consultation*. Department of Health, London.

Department of Health (April 2001). *Establishing the New Health Professions Council*. Department of Health, London.

Department of Health (July 2001a). *Learning From Bristol: The Report of the Public Enquiry into Children's Heart Surgery at the Bristol Royal Infirmary. 1984–1995*. Department of Health, London.

Department of Health (July 2001b). *Shifting the Balance of Power within the NHS: Securing Delivery*. Department of Health, London.

Department of Health (November 2001). *Working Together, Learning Together: A Framework for Lifelong Learning in the NHS*. Department of Health, London.

Department of Health (January 2002). *Shifting the Balance of Power: The Next Steps*. Department of Health, London.

Department of Health (April 2002). *Workforce Development Confederations*. Department of Health, London.

Department of Health (July 2002a). *Shifting the Balance of Power: Delivering the NHS Plan*. Department of Health, London.

Department of Health (July 2002b). *Funding Learning and Development for the Healthcare Workforce*: Consultation on the Review of NHS Education and Training Funding and the Review of Contract Benchmarking for NHS Funded Education and Training. Department of Health, London.

Department of Health (November 2002a). *Improving Working Lives for the Allied Health Professions and Healthcare Scientists*. Department of Health, London.

Department of Health (November 2002b). *Agenda for Change: A Modernised Pay System*; Letter to all NHS Chief Executives and HR Directors. Department of Health, London.

Department of Health (February 2003). *Funding Learning and Development for the Healthcare Workforce*: Summarised Responses on the Consultation of Funding Learning and Development for the Healthcare Workforce. Department of Health, London.

Department of Health (March 2003a). *Agenda for Change: Proposed Agreement*. Department of Health, London.

Department of Health (March 2003b). *The NHS Knowledge and Skill Framework and Related Development Review: Working Draft*. Department of Health, London.

Department of Health (July 2003). *Developing a Shared Framework for all Health Professional Learning Beyond Registration*. Department of Health, London.

Department of Health (August 2003). *The NHS Plan: System Reform*. Department of Health, London.

Department of Health (July 2004). *Organising and Delivering Psychological Therapies*. Department of Health, London.

Department of Health (August 2004). *The Ten Essential Shared Capabilities. A Framework for the Whole of the Mental Health Workforce*. Department of Health, London.

Department of Health (October 2004). *The NHS Knowledge and Skills Framework (NHS KSF) and the Development Review Process (October 2004)*. Department of Health, London.

Department of Health (2005). *Enhancing Public Protection: Proposals for the Statutory Regulation of Applied Psychologists*. Department of Health, London.

Golding, L. (2003). *Clinical Psychology Continuing Professional Development Project: Final Project Report*. Greater Manchester Strategic Health Authority.

Health Professions Council (2003). *Annual Report of the Health Professions Council*.

Health Professions Council (April 2003a). *An Introduction to the Education and Training Committee 021/ET/A5*.

Health Professions Council (April 2003b). *Continuing Professional Development*. 031/TR/A5.

Health Professions Council (June 2003). *Healthcare and Associated Health Professions*. The Health Professions Order 2001 (Consequential Amendments) Order 2003. SI 2003 No. 1590.

Health Professions Council (July 2003). *Standards of Proficiency, Clinical Scientists*, 037/SOP/CS/A5.

Health Professions Council (September 2004). *Continuing Professional Development: Consultation Paper*. Health Professions Council.

House of Commons Health Select Committee (February 1999). *Developing the NHS Workforce*.

Manufacturing, Science, Finance (June 2000). *A Health Service of all the Talents: Developing the NHS Workforce*. A response from MSF.

Manufacturing, Science Finance (August 2000). *The NHS Plan for England: An Initial MSF Response*.

National Audit Office (February 2001). *Educating and Training the Future Health Professional Workforce for England*.

NHS Executive (October 2000). *Human Resources Performance Framework* HSC 2000/030.

Pearson, M. (July 2002). *Developing a Shared Framework for Health Professional Training Beyond Registration*. Department of Health, London.

The North West Clinical Psychology Continuing Professional Development Scheme – http://www.gmsha.nhs.uk/core/psychology/

Chapter 4

A Practical Guide to Meeting CPD Needs

Gundi Kiemle (with special contributions by *Ian Gray, Polly Kaiser, Laura Golding* and *Carol Collins*)

Introduction and Acknowledgements

This chapter aims to provide practical ideas regarding how best to identify, meet, monitor and organize CPD needs and activities, whether for ourselves or for others. It is intended to be a 'hands-on', rather than an evidence-based, referenced guide. Where appropriate, the national and professional context relating to the main sections will be briefly outlined for clarification.

The suggestions proposed are based on personal and colleagues' practical experience as NHS clinicians, as well as guidance from the BPS Division of Clinical Psychology. Some of the ideas and issues in this chapter on how best to meet CPD needs within clinical psychology services are based on two workshops held in the North West of England in early 2004 ('Meeting Continuing Professional Development Needs in Psychology Services': Workshops organized by the North West Clinical Psychology CPD Scheme, 29.1.04 Preston and 10.2.04 Warrington). Approximately 50 clinical psychologists attended these workshops. They came from a range of specialisms and services and varied considerably in clinical and managerial experience. Their thoughts and ideas have – with their permission – provided a valuable contribution to the section on CPD needs identification.

In addition, this chapter is informed by a number of recent surveys of clinical psychologists and clinical psychology service managers, which were undertaken in the North West (Golding, 2003a, b) and nationally (Gray, 2004) in relation to CPD activities, and CPD funding and allocation.

The help and support of all these contributors is gratefully acknowledged.

Chapter Plan

Starting with a brief overview of CPD in the national context, the chapter looks at key stages in the CPD process. Practical guidance on the process of analysing CPD needs is presented with examples. This is followed by a more detailed look at meeting CPD needs including issues of funding and addressing CPD needs where funding might not be available and/or needed. The chapter concludes with a discussion of future directions in CPD and offers practical guidance in organizing CPD events.

CPD in the NHS: The National Context

The government is focusing on a strategic approach to post-qualification learning and development to deliver a modernized NHS (see various reports by the Department of Health (DoH) 1997, 1998, 2001). CPD is defined as a process of lifelong learning for all individuals and teams, which meets the needs of patients and delivers the health outcomes and healthcare priorities of the NHS. Professionals are encouraged to expand and fulfil their potential, supported in the principle that lifelong learning should be designed to meet service needs as well as individual needs and aspirations. At the core of these developments is patient-focused care/services which is the driving force behind the modernization agenda. This has been addressed, among other things, via the National Service Frameworks (DoH, 1999a). The aim is to encourage integrated service and workforce development based on the needs of patients, rather than on the needs of separate professional groupings.

Therefore, a whole-systems approach and multiprofessional learning is required, which in turn necessitates appropriate workforce planning and has issues for workforce development (see for example, DoH 2001a, 2001b).

The workforce issues to meet the needs of patients, as outlined in the NSFs, are drawn together in the Local Delivery Plans (LDPs), which outline the service priorities for a particular health community. In order for CPD needs to be met by an individual's employers, they must be linked to service delivery plans. The Personal Development Plan (PDP) thus needs to look at a clinical psychologist's development needs and CPD goals in the overall context of the needs of the service.

Identifying CPD Needs: British Psychological Society (BPS)/Division of Clinical Psychology (DCP) Guidance

The British Psychological Society's (2000) guidelines on continuing professional development aim to provide broad, enabling guidance that will facilitate the CPD of all qualified clinical psychologists, whatever their current career stage or specialist interest might be. The start of this process is linked to the identification of CPD needs (our own, and those of colleagues whom we manage, supervise or mentor), which aims to highlight those areas of work that would benefit from professional development (BPS CPD Logbook, 2001, 2004). As clinical psychologists, we apply a range of skills and knowledge across diverse client groups (individuals, systems, and organizations). New developments and an adherence to evidence-based practice require us to extend our repertoire of therapeutic skills and increase our knowledge of underpinning theoretical frameworks, while existing areas of practice also need to be developed and updated.

As with any developmental activity, the process of identification, action, reflection and implementation must be structured in a meaningful way (see Figure 4.1). Evaluation and reflective practice are particularly important elements in this cyclical process.

Recent BPS guidance (2001, 2004) emphasizes the link between actual practice and the CPD needs identified. Thus, we can begin the process of identifying CPD needs by thinking about:

- the services we are currently delivering;
- the likely demands for new services in the near future;
- the key areas of these services that require development;
- the local, regional and national priority objectives for these key areas; and
- the expected outcomes and benefits (to the individual, service, service user, employer, and relevant others).

The BPS guidelines on CPD (2002) remind us that CPD can encompass a broad range of activities, both formal and informal. The majority of psychologists are already undertaking many recognized CPD activities as a normal part of their professional life. The nature and balance of these will vary at different stages of a psychologist's career and practice, depending on the particular CPD needs at the time in relation to one's role, job description, and service needs. For example, few clinical psychologists will undertake management and leadership training

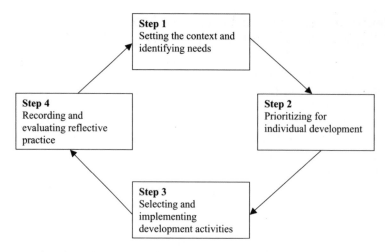

Source: Taken from the Division of Clinical Psychology (2001)
Figure 4.1   Cyclical four-step model of CPD

when newly qualified, but skills training in relation to these areas has consistently been identified as a CPD need among more experienced clinical psychologists in the North West of England, particularly in preparation for B/consultant grade posts. There is national recognition of this within the profession, as evidenced at the BPS/DCP/NIMHE Birmingham conference in February 2005. The North West Clinical Psychology CPD Scheme has responded to this identified need by planning the delivery in 2006 of a regional 'Aspiring Bs/Consultants' programme which will include generic as well as uniprofessional and specialist elements, mapping directly on to the NHS Knowledge and Skills Framework.

Clinical Psychologists and CPD: Needs Identification in Practice

A number of different methods can be employed to aid the process of identifying CPD needs, such as informal discussion with colleagues, or in a more formal relationship, with one's professional line manager, clinical supervisor, or mentor. Often these discussions will arise in the context of current clinical or professional activity, although the identification of CPD needs should also occur as part of an – usually annual – appraisal.

The Division of Clinical Psychology Guidelines for conducting appraisals (DCP, 2001) includes practical tips to aid the identification of development needs. They have been piloted and found to be effective by the North West Clinical Psychology CPD Scheme. However, each NHS Trust may have its own appraisal system in place; appraisal and personal development guidelines and templates (for appraisers and appraisees) are usually available from human resources departments, in most cases on the organization's intranet. An appraisal should cover the following points in a balanced way:

- reviews of previous performance;
- assessment of the appraisee's aspirations;
- identification of the goals for the job over the next year;
- identification of a plan for professional development which affects training needs that are required to help the appraisee to do the job effectively, and will also meet some of their personal professional development needs; and
- identification of a longer-term career plan (if appropriate).

A survey of 30 service managers (response rate 66 per cent) in the North West of England by Golding (2003a) found that the most common way CPD needs for services were identified was through a system of individual appraisal. This method was cited by 26 respondents. Additional methods included team 'away days' (2 respondents), directorate strategic objectives (2 respondents), consultation with general manager/head of service (4 respondents), and supervision (5 respondents).

Specific Ways of Identifying CPD Needs at Individual and Service Level

As part of the preparations for appraisal, CPD needs can be identified in a number of different ways. All too often, we are of course aware of our *unmet* needs. One commonly used approach to examine our CPD needs within the context of our overall professional practice is to conduct a SWOT analysis: Strengths, Weaknesses, Opportunities and Threats (see Atkinson, 1998, for a description of SWOT analysis in CPD for professionals working in health and social care), or in line with recent changes in terminology, replacing the term 'Weaknesses' with 'Needs', thereby producing a SNOT analysis! The purpose of this is to help identify CPD needs in relation to current performance, anticipated changes within one's role, and long-term career and personal aspirations.

The above-mentioned North West workshops on CPD in psychology services utilized this approach as a way of thinking about a number of questions or themes, including 'What is the range of CPD activities and how do we address these?', 'How is CPD identified and who decides?'(see Tables 4.1 and 4.2 as illustrative examples of this), and also 'The CPD needs and priorities of the individual, service and organization'.

As can be seen from Table 4.1, psychologists felt that there are a number of different strengths. A strong professional identity, along with links to local university departments, and prevailing supervision arrangements were cited as examples. CONTACT refers to the North West England post-qualification training scheme provided for clinical psychologists in their first two years post qualification. As one of the few examples of its kind in the country, this was recognized as a positive asset to the region. Given the excellent CPD provision for newly qualified clinical psychologists, a need was expressed for the continued provision of CPD activities across the post-qualified spectrum, in order to meet requirements at different levels. B/consultant grades particularly felt that there was a lack of suitable training around management and leadership.

The opportunities column speaks for itself, and is expanded upon in this chapter. The one comment to clarify, concerns the role of SIGs (Special Interest Groups). On the one hand, SIGs appear as an opportunity, and on the other hand, as a threat. Workshop participants reported that some special interest groups in the region were meeting regularly, and had been fairly successful at obtaining bids for CPD activities. These included, for example, the Race and Culture SIG, Learning Difficulties SIG and Older Adults SIG (PSIGE). Strong and successful SIGs like these were seen as a strength in terms of providing a collaborative forum in which to meet CPD needs.

However, psychologists also commented on the absence of any active Adult SIGs; even a previously active Primary Care SIG had stopped meeting. Given the predominance of clinical psychologists who work with adults, and the 'dissolution' of such SIGs, this was seen as a possible threat to CPD activities. Other participants commented that as activities in general clinical psychology departments tended to be more orientated towards adult work, perhaps there was not such a perceived need for an Adult SIG. It is interesting to note that it is the SIGs of marginalized and often devalued client groups that seemed to

Table 4.1   SNOT analysis example 'What is the range of CPD activity and how do we address this?'

STRENGTHS	NEEDS
Existing knowledge base and expertise	Clinical: specific therapy skills, providing supervision
Networks	Professional: providing consultation
Links with university training courses and departments	Managerial: progression along A and B scale, management and leadership skills
Supervision (quantity, quality, variety)	Meeting post-qualification needs at different levels
Diversity of roles	
CONTACT scheme	
Audit	
Professional identity	

OPPORTUNITIES	THREATS
'In-house' provision	How valued are we as a profession? – feeling devalued/feeling abused
CPD exchange between Trusts	Pressure of clinical and service needs
CPD audit to determine extent of need	Part-time status and priorities
Shadowing/ joint work	Career routes and specialisms: too limiting/ too soon?
CONTACT and mentor schemes years 1 and 2 post-qualification	Lack of funding
Mentor scheme expansion to include whole career span	Lack of supportive management structures
SIGs	Feelings of professional isolation
University training courses and departments (under-utilized)	Competing with other professionals
Workforce Development Confederations/ Strategic Health Authorities	Agenda for change
	Fragmentation of clinical psychology services
Agenda for Change	Dissolution of SIGs
Increase in numbers being trained	'Lost' posts/money for posts 'evaporated'
	Lower starting levels – realistic

Source: Preston and Warrington CPD Scheme workshops, 2004.

be the strongest (i.e., most successful in terms of active membership and activities).

As some traditional psychology departments with traditional district heads are 'fragmenting' into service directorates, this was also seen as a threat to professional identity and professional structures.

Table 4.2   SNOT analysis example: 'How is CPD identified and who decides?'

STRENGTHS	NEEDS
Knowledgeable profession – able to negotiate CPD needs	Consistent holistic appraisal system Appraisal training for managers
OPPORTUNITIES	**THREATS**
Statutory regulation Registration with HPC Guidance for employers (DCP, Workforce Development Confederation) Management structure	Management versus professional roles: role conflict? Management structure

Source: Preston and Warrington CPD Scheme workshops, 2004.

Table 4.2 describes the themes that emerged from looking at a different question, namely: 'How is CPD identified, and who decides what and how it is identified?' On the one hand, participants felt that our main strength related to the fact that we are a knowledgeable profession and should, therefore, hopefully also have the necessary skills to negotiate what type of CPD activities are needed. It is necessary, however, for this process to take place within a consistent system, one which is seen as equitable and transparent and not one of 'the ones who shout loudest get their needs met'. In order to identify CPD needs that are consistent with patient needs and service needs, it was felt that additional training would be necessary for managers to enable the implementation of personal development plans in a consistent manner.

Opportunities in the form of current drivers for CPD included the profession's possible statutory regulation and registration with the Health Professions Council (HPC), and relevant workforce guidance which would put the onus on employers to provide certain types of CPD, particularly for clinical psychologists with managerial or leadership roles. Management structure was perceived to be an opportunity as well as a threat, largely due to the variations in management arrangements across different services. Those managed by clinical psychologists still considered this an opportunity, while those managed by other professionals saw this as a potential threat. The latter was based on fears that other professionals may not have an adequate understanding of our professional role; the question 'Why do psychologists need so much supervision, when other professionals in similar jobs just get on

with it?' was cited as an example of this. Irrespective of line management arrangements, participants felt that there may still be a potential
role conflict in terms of wanting staff to be competent managers (and
therefore releasing them for appropriate periods of time to fulfil this
function), but also needing them to be available to provide a clinical
service to patients.

SWOT analysis is commonly used by many professions and organizations as part of personal and professional development, and more
specifically it is often used in relation to CPD (see, for example, The
Institute of Administrative Management website for downloadable
information and recording tools, utilizing SWOT analysis in CPD:
www.instam.org, and also www.mindtools.com, which includes downloadable information on a range of occupational skills, including SWOT
analysis which is listed in the Problem Solving section).

The development of a personal development plan can be based on
a SWOT analysis. Its purpose is to assist in formulating a set of development activities covering a period of one year. Long-term career plans
should cover development activities for the next twelve months in the
light of one's intentions over the next three years.

Critical Incident Analysis is used by many healthcare professionals
as an aid to reflection within CPD (see Brocklehurst and Walshe (2000)
for a description of critical incident analysis in relation to clinical governance in the NHS, and also *share-net-Introduction* for a downloadable
selected bibliography on critical incident technique). It is used for both
evaluative and developmental purposes, and refers to the critical reflection (usually in writing) of an action, incident or activity carried out at
some point in the not too distant past, which has left the person feeling
that they could have handled the situation better. Writing a brief
description of the incident, and (alone, or better still with others) reflecting on and identifying the skills, knowledge or attitude change that
may have been needed to deal with the situation better, should result
in a list of CPD objectives. For instance, this might include updating
one's knowledge in relation to a specific clinical area, attending appropriate training to improve presentation skills, or undertaking any other
professional activity which would be considered essential in being able
to deal with the same situation more effectively, should it arise again
in the future.

The use of critical reflection and reflective practice has been a cornerstone of education and training in many professions, particularly
within healthcare (Tate and Sills, 2004). It includes elements such as the
use of professional portfolios, and clinical and reflective learning journals. In recent years, it has also commanded increasing attention within

clinical psychology (see *Clinical Psychology Special Issue July 2003: Reflective Practice*) within pre- and post-qualification training and practice, all of which is relevant to CPD. Lavender (2003), in asking why reflective practice is important, poses the pertinent question: 'What would it be like to be an *un*reflective practitioner and, if you were, what would that mean for your practice, and do you think anybody would want to see you?' Developing one's skills as a reflective practitioner through reflective writing, for instance in a learning journal, has been described by Bolton (2001) as a way of linking together different CPD activities. This process can be greatly enhanced if it is linked to the discussion and sharing of material in groups.

Meeting CPD Needs: BPS/DCP Guidance

Recent BPS/DCP guidance (2001, 2004) on the implementation of CPD activities suggests the following methods:

- trying out new aspects 'on the job' in a small way;
- paired work with a colleague;
- secondment to another situation providing relevant learning experiences;
- joining a working group;
- simulation or role-play activities;
- reading;
- attending courses or workshops;
- delivering courses or workshops to those with less knowledge;
- consulting or working with a colleague who has specialist knowledge;
- research, reading, writing in order to publish distance learning courses; and
- visiting examples of good practice.

The implementation of your CPD plan does not imply that you cannot or should not change it once implementation is under way. Situations and circumstances can change and often do, while new opportunities as well as threats may emerge that could not have been foreseen. Your plan in action should be regularly reviewed, and changes made in the light of recent or forthcoming events, as appropriate. There is appropriate reference in the above BPS/DCP guidance to factors such as cost and time available, as well as psychological considerations such as your own preferred learning style.

CPD Funding for Clinical Psychology: The Strategic and Organizational Context

Funding Learning and Development for the Healthcare Workforce (DoH, 2002) considers how the NHS should use its £3 billion annual budget for learning and personal development to support better the development of staff, and to deliver the necessary skills to support patient-centred services and public health strategies. It is essential that the planning for education commissioning and service planning be closely integrated. This is especially the case for specialized services and specialized education, and small and/or specialist groups such as clinical psychologists. Commissioning post-qualification learning/CPD for such groups raises a very complex set of issues, including the definition of 'small' for professional groups, and the importance of flexibility – a model suitable for one group may not be appropriate for another (WDC CPD Network, 2004). Funding arrangements for CPD seem to vary from one strategic health authority (SHA) to another. For example, in the North West, the Cumbria and Lancashire SHA's allocation of CPD monies for smaller professions is currently dealt with in a number of ways. Each Workforce Development Group (WDG) is allocated a budget to spend on its priorities, and some smaller professions have benefited from this. The WDGs are client-group related, for example Children, Mental Health, Learning Disability, Older Persons, Long-term Conditions. Each Health Economy also has a budget to support LDP delivery, and this has benefited some of the smaller professions on a local basis. Elsewhere in the country for instance, Durham and Tees Valley SHA allocates monies to contracts with Higher Education Institutions for CPD provision, top-slice funding for patch-wide projects, and allocate any residual funding to Trusts and PCTs for local priorities.

The key issues that influence the success or otherwise of implementing post-qualification learning/CPD commissioning models for 'small' professional groups include: equity of access to learning opportunities, equity of access to funding, formal accreditation of learning, and supporting multidisciplinary learning.

At the level of individual Trusts or PCTs, CPD funding is often agreed by Human Resources/Education and Training departments, based on information contained in personal development plans. It is important that accurate PDPs are carried out and fed back through the appropriate channels for these to be collated. Therefore it is crucial that psychologists have an appropriate understanding of and possible training in putting together effective PDPs. While senior psychologists may carry these out for junior members of staff, it is not always apparent who would conduct these for the more senior members of the profession – and in some cases, this may not be a clinical psychologist (see Table 4.2 – Threats).

CPD Funding and Allocation: The Views of Clinical Psychologists and Service Managers

A survey by Golding (2003b) of half the qualified clinical psychologists in North West England (224 respondents, 49.7 per cent response rate) examined in more detail the CPD needs of this group. Respondents ranged in age from 26 to 64 years (mean age 40 years). Consistent with the gender split in the profession nationally was a high proportion of female respondents (71.3 per cent). The majority (86.4 per cent) were BPS members, and 65 per cent also belonged to the DCP. In addition, 59.7 per cent also stated that they were Chartered Clinical Psychologists.

Participants were asked to indicate how much money and time had been spent on their CPD activities during 2001. The results showed that a mean of £565 (median = £300) was spent on CPD activity by respondents' employers during 2001 (range = £0–£4,000).

The survey also found that respondents spent half their employers' CPD contribution again, by paying a mean of £287 (median = £200) of their own money to fund CPD activity during 2001 (range = £0–£2,000). Over the same period of time (2001), respondents spent an average of nine days of their work time (median = 6), and additionally an average of 8 days (median = 5) of their own time, on CPD activity.

The North West CPD workshops referred to above discussed the issue of meeting CPD needs directly in relation to funding and resources, and finding creative solutions to CPD. Strengths and opportunities listed included the profession's strong organizational structure, statutory registration, Agenda For Change, and income generation. On the other hand, our needs concerned the identification of what could be considered a reasonable level of CPD, to develop service links and identify CPD protocols from other areas (thus sharing good practice), and to develop skills to negotiate CPD and training strategies.

The issue of resources (time and money) is at the heart of many of the questions that relate to CPD. In addition to the clinical psychology service managers survey by Golding (2003a) cited above, two further surveys have examined issues in relation to CPD funding in more depth. The first of these, a recent electronic national survey via the DCP Managers Faculty (Gray, 2004) produced detailed responses from 25 clinical psychology managers (approximately 20 per cent response rate). The questions and results are produced in Table 4.3 below.

Gray's (2004) national survey of clinical psychology managers must be interpreted with caution due to the small number of respondents. With this limitation in mind, however, we can see that approximately half the managers who replied were managing a CPD budget, averaging approximately £10,000 per annum or £344 per whole-time equivalent (wte) member of staff. These services ranged in size from 1.8 to 100 or more staff, averaging 30 wte staff. By contrast, services where managers did not have their own departmental CPD budget, on average only about half (£5,000) the annual funding for CPD was accessed, resulting in a CPD allowance of only £150 per annum, per wte. A realistic CPD allocation would appear to be around £850 per wte member of staff.

It is interesting to note that the majority of services employed a range of applied psychologists, and only in 9 of the 25 services were clinical psychologists the only health professional in the service.

In Clinical Psychology services where managers did not have their own CPD budget, all respondents managed to access monies via central Trust funds, but Workforce Development Confederations/Strategic Health Authorities were also emerging as potentially fruitful sources of additional CPD funding. Personal development plans allied to service needs appeared to be the main principle underlying the allocation of CPD monies in these services.

Almost all services could retain earned income for CPD purposes, although some managers expressed doubts as to whether income generation was an appropriate activity. Two respondents commented that although they could retain generated income, they felt that income generation should not be a departmental activity.

In line with BPS/DCP recommendations that minimum requirements for CPD should be the same for part-time and full-time staff, the survey found that in the main, part-time staff had equal access to CPD monies. However, several respondents commented on a need for guidance on this issue.

In conclusion, the accountability arrangements for CPD budgets and completed CPD activities were extremely varied, although the most frequent line of accountability was with respondents' employing Trust. The range of responses illustrates the variation in individual accountability arrangements, in line with local or regional policy,

Table 4.3 DCP Managers Faculty CPD Funding Survey

1   *Do you manage a CPD budget?*

Yes   12
No   13

One or two respondents managed tiny CPD budgets relying on central Trust funds and/or income generation to make up the rest.

2   *If yes, how much per annum?*

Range   £300 to £45,000
Mean   £9,794

Using whole-time equivalent (wte) figures below:

Range   £83 to £1,639 per wte member of staff per annum
Mean   £344 per wte member of staff per annum.

3   *What are wte staff numbers for whom you have CPD responsibilities?*

Yes to CPD Budget

  Range   2.2 to 100
  Mean   30.3

No to CPD Budget

  Range   1.8 to 100
  Mean   29.9

4   *What professions make up the staff for whom you have CPD responsibilities?*

Clinical Psychologists featured in all	25 Services
Assistants in	13 Services
Counselling Psychologists in	13 Services
Nurse Therapists in	8 Services
Psychotherapists in	5 Services
Counsellors in	4 Services
Health Psychologists in	2 Services
Forensic Psychologists in	3 Services
Admin/Office staff in	3 Services
Primary Care Mental Health Workers in	1 Service
Dietician in	1 Service

5   *If No, how do you access CPD money?*

Of the 12 *No* CPD budget responses:

Central Trust Funds	12 Services
Workforce Development Confederation/SHA	5 Services

Continued

Table 4.3 *Continued*

Income generation including legal work	3 Services
Department underspends including vacancies	3 Services
Charities	1 Service
Home Office	1 Service
Locality Team Manager	1 Service

6 *If No, how much did you access last year?*

Range	£500 to £15,000
Mean	£4,857
Mean	£130 per wte member of staff

Three services reported that they had no CPD budget but accessed Trust budget to an unspecified but adequate level.

7 *Can you retain monies that you 'earn' (e.g. through teaching) for CPD activities?*

Yes	22
No	2
Don't know	1

8 *What principles underpin the allocation of monies to CPD activity?*
   (E.g., equal amount to each member of staff? As per CPD needs based on PDP?
   Other?)

Personal Development Plan	17 Services
Trust Policy/Service Need/Business Plan	10 Services
Equal allocation	2 Services
DCP policy	2 Services
No control	2 Services
Equal Opportunities Policy	1 Service

9 *How do allocate monies with regard to full time v part time staff?*

Treated no differently	13 Services
Pro rata basis	3 Services
Personal development plan	3 Services
Trust protocol	1 Service
Equal opportunity policy	1 Service
Discussion	1 Service

10 *What do you feel would be a realistic allocation of monies per whole-time*
    equivalent member of staff for you service?

Range	£200 to £3,000
Mean	£870
Majority response	£500 to £1,000

Continued

Table 4.3 *Continued*

---

11 Who are you accountable to regarding your CPD budget?

Trust Director	8 Services
WDC/SHA	3 Services
Trust Training Committee	2 Services
Training Manager	1 Service
Locality Manager	1 Service
No-one	1 Service
Business Manager	1 Service

12 Who are you accountable to regarding completed staff CPD activities?

Trust Director	4 Services
No-one	4 Services
Line Manager	2 Service
Self	2 Services
Trust Training Committee	2 Services
Line Manager	2 Services
HR	1 Service
Medical Director	1 Service
WDC/SHA	1 Service
Locality Manager	1 Service
Governance Committee	1 Service
Appraiser	1 Service
Executive Team	1 Service

Source: Gray (2004).

and it makes it difficult therefore to generalize to the majority of services.

Finally, in Golding's (2003a) survey of clinical psychology managers, the size and type of service managed by respondents ranged from one psychologist working alone in a specialist area, to more than 100 staff, including non-psychologists, across a range of specialties. One-third of the 30 respondents managed services of between 40 and 100 staff.

In response to questions about how CPD funding operated in their services, almost half (14) stated that limited funding was available. Six respondents referred to funds being allocated for CPD resources. Two noted that no CPD requests had been refused/or rarely refused, and a further two stated that appropriate bids made were usually funded or part funded. One person remarked that resources were limited and available on a competitive basis, and another stated that there was no money available to fund CPD activity in their service. Three respondents stated that the funding situation for CPD activity was currently uncertain due to the organizational changes that took place within the NHS in April 2002.

Meeting CPD Needs at No Cost or Low Cost

There are possibilities for obtaining 'free' CPD – by which we usually mean free of charge, although there is of course always a cost in terms of time, and the 'service' cost to the employer if the 'free' CPD activity is carried out within work time, at the expense of another (service-related) activity. Nevertheless, there is a range of professional development activities, which can be undertaken at little or no cost, as listed in Table 4.4. Some of these activities rely on a quid pro quo system (e.g., peer supervision, supervisor training), while others may not require any reciprocal participation (e.g., listening to 'public' lectures or presentations). In the North West, the three doctoral clinical psychology training courses have promoted positive pre- and post-qualification links in relation to CPD in a number of different ways, for example via free supervisor training and workshops, and by ensuring that the regional CPD Scheme Tutor for each of the three SHA areas (Greater Manchester, Cheshire & Mersey, Cumbria & Lancashire) attends and contributes to the relevant Clinical Psychology training course stakeholder/executive committee (Manchester, Liverpool and Lancaster D.Clin.Psy. courses respectively). Many clinical psychologists have also identified a need for management and leadership training. Some of this could be gained indirectly (i.e., experientially) by joining one or more local, regional or national committees which have a management or leadership function, as one's participation in, and observation of, the structure and work of such a committee could definitely be described as 'on the job' training. Finally, although one has to adopt a critical stance, the Internet is a great source of free CPD (apart from the cost of one's internet connection). A simple search on CPD and related terms will yield a lot of useful websites, many of whom will offer free, downloadable resources. For example, www.parn.org.uk, the Professional Associations Research Network, includes a substantial amount of information on CPD, as does Training ZONE, the Institute of Continuing Professional Development, at www.trainingzone.co.uk.

Table 4.4 lists other suggestions for 'free' CPD, and it might be helpful for every clinical psychology service to have such a list (with specific details attached), prominently displayed on a notice board or in a meeting room, alongside notices of forthcoming courses and conferences. This way, a positive emphasis and culture of CPD within

Table 4.4 Meeting your CPD needs for free

CPD provided by your local NHS Trust or Higher Education Institutions:

- Find out about free 'in-house' training events being organized by your Trust's training department.
- Visit your Trust or local university library regularly and read the most recent journals in your area of work.
- Find out about clinical or research presentations at your local post-graduate/medical education centre – these are usually held during a weekday lunchtime, or early evenings. Presentations tend to be organized by medical staff, but selected topics are often useful and relevant to clinical psychology. Ask to be put on the mailing list, if the programme cannot easily be accessed electronically.
- Ask if you can attend any relevant departmental lectures/presentations/ seminars organized by your local university psychology or psychiatry departments (especially post-graduate clinical and research presentations). Ask if your department can be put on the mailing list, if the programme cannot easily be accessed electronically.
- Contact the module co-ordinators for a contents list of relevant teaching modules on your local Doctorate in Clinical Psychology training course. In return for attending some of the teaching sessions, you could offer to provide systematic peer observation and feedback to the lecturer/course (all HEIs will soon be required to institute this).
- Many Clinical Psychology Doctoral Training Courses offer free training and workshops for clinical supervisors, with programmes tailored to new as well as more experienced supervisors.

CPD to improve clinical and other professional competencies:

- Join a peer supervision group (or set one up, if there isn't one).
- Set up a case discussion group in your workplace.
- Set up a journal club in your workplace.
- Arrange to shadow a more experienced colleague who works in your specialty for a day.
- Agree to do some co-working with a colleague (e.g. couple/family systemic work with a co-therapist).
- Visit a neighbouring example of good practice related to your field of work.
- Supervise trainees (they always have access to the most up to date information in your specialty).
- Improve your supervisory skills by taking up free supervisor training (usually organized by your local clinical psychology training course).
- Identify a colleague whose work you admire and is more experienced than you. Ask them to be your mentor!

Continued

Table 4.4 *Continued*

- Explore multiprofessional working together and learning together, as much as possible.
- Find out about any local or regional clinical research groups in your area. They usually meet on a regular basis to report on research in progress, or completed research projects which may be relevant to you clinically and for networking.
- Update yourself on clinical issues by attending a local Special Interest Group or Faculty meeting.
- Update yourself on professional issues by attending a local Division of Clinical Psychology meeting.

CPD via committee involvement:

- Join a conference organizing committee – in return for organizing some aspects of the conference, you'll be able to attend for free.
- Join your local Special Interest Group, or one of the national Faculty executive committees. Any CPD activities organized by SIGs/Faculties are usually free for the organizers, and expenses are usually met for committee officers.
- Join your local Division of Clinical Psychology (DCP), or one of the national DCP committees. Any expenses associated with such work are usually met by the DCP.
- Increase your practical and critical research skills by joining your Local Research Ethics Committee, or the Trust's Research Governance committees, when vacancies come up.
- Improve your leadership and management skills by joining a relevant committee within your Trust as the clinical psychology representative (e.g., Clinical Governance Committee, Improving Working Lives Committee).

Reciprocal benefits:

- Organize a CPD event within your own service, and utilize the income generated to support further CPD.
- Arrange reciprocal arrangements with other local services – e.g., seminars, lectures, case discussions, supervision, consultation, etc.
- When asked to teach or provide training on courses or workshops, or when presenting at conferences, ask if you can stay for the rest of the day to listen to other people's presentations.
- Write a book review: you get to keep the book, and it counts as part of your publications.
- Any teaching/supervision/assessment of trainees, assistants or qualified staff (including non-psychologists) should result in you gaining from the preparation and the process as much as you are putting into it.

Continued

Table 4.4   *Continued*

Regional opportunities:

- Find out about your Strategic Health Authority's Education and Train-ing/CPD priorities (much of this information should be available on their website). Your clinical or professional skills maybe useful for certain SHA supported projects, or strategic committees/subgroups which have clinical psychology representation.
- Find out about any free Strategic Health Authority funded training events. These often fit around national training agendas (e.g., leadership and management training, mentor training).

E-learning:

- Visit relevant websites at least once a week to keep up to date with professional developments (e.g., Department of Health, the BPS).
- Take part in e-discussions within your specialty via SIG discussion groups etc.
- Find out about your Trust's/your SHA's e-learning strategy, and the (free) CPD opportunities this entails.
- Search for 'Continuing Professional Development' and look for free downloadable resources and forthcoming events

the service may help to improve recruitment and retention, particularly in hard-to-recruit areas.

Future Directions in CPD Provision

Two recent national developments require further elaboration in rela-tion to current and future CPD practice, namely the NHS University[1] (NHSU, 2003; www.nhsu.nhs.uk) and the government's e-learning strategy which aims to deliver CPD by remote access i.e., by distance learning or e-learning. Usually such learning is accessed through formal partnership links between the NHS as the main employer, and an appropriate higher education institution which could be sited locally, regionally or nationally. The NHSU is working with the SHAs to develop a shared strategy for e-learning across the whole of the NHS. The strategy will embrace e-learning, knowledge management and network technology, and provide local guidance to help bring coher-ence to the many initiatives already underway across the NHS.

The Department for Education and Skills' e-learning strategy (2004) aims to embed e-learning across the education and skills sector. It provides the framework within which the Department and partners will work to utilize the effective use of e-learning to improve the experience of learning. Future investment in technology focuses on three priorities: tailored learning or support for individual citizens, support to front line professionals, to assess and monitor learners – and to develop their own skills, and integrated systems to facilitate the exchange of information and learning materials between institutions and sectors. An example of a national resource particularly useful for clinical psychologists working in mental health is found at http://kc.nimhe.org.uk, the NIMHE online knowledge community which is a shared space where people can exchange knowledge, information and experiences relating to any aspect of mental health.

Across the country, each organization should have a learning strategy in place that includes e-learning with action plans to support organizational development, taking into consideration the increasing choice of delivery media available for learning. A joint national project between the SHAs and the NHSU 'Common Approaches to E-Learning' (2004) includes a number of proposed developments, such as the establishment of a national e-learning strategy, and the creation of a national e-learning database to share details of e-learning projects/activity currently being developed for the NHS. The NHS Leadership Centre (2004) is currently undertaking research among senior NHS stakeholders to find out the leadership development needs of senior staff involved in the implementation of new Information Technology systems, including the National Programme for IT (NPFIT; see www.npfit.nhs.uk).

The development and application of e-learning is obviously at the heart of the NHSU. This 'virtual university' has been set up to develop and improve the skills of the health and social care workforce, thus contributing to the NHS Plan, the modernization of social care, and the nation's Skills Strategy (NHSU, 2003). It aims to improve standards of service for patients, and to give everyone in health and social care the opportunity to learn and develop personally and professionally. Although designed for staff, it endeavours also to involve volunteers, carers, patients and the public. The NHSU intends to create and nurture learning environments and learning cultures that makes learning a central part of everyone's working life. Additionally, it aspires to influence and help develop education and training policy for healthcare, both locally and nationally. Core funding will come from the Department of Health, and learning programmes and services will be charged out to workforce development groups, SHAs and employers, with costs calculated on a 'whole useful life' basis. The NHSU will concentrate on the key priorities set out in major NHS policy statements initially. Longer term, it plans to set up a Learning Needs Observatory to identify learning needs, and a Learning Advisory Committee to advise on the relevance of proposed programmes. It is intended for most learning to take place in the work environment, with a strong emphasis on e-learning, including support online, over the phone, at local resource centres and through the NHSU virtual campus. Objective performance measures focusing on the NHSU's reach, the impact of learning on staff, and the impact of learning on healthcare delivery will complement external benchmarking involving learners, staff, employers and service users.

All clinical psychologists have a minimum of two university degrees, and many have additional degrees (Masters and PhD) acquired either before or after qualifying training. To date, clinical psychology is the only healthcare profession in the NHS requiring a professional doctorate as its vocational qualification. The impact and benefit of the NHSU to the profession as a whole remains to be seen, therefore, as achieving degree-level higher education is obviously not a relevant goal for most psychologists. Furthermore, much of our post-qualification CPD involves the practice and maintenance of existing therapeutic skills, as well as the acquisition of new techniques. It will be challenging to combine the benefits of a virtual learning environment with the challenges inherent in translating what we have learned to everyday 'real' clinical situations. The success of this will depend, at least in part, on the quality of the learning resources, which must enable interactive e-*learning* as opposed to passive e-*reading*.

Monitoring CPD

As Chapters 8 and 9 specifically address issues around recording, monitoring and evaluating CPD activity, this section is very brief in the interests of avoiding unnecessary overlap.

BPS/DCP Guidance

An important aspect of monitoring CPD concerns the use of reflection, which has already been mentioned above in relation to the initial identification of CPD needs. Reflection that takes place after CPD needs have been met will help to identify what has been learned and where relevant, identify how this learning has been used, or will be used (BPS, 2002). Psychologists may therefore wish to consider:

- whether the activity has been successful and has met the desired outcomes;
- how their knowledge, skills and/or understanding has changed;
- whether their perspective or approach has changed in any way;
- how it has helped them to develop in relation to their professional activity;
- what they can do that is different; and
- whether new objectives that have arisen have augmented or replaced the original plan.

The appraisal cycle which begins with (1) *identification* of CPD needs, followed by (2) *prioritizing* for individual development, and (3) selecting and implementing (*meeting*) CPD activities, thus ends with (4) *monitoring*, which includes the processes of recording and evaluating. This last stage will focus on learning outcomes (actual versus intended) and the processes that were necessary for the achievement of such outcomes. It must also include the provision of evidence of accomplishment of identified learning objectives. Finally, no CPD record is complete without the identification of further development needs, and thus the cycle begins again. Some evaluation is necessary after each new development activity has been undertaken.

Participants at the two CPD workshops mentioned above strongly emphasized the need for recording and auditing CPD, within the context of individual performance review (IPR) or appraisal, mandatory CPD and statutory registration, while making the whole monitoring process helpful and meaningful. By monitoring, recording and evaluating our activities on an ongoing basis, we are able to build a cumulative record of our personal and professional development that can form the basis for long-term career progression.

Practical Issues in Organizing CPD Events

It is important to remember that some of our CPD activity relates to the provision of CPD for others. It has already been mentioned that an individual or service involved in organizing a CPD event would usually be able to attend this CPD activity free of charge, and the income generated from such events may be 'recycled' back into the CPD budget to fund further professional development training. There are a number

Table 4.5 Practical suggestions for organizing a CPD event

Planning an event

Once you have decided on the CPD event you are planning, perhaps
consider the following . . .

Budget

Put a 'ceiling limit' on the amount of money available and monitor this as
you go along. Your budget must include the cost of the venue and
catering, speakers' fees and expenses, advertising, administrative costs in
terms of processing applications (secretarial time, paper, photocopying,
postage, telephone), and costs associated with producing delegate packs.

Dates

Try to have options when contacting venues/speakers and give yourself
plenty of time to arrange advertising and speakers.
Check out if there are other events already organized/advertised which may
clash with your date.

Location

Consider the location and travelling time, and possibilities for parking and
public transport. Popular venues are near major motorways, or not too far
from the nearest train station.

The venue

Apart from NHS facilities, you could consider university conference
facilities, local authority training venues, and hotels or even sports and
leisure centres. How accessible is your venue for people with disabilities?
Consider 'delegate packages' for commercial venues which can sometimes
work out cheaper, but you may have to have a guaranteed 'minimum
number'.

Rooms and equipment

Conference rooms come in all shapes and sizes – if possible, pay the venue
a visit to check out facilities and check out the maximum number of
delegates that are permitted.
Are there facilities for people who are hard of hearing (e.g., induction loops),
if required? Are all the rooms and toilets wheelchair accessible?
Do you need one room for the entire event, or additional 'break-out' rooms
for small group work?
The cost of equipment hire such as flipcharts and overhead projectors varies,
and not all venues offer power-point projectors.

Catering

Costs can vary widely. Some conference facilities can serve a simple buffet
lunch within the room, while some hotels can only offer food that is
served in their own restaurant.
Some venues will provide just sandwiches – discuss your requirements and
ask if they will cater to your needs, rather than use their menu.

Continued

Table 4.5 *Continued*

It is better to over cater for vegetarians than carnivores – the latter will always eat food that has been ordered for the former, but it never works the other way round!

Don't forget to include speakers and presenters in your catering requirements.

Speakers

Make provisional enquiries with potential speakers.

How much would they expect to be paid? What about travel, accommodation, and any other expenses?

What are their requirements in terms of equipment on the day for teaching/presenting?

It would be useful to ask them for a copy of their presentation to include in your Delegate Packs.

Registration

Register all delegates as they respond.

A text list for registration is ok – but why not try a simple database (e.g., Access).

This can be added to and altered as your event grows and can be used to generate mailing labels, confirmation letters and name labels for the event.

Make sure your applicants give you the information you require for registration.

Some people may have special needs in order to be able to attend – make sure there is space on the registration form for these things to be identified.

A simple letter of 'thanks for registering' seems to suffice, with the promise of further details being sent at a later date.

Delegates

How large is your audience size?

Assess the situation as numbers grow and liaise with your venue if numbers change massively.

Do any delegates have special needs that you need to be aware of?

Provisional bookings

Some hotels and conference venues will 'hold' your provisional booking for a couple of weeks, until you are ready to confirm. This gives you time to make other enquires.

The contract

You may well find yourself with additional delegates on the day, or a number of delegates who do not attend but have failed to cancel. Generally it is better to overestimate than underestimate the amount of seating and/or lunches and refreshments that are actually available.

Confirmation of your booking should be in writing, and although you may not want to think about your event having to be cancelled – it is well worth checking out the cancellation fee!

Continued

Table 4.5 *Continued*

Advertising

Consider the most appropriate ways and means of advertising your event, including any free distribution channels (e.g., attaching your information to other items which are already being distributed through professional networks).

Advertise your event as soon as possible – something eye-catching, but clear. Decide upon your contact person for the event and make this clear on your flyer.

Get artistic with your software!

Delegate packs

These should include a programme, participant list, evaluation form, certificate of attendance and any other relevant information (e.g., information about your organization, advance notice of future training events, leaflets concerning other relevant events or services etc.).

Participants usually appreciate copies of the presentations included in the packs.

And finally . . .

on the day, here are some handy DOs and DON'Ts.

Do visit the hotel/venue (preferably the day before) to make sure the facilities are as expected.

Don't be surprised if not everything is as you wanted it.

Do confirm your arrangements/requirements with the venue prior to the event.

Do arrive early on the day.

Do check the timings for the day with the venue representative upon arrival.

Do check that the electrical equipment is plugged in and working.

Don't wait until delegates begin to arrive before unpacking or setting up.

Don't be surprised if unregistered people attend your event.

Do meet and greet delegates – have delegate packs ready and in order.

Do take supplies of pens, paper, post-its, etc.

---

of practical issues to consider when organizing a CPD event, as suggested in Table 4.5.

It is helpful to prepare a pro forma for your planned event in terms of choosing a venue and speakers. Not only will this organize and structure your planning, but in the event of you having to hand over to another organizer (perhaps unexpectedly and without an opportunity to brief them), they should be able to see at a glance where things are up to. Figures 4.2 and 4.3 are examples of such templates.

SPEAKER FEES – PRO FORMA
(Complete one form per speaker)

CPD Event: Title and Date
Organized by:

Speaker's name:_____

Speaker's address:_____

_____

_____

Telephone:_____

Email:_____

Title of presentation:_____

Duration of presentation:_____

Preferred time slot:_____

Travel:_____miles @   per mile:_____

Other travel costs (train/taxi/tube):_____

Speaker fees:_____

Other expenses:_____

Speaker contacted on (date) _____

by (organizer's name):_____

Further action?_____

Figure 4.2 Speaker cost pro forma

In terms of a programme, to be sent out on application and also to be included in the delegate pack on the day, it is important to remember the essentials such as starting and finishing times, the times and titles of each presentation, and the times of tea/coffee and lunch breaks. The programme should clearly state the title, date, venue and organizers of the event. A good starting point is to find actual programmes of CPD events you have attended, and copy the format of those that seem the most effective.

It is essential to include an evaluation form of your event, as this will help both your delegates and you to reflect on and critically

VENUE COST – PRO FORMA
(Complete one form per venue)

CPD Event: Title and Date
Organized by:

Name of venue:_____

Venue address:_____

_____

Contact person:_____

Telephone:_____

Email:_____

Venue facilities (number and size of rooms):_____

_____

Any comments re. venue location:_____

Is the venue accessible for people with disabilities?_____

Cost of venue:_____

Catering – options:_____

Catering costs per delegate:_____

Additional information: _____

Venue contacted on (date)

_____

by (organizer's name):_____

Further action?_____

Figure 4.3   Venue and catering costs pro forma

evaluate the training they have attended. Figure 4.4 is a specimen copy of a standard evaluation form used by the North West Clinical Psychology CPD Scheme. The advantage of quantitative ratings is that successive training events can be compared with each other, while more qualitative data helps to inform reflection and future planning of events.

For events which aim to increase participants' knowledge, skills or confidence in a certain area, a pre- and post-evaluation form can be

North West Clinical Psychology CPD Scheme
Evaluation Form
Title of CPD Event
Date
Venue
Specialty of Participant: ....

Guidelines for completion of this Evaluation Form
Various aspects of the event you have just attended are covered in the questions that
follow.
Please *circle* the rating that *best* represents your opinion.
The final 3 questions overleaf are more open-ended.
Please try to give some kind of response to all 3 questions.

Content of Event

What was your general opinion of the Event as a whole?

1	2	3	4	5
Very low	Low	Average	High	Very high

Did the Event achieve its aims? (e.g., as set out in the programme/timetable for the
day.)

1	2	3	4	5
Very low achievement	Low achievement	Average achievement	High achievement	Very high achievement

Were appropriate topics covered?

1	2	3	4	5
All topics very inappropriate	All topics inappropriate	Most topics appropriate	All topics appropriate	All topics very appropriate

Facilitator(s)

What was your general opinion of the workshop speakers/facilitators?

1	2	3	4	5
Very low	Low	Average	High	Very high

What did you think of the facilitator(s) use of instructional methods? (e.g.,
effectiveness of small group exercises, didactic teaching, small workshops.)

1	2	3	4	5
Very unsuccessful	Unsuccessful	Reasonably successful	Successful	Very successful

Continued

designed which asks delegates to rate themselves on a number of
dimensions just before the start of the event, and immediately at the
end. Although very subjective, such evaluations do at least provide
some 'value-added' measure of the training delivered on the day.
A longer-term follow-up could be introduced by sending participants
questionnaires 6–12 months after completion of the training event in

Did the facilitator(s) make sufficient use of teaching aids? (e.g., audio-visual equipment, overheads, flip charts.)

1	2	3	4	5
Very inadequate use	Poor use	Average use	Good use	Very good use

Was the event on the day(s) properly organized?

1	2	3	4	5
Very badly organized	Badly organized	Organized	Well organized	Very well organized

How do you feel about the length of the event?

1	2	3	4	5
Much too short	Too short	About right	Too long	Much too long

Resources related to the Event

How would you rate the facilities in general ? (e.g., venue, parking, general ambience, lunch arrangements.)

1	2	3	4	5
Unacceptable	Very poor	Acceptable	Good	Very good

How would you rate the 'teaching space' itself? (e.g., room in terms of size, general ambience, level of comfort.)

1	2	3	4	5
Unacceptable	Very poor	Acceptable	Good	Very good

Communication related to the Event

What kind of notice were you given for this event?

1	2	3	4	5
Very short	Short	Adequate	Long	Very long

How would you rate the information circulated to you in advance about the event? (e.g., map, delegate list, programme for the day.)

1	2	3	4	5
Very unclear	Unclear	Reasonably clear	Clear	Very clear

Personal/Professional Development

Based on the ratings you've given so far, to what extent were your specific aims met?

1	2	3	4	5
Not at all	Very little	Average	Highly met	Very highly met

Continued

Continued

If you feel able, please state at least one aspect of the day that you found helpful in terms of your own personal/professional development:

_____

_____

_____

If appropriate, please state any aspects of the day you found unhelpful to or hindered your personal/professional development?

_____

_____

_____

Finally, do you have any ideas for future CPD events? These may be a development of a theme covered today or be of a completely different nature.

_____

_____

_____

Any other comments

_____

_____

_____

Thank you very much for taking the time to complete this Evaluation Form.

Source: Adapted from version provided by Garfield Harmon

Figure 4.4   Pro forma evaluation form for a CPD event

order to assess the transfer of new skills and knowledge into practice. This can be a useful exercise to do as it encourages reflection on the part of the participant. Also, the benefit of many training events is not always immediately apparent, and a more true evaluation in terms of benefits and outcome may only happen after a period of time.

There are many different ways of organizing training events, and the relevant documentation necessary to do this. A useful way of thinking about the requirements for your planned event is to reflect on courses and conferences you have attended where everything has gone smoothly, from application through to registration and final evaluation, and also events where things have gone wrong. What has made the good training events successful, and the bad ones experiences you would rather forget? If you can put your own experience as a delegate to good use as an organizer, then you are far more likely to avoid obvious mistakes.

Conclusion

As can be seen from the information in the above sections, the practical aspects of CPD are best thought about in terms of a learning cycle model. We start with the identification of development needs and activities, and then move on to carrying out the activities in practice. We monitor and record what we have achieved (as well as what we have not managed to achieve), and evaluate the CPD activity by critically reflecting on all aspects of the process, and finally implement what we have learned into everyday practice before progressing to the next CPD need identified.

Meeting our professional development needs can be challenging, particularly when resources appear to become more scarce or, at least, their allocation may seem to be more tightly controlled. However, creative and innovative approaches to CPD can enable us to meet at least some of our needs at low cost, or even for free. New technologies utilizing e-learning and virtual learning environments, and the establishment of the NHSU, may facilitate our professional development, particularly for clinical psychologists working in more geographically remote areas, part-time staff, and for those who may have difficulty accessing 'live' CPD due to budgetary constraints. Providing CPD activities for others is an excellent way of obtaining free and 'tailor-made' professional development for ourselves, as well as facilitating essential networking with colleagues.

Above all, when we reflect on past, present and future CPD needs and activities, we should always ask ourselves for whom we are undertaking professional development. Although the benefits to ourselves may be more readily identifiable, we need to remember that our focus – in terms of outcome – must ultimately be on our clients, as the recipients of our services. User involvement, which we are urged to consider more and more within our professional life, also has a meaningful part to play in this process when we remember to keep our clients firmly in mind at all stages of continuing professional development.

NOTE

1 The NHSU was dissolved on 31 July 2005. A new organization, the NHS Institute for Innovation and Improvement (www.institute.nhs.uk), will take forward strategic advice and direction concerning learning. The delivery of the NHSU's programmes and services, meanwhile, will be taken forward by host organizations across the NHS.

REFERENCES

Atkinson, K. (1998). Education and research – SWOT analysis: A tool for continuing professional development. *British Journal of Therapy Rehabilitation*, 5(8), 433–5.

Bolton, G. (2001). *Reflective Practice – Writing and Professional Development*. Paul Chapman Publishing Limited, London.

British Psychological Society (2000). *Guidelines for Continuing Professional Development for Clinical Psychologists*. The British Psychological Society, Leicester.

British Psychological Society (2001). *CPD Logbook*. The British Psychological Society, Leicester.

British Psychological Society (2002). *Society CPD Guidelines*. The British Psychological Society, Leicester.

British Psychological Society (2004). *Continuing Professional Development*. The British Psychological Society, Leicester.

Brocklehurst, N. and Walshe, K. (2000). Quality and the new NHS. *Emergency Nurse*, 8 (2), 26–33.

Department of Health (1997). *The New NHS: Modern and Dependable*. Department of Health, London.

Department of Health (1998). *A First Class Service: Quality in the New NHS*. Department of Health, Leeds.

Department of Health (1999a). *National Service Framework for Mental Health*. Department of Health, Leeds.

Department of Health (1999b). *Continuing Professional Development: Quality in the New NHS*. Department of Health, London.

Department of Health (2001a). *A Health Service of All the Talents: Developing the NHS Workforce*. Department of Health, London.

Department of Health (2001b). *Working Together, Learning Together: A Framework for Lifelong Learning for the NHS*. Department of Health, London.

Department of Health (2002). *Funding Learning and Development for the Healthcare Workforce*. Department of Health, London.

Division of Clinical Psychology (2001) *Guidelines for CPD*. British Psychological Society, Leicester.

e-learning Strategy Unit: Strategy Update Bulletin (July 2004).

Golding, L (2003a). *Final Report of the Continuing Professional Development Survey of NHS Clinical Psychology Service Managers Working in the North West of England*. Unpublished report (North West Clinical Psychology CPD Scheme).

Golding, L. (2003b). The continuing professional development needs of clinical psychologists in the North West of England. *Clinical Psychology*, 26, 23–7.

Gray, I (2004). *DCP Managers Faculty CPD Funding Survey*. Unpublished report.

Lavender, T. (2003). Redressing the balance: The place, history and future of reflective practice in clinical training. *Clinical Psychology*, 27, 11–15.

NHS Modernization Agency Leadership Centre (2004). *Leadership Centre Work Review.* Department of Health, London.

NHSU (2003) *NHSU Towards Delivery: Draft Strategic Plan 2003–3008.* NHS, London.

Tate, S. and Sills, M. (eds) (2004). *The Development of Critical Reflection in the Health Professions.* Higher Education Academy, King's College, London. (Also available onlie at: www.health.Itsn.ac.uk)

WDC CPD Network (2004). *Discussion Paper: Commissioning Post-qualification Learning/CPD for Small and/ or Specialist Professional Groups.* Department of Health, London.

WEBSITES

www.dfes.gov.uk/elearningstrategy

Institute of Administrative Management: www.instam.org

NIMHE Knowledge Community: http://kc.nimhe.org.uk

Downloadable skills-based career tools: www.mindtools.com

Professional Associations Research Network: www.parn.org.uk

share-net-introduction: type in share-net-introduction via www.google.co.uk

website for the Institute of Continuing Professional Development: www. trainingZONE.co.uk

Chapter 5

CPD and Newly Qualified Clinical Psychologists

Angela Latham and Karla Toye

Continuing Professional Development (CPD) is a particularly important consideration for newly qualified psychologists. Drawing on both personal experience and the available literature, this chapter explores some of the reasons why the period immediately following qualification is a particularly important phase with regard to CPD needs.

The chapter begins by addressing why CPD is an important consideration for newly qualified clinical psychologists. Increasingly there are fewer full time generic posts available, forcing newly qualified clinical psychologists to specialize earlier in their careers. The implications for this within the context of CPD will be discussed.

Following on from this discussion, the next section considers the transition from trainee to qualified status. We will attempt to answer the question of how well an individual's pre-qualification experiences prepares them for their future careers and CPD needs once qualified. This section outlines the mythical concepts that emerge during the pre-qualification years and also describes how the progression from undergraduate to qualified status takes the individual through a number of developmental cycles, involving the acquisition of a variety of skills.

In the following section we move on to list the specific CPD needs that are identified as particularly important for the newly qualified clinical psychologist. The section focuses on the comparison between trainee and newly qualified status and considers both the positive and negative aspects involved in this transition. The role played by supervision in CPD, both as a supervisor and a supervisee, is recognized in line with DCP guidelines. In addition, we highlight the need for newly qualified psychologists to maintain their generic skill base while at the same time developing an ever increasing specialist role. The challenges of increased case load management and the importance of harnessing skills gained during training, such as research skills, are also high-lighted. The section ends with a summary table comparing the key points of change made during the transition from trainee to newly qualified clinical psychologist.

The chapter moves on to outline methods of how to identify and monitor the newly qualified clinical psychologist's CPD needs. Here the role of the manager becomes more of a focus with the identification of CPD needs within a job description and employment contract. The importance of an annual appraisal is discussed, and comparisons are drawn with the change that the newly qualified clinical psychologist makes from frequent appraisal and feedback through training to a reduced level once qualified. We describe a number of practical solutions to meeting CPD needs including discussing some examples of good practice existing nationally that endeavour to meet and support these needs.

The chapter ends with a summary to guide employers and employees and a checklist to aid in the monitoring and development of CPD practices.

Why is CPD a Particularly Important Consideration for Newly Qualified Clinical Psychologists?

Newly qualified clinical psychologists graduate with the skills and strengths of a generic training. The first job/specialty they enter may not be where they remain for the rest of their career. As funding increasingly becomes available for posts through specific funding lines, clinical psychologists may be forced to take on less generic and more specialist posts earlier in their careers.

The fine balance between maintaining and further developing the generic role while establishing specialist skills within specialist posts needs careful monitoring and support, and will be outlined more clearly later in the chapter. The responsibility for this balance may need to be supervisor-led in the first instance while the newly qualified clinical psychologist finds their own identity within the workplace. Increasingly, clinical psychology posts are becoming less generic. Using the first jobs of the authors of this chapter as an example of this; Karla Toye took on the role of clinical psychologist within a specialist pain service and Angela Latham took a first job half time community-based early intervention and half time generic. Our roles within our employment are poles apart early in our career, yet we graduated from the same course in the same year!

The core competencies outlined by the DCP are a useful tool upon which to assess the needs that may be more relevant to the newly qualified clinical psychologist (see Figure 5.1). Although the competencies are relevant to all clinical psychologists, for the purpose of this chapter only those directly applicable to the newly qualified clinical psychologist will be outlined here.

How Well Do Pre-Qualification Training Experiences Prepare Trainees for their Future Careers and CPD Needs?

The mythical concept that once qualified things will be different and that we will become 'super psychologists' needs addressing (Corrie and Harmon, 2001; Deeley et al., 1998). Rudkin (2000) describes it as a fantasy, that on 'graduating from clinical training, we shall be presented with an envelope inside of which The Secret will be written, and forever more we shall know we are doing the right thing'. We know that such concepts exist and in order to prepare the newly qualified clinical psychologist, its existence needs to be made more explicit and open to discussion during the training phase.

Pre-Qualification Training Experiences

If we consider the path an individual has followed to reach the point of qualification, it consists of the transition of numerous developmental cycles. For the majority of individuals, the first of these cycles will have been the transition into undergraduate studies. From this point onwards the ultimate goal is to reach qualified status as a clinical psychologist. With the acquisition of an undergraduate degree, classed suitably high enough to be considered for clinical training, the next cycle is the transition into the working practices, usually in the NHS, as an assistant psychologist. For some, this stage might be more researched focused if the first position is one of research assistant. Either way, the perceived wealth of knowledge gained from three years of undergraduate study, is put into stark perspective when working within a highly specialized field. Work then begins to acquire the relevant skills that will gain the individual a place on a training course, which for many involves numerous applications to the Clearing House for Postgraduate Courses in Clinical Psychology. Throughout this cycle the individual may hold a number of different assistant

3.1.1 *Immediate post qualification* It is clear that training must be seen as a first step in enabling the clinical psychologist to establish expertise throughout their career. The first job after qualification will provide opportunity for consolidation of skills. Further courses (such as in specialist therapeutic techniques) are often taken. If a first (or subsequent post) entails working in an area not covered within the original three year training, clearly it is essential for the psychologist to attend courses to acquire necessary skills through further learning. Clear examples of this are in the areas of neuropsychology; clinical psychology within a physical health or forensic setting; and drug/alcohol rehabilitation.

If the first years can be viewed as a time for consolidation of skills and expertise, they may also be seen as a period where psychologists broaden their perspectives regarding their profession. For example, successful training and ensuring recruitment and retention is to a large extent dependent on the availability of placements. If newly trained psychologists 'team' with more experienced supervisors, they can go on to support training initiatives by providing placements for trainees once they themselves have acquired necessary supervision skills.

Other ways in which psychologists go on to amalgamate individual interests and professional advancement include research (including 'top up' doctorate qualification) acquisition of managerial skills in relation to both Trust/Regional work; and wider professional work (for example, involvement with national bodies, such as the DCP).

3.1.3 *Conclusion* It is useful to conceptualise the completion of the three year clinical psychology training as just the beginning of professional and personal development, which continues throughout the entire time that an individual is involved with the clinical profession.

Source: The Division of Clinical Psychology (2001, Chapter 3)

Figure 5.1 The Division of Clinical Psychology guidelines for CPD throughout the career

psychologist posts in a range of different specialties, requiring the challenge of continually adapting to a new working environment. These different posts will bring with them varied roles and levels of autonomy. The next transitional cycle is that to trainee clinical psychologist. During this cycle the individual is required to adapt on a six monthly basis not only to a new working environment with each new placement, but also having to face the continued challenge of working with different client groups and experiencing the feeling of being deskilled on a regular basis! Throughout all of these challenges and cycles the individual has the motivation that it is all a means to one end, that of qualification. Once that end is reached, the forced striving has gone and the newly qualified clinical psychologist may experience the sense of a feeling of loss or anticlimax. Once the end is reached – what then?

Clinical Training

During the three years of a doctoral clinical psychology training programme, the focus is essentially and, necessarily, on acquiring the core skills and experiences needed to practice as a clinical psychologist. It could be viewed that this is a period where every activity is one focused on CPD; with new skills being continually acquired, specific time being allocated for research and reading of current relevant academic material, and a continual process of assessment. This, in theory, should prepare the newly qualified psychologist with the skills on which to base their CPD activities once qualified. The truth remains, however, that transition into qualified practice brings with it a range of other pressures that, unless monitored, can override basic CPD needs.

Managing the changes, both positive and negative, that come with qualification is likely to be challenging. Positive changes may include increased autonomy and income, continuity of staying in one place for more than six months and a decrease in the continuous demands of academia (also known as getting your life back or the rediscovery of weekends!). Some of the less positive changes, however, may include increased pressure on clinical skills, less supervision and a natural decrease in informal peer support. Although it is hoped that many of the skills required to manage this transition on the developmental trajectory of the clinical psychologist will have been gained throughout training, it may take some careful thought and consideration in order to apply them successfully to qualified practice.

One of the biggest impacts of qualification is the loss of the close peer support network that is implicit in training courses. For many, the natural support that is gained from weekly contact with peers is lost immediately upon qualification. Once qualified this support needs to be gained in a more formal and structured way, especially for individuals who accept posts in smaller psychology departments where there will be less natural peer support.

How this is dealt with during the training years may have a direct impact on how an individual looks to establish such support post-qualification. Some courses, for example set up 'buddy systems', where each trainee is paired with a trainee from the year above, while other courses have therapy networks, providing a more formal level of support. Training schemes should promote discussion around the issues of transition during the final year of training to prepare them more and normalize the experience. With the Quality Assurance Agency's (QAA) increasing control over the NHS training schemes (The Quality Assurance Agency for Higher Education, 2003) hopefully these issues will be addressed more explicitly in the future. This preparation would do well to assist trainees in planning how they are going to seek the support they may require once their natural peer support network has gone.

The focus on learning during training is essentially on the learning of blocks of knowledge required to perform successful therapy. This knowledge needs to be learned at a level where the intricacies of various models are known in order to answer an exam question. There is also the pressure of developing skills in the art of research in order to complete numerous research projects. With the transition to qualified status this knowledge needs to be applied to the ever increasing numbers of people coming through our doors and the ever increasing complexity of the cases seen, while placing this within changing government and local policies and continuing organizational restructures. The emotional and intellectual burden that this brings can weigh heavy on the newly qualified clinical psychologist. The scientist-practitioner focus of training, which remains important post-qualification, will receive a different emphasis in the work place. Once the individual is carrying and managing a clinical caseload, the importance of the process of therapeutic skills tends to move ahead of the theory.

The training programmes, under the guidelines of the QAA, have the responsibility to provide individuals who are 'fit for practice' and 'fit for purpose' as well as to obtain their degree status (fit for award) (The Quality Assurance Agency for Higher Education, 2003). As the trainee goes through the process of qualification, the feedback they receive changes from the person who is going to award their qualification, to the whole organization that is the NHS. The benefit of the QAA major reviews should ensure that individuals leaving training will not only be qualified in processes such as audit, but also well prepared for the demands that user groups and wider organizations beyond direct departmental management, can have on working practice.

The importance of preparing trainees for the transition to newly qualified status was outlined by Corrie and Harmon (2001). They reported on the outcome of a series of one-day workshops organized for final year clinical psychology trainees on the South Thames clinical psychology training programme. One of the main aims of the workshop was to facilitate the transition from trainee to newly qualified clinical psychologist. The authors generated specific recommendations based on their experience of running these workshops. They stated that the responsibility for facilitating this transition lies not only with the clinical training courses, but also prospective employers and the wider field of other networks such as the DCP, its local branches and special interest groups/faculties.

Clare and Porter's survey (Clare and Porter, 2000) highlighted the need for doctoral clinical psychology training programmes to address the issues that arise in transition from pre- to post-qualification. The recent introduction of a core competency model within the UK's clinical psychology training programmes has been a significant move towards ensuring that trainees receive placements and training which provides them with experiences enabling the achievement of core skills rather than the more traditional generic placement experience. This move towards a model of being trained to achieve core competencies should assist in the long term in preparing trainees to take on the ever-changing role of the clinical psychologist.

What are the CPD Needs of Newly Qualified Psychologists?

There have been a number of studies that have attempted to identify the CPD needs of newly qualified clinical psychologists through the process of asking psychologists to reflect on their experience of this transition. This section will attempt to outline some of these needs as identified in the relevant studies. Primarily, the needs can be categorized as; issues relating to taking on a more autonomous role, supervision, the need to maintain and develop generic skills, the development of specialist skills, and issues relating to case load management and research. Supervision can be further broken down into mentorship and clinical supervision. This section concludes with a table summarizing the comparisons of the key points of change made in the transition from trainee to newly qualified clinical psychologist.

Autonomy

The increased autonomy of being newly qualified is generally regarded as an enjoyable aspect of qualification. A survey conducted by Clare and Porter (2000) found that it was the most frequently reported enjoyable aspect of qualification. Despite the positive aspects of increased autonomy however, it should be noted that this change can also bring with it a range of anxieties.

Gelsthorpe and Allen (1989) identified the need for support as the most important factor in assisting the transition phase. There is no doubt that peer support provides an essential base on which to explore demands such as those brought on by increased autonomy. This support network can be found naturally in larger psychology departments where there may be more than one or two psychologists within their first years of qualification. In smaller departments, however, newly qualified psychologists may find themselves feeling more alone and isolated. This may be a particularly important issue for psychologists who have taken up posts outside the region where they trained.

The period immediately following training has been highlighted by Skovholt and Ronnestad (1992). They reported that during an individual's training years, feelings of a 'comforting dependency' naturally form. They stated that in order for the individual to assume a more autonomous role this needs to be lost, which will then help them cope with the complexities of working as a qualified practitioner. In a similar vein, Corrie (1998) identified how learning to *feel* qualified is a fundamentally different task from being *pronounced* qualified.

This transition can also provide the newly qualified clinical psychologist with a cognitive challenge! They may (and it could be argued after three years' hard slog, should) enter the workplace with a positive view of themselves through having successfully completed a three year training programme. This perceived sound knowledge base however, can be quickly challenged once having to work more independently and face the task of higher numbers of cases with increasing complexity. Skovjolt and Ronnestad (1992) identified this process and suggested that the conflicting message that this provides causes a fluctuation between states of confidence and anxiety, a process that requires careful monitoring during supervision.

Clare and Porter (2000) reported on the results of a questionnaire survey of clinical psychology graduates from three training courses in the Northern and Yorkshire region. The questionnaire was designed to elicit information regarding their experience of the transition from trainee to newly qualified status. The authors reported that 'support' factors (e.g., support from colleagues, supportive department, supervision) were rated most highly as factors which aided the transition from trainee to newly qualified.

Supervision

Supervision is often highlighted as a concern for newly qualified clinical psychologists (Lavender and Thompson, 2000). This concern is two fold; there is primarily the need to receive one's own personal supervision, while also taking on the new role of being a supervisor to others. This supervisory role may be initially to assistant psychologists and later (though increasingly less later with the increase on training places and the demands placed on departments for training placements) to trainees. Depending on the first post taken, there may also be the demand to supervise non-psychologists in their roles within multi-agency and multidisciplinary teams.

Personal supervision   The Division of Clinical Psychology (DCP) supervision guidelines document states that: 'it is expected that all clinical psychologists, at all stages of their career and in all work contexts, will engage in regular supervision of their own work' (DCP, 2003). It also states that: 'all supervision should be needs led and appropriate to the level of experience, caseload and managerial responsibility.' The guidelines also state that the minimum standard of supervision should be 60–90 minutes for every 20 sessions worked and clearly states that newly qualified clinical psychologists will require more than this. If we consider the reality of this amount of supervision, it equates to approximately 1½ hours supervision per fortnight. As previously mentioned, newly qualified clinical psychologists are taking on more specialist roles much earlier than historically, which should surely be an argument for having more supervision, especially during the early stages of qualification.

The newly qualified clinical psychologist may also find the feedback they receive on their work to be significantly less frequent and forthcoming than during their training years. They may therefore find it difficult to evaluate their own practice. When the changes are so new and their anxieties high, finding the reference point at which to work out how well they're doing may be difficult. It may be important during this stage for the supervisor of a newly qualified clinical psychologist to place the issue of the anxieties of the new role on the agenda for supervision. It should also be noted that it may be difficult for the newly qualified clinical psychologist to bring issues such as these to supervision for fear of being negatively evaluated by their new employers.

Supervision of others – Psychologists   The DCP Supervision Guidelines (DCP, 2003) state that: 'it is expected that clinical psychologists provide supervision, particularly to trainees and newer members of the profession. This activity should be regarded as a core part of all clinical psychologists' work and will require its own training and development.' The guidelines also state that: 'every clinical psychologist should seek basic training in supervision before undertaking the role of clinical supervisor.' In the first few years post-qualification, it is likely that this supervision will take the role of supervising assistant psychologists and trainees. Some of the anxieties that supervising others may bring will be highlighted in the next section on supervising non-psychologists, however, there are some issues which may be more pertinent to the supervising of psychologists. Working from the same model may make the process of supervision easier as the supervisor and supervisee will have some shared knowledge base. However, when first embarking on the role of supervisor, there are many skills to gain. Newly qualified clinical psychologists will be in a position of having recently experienced a number of models of supervision through their numerous training placements. They may choose to draw on their more favoured aspects of these models to form their own personal supervisory style. They must note at this point though the importance of using external factors to shape and develop this style. This may be done through accessing specific training on supervision and also by taking supervision issues to their own supervision sessions.

Supervision of others – Non-psychologists   It is commonplace for clinical psychologists to provide supervision to non-psychologists. This supervision can take a variety of forms. Sometimes it may be supervision of therapeutic based practice, or it may be on a more consulting role. We have already discussed the dichotomy we experience as newly qualified clinical psychologists feeling like we should have a large knowledge base having just qualified versus the feelings of being deskilled by the wealth of new challenges. To be placed in a role where the knowledge we do not think we have is being tested can be highly anxiety provoking and may need a significant level of support. The title of doctor received at qualification may also have an impact on how the individual is perceived by others, particularly in professions outside psychology. In light of the individual feeling deskilled, others considering them highly skilled 'doctors' may arouse feelings of anxiety. On a more positive note however, with adequate supervision and support, this role may be particularly empowering for the newly qualified clinical psychologist. They will, of course, have the knowledge to provide this supervision/consultation and being placed in a position where they may exercise this knowledge should be both rewarding and reinforcing.

Need to Maintain and Develop Generic Knowledge and Skills

The DCP's CPD guidelines (DCP, 2001) describe the first years after qualification as a time for 'consolidation of skills and expertise'. In order for individuals to maintain and develop their generic knowledge and skill base, both training and the time to participate in this training needs to be made available. Anecdotally, many newly qualified clinical psychologists state that they feel the clinical demands expected of them do not allow them to pursue training events, especially where the training event may be of a more generic nature and less directly applicable to their post. It should be noted that one of the important strengths of clinical psychology training is its generic nature. To lose this focus in the first years post-qualification would seem to be a waste of the valuable experiences acquired during training.

Development of Specialist Knowledge and Skills

Following clinical psychology training, individuals may choose to work in an area that was not one of the core areas within this training (i.e., work with adults, children, older adults and people who are learning disabled). As outlined by the DCP: 'If a first post entails working in an area not covered within the original three-year training, clearly it is essential for the psychologist to attend courses and acquire necessary skills through further learning' (DCP, 2001). Time therefore needs to be allocated to individuals accepting these more specialist roles to allow for their skill development and where necessary, skill acquisition.

Case Load Management

Newly qualified clinical psychologists' case loads are likely to be significantly larger post-qualification and do, of course, require managing for a period longer than six months! Clare and Porter (2000) reported that issues relating to case load management were found to be the most stressful aspect of recent qualification. Services work to different guidelines in terms of the number of contacts required per week, number of open cases held on a case load and length of waiting list. During training, individuals maintain a small case load where they have time to discuss every case weekly. The shift to a large and often ever increasing case load where only priority cases can be taken to supervision may feel, at times, overwhelming.

Research

Throughout the training period there is a significant focus on research. Within the health professions the research skills of clinical psychologist are generally held in high regard and therefore it is essential that these skills be harnessed early in a career while they are still fresh. The DCP's CPD guidelines state that CPD should go beyond clinical skills and should: 'include the development of skills and knowledge such as research and development, audit and evaluation, management and organisational issues' (DCP, 2001). Some posts allow for specific time to be allocated to research, and the time allowed for it should be negotiated when discussing employment terms.

Table 5.1 provides a comparison of the key points of change made in the transition from trainee to newly qualified clinical psychologist.

How to Identify the Needs of Newly Qualified Clinical Psychologists

The previous section outlined some of the needs of newly qualified clinical psychologists as identified through personal experience and existing literature. This section will move on to consider methods of how to identify one's needs in the first place and also how to monitor the change in needs.

Identification of CPD Needs

Employment contract   Housten et al. (1989) identified the lack of a clear job description as one of the main difficulties rated highly by individuals during their first few years post-qualification. It is probably true to say that for most individuals accepting their first post following

Table 5.1 A comparison of trainee versus newly qualified clinical psychologist

Factor	Trainee	Newly Qualified
Supervision	Regular – stipulated at least one hour weekly for clinical supervision. Supervision will also be received through course staff.	DCP guidelines stipulate 60–90 minutes fortnightly. Depending on job the amount of supervision received may decrease significantly. Supervision received solely through employment (unless external supervision has been negotiated).
Case load	Limited by course requirements to approximately 6 to 8 cases at any one time.	May be unlimited in some settings. Guaranteed to be higher than during qualification.
Case management	Opportunity to discuss each case weekly, number of cases closely monitored by supervisor and course team.	Cases discussed on priority basis due to time constraint. Responsibility shifted to individual.
Skill focus	General focus on the development of skills – with some specialism in final year of training.	Increased need to focus on specialist skills.
Negotiation of need	Assistance in the negotiation of need through clinical tutor.	Necessity to negotiate all need for self.
Peer support	Natural support network established involving peers in year group.	Depending on size of department peer support networks need to be more formally established.
Autonomy	Some level of autonomy, but primarily answerable to supervisor/course team.	Increased levels of autonomy.
Accountability	Accountability lies ultimately with supervisor.	Accountability lies with self.
Research	Closely guided and supervised research. Specific time allocated to conduct.	Pressures if clinical time likely to maker the conducting of research difficult.

qualification the main focus is likely to be around the clinical aspects of the job, rather than thinking about how the post may help them meet their CPD needs. It should be noted however, that this can be a crucial time for negotiating things such as research time, clear CPD time, and CPD opportunities which can be offered by an employer, so that one's CPD needs do not go overlooked. The DCP's CPD guidelines (DCP, 2001) state: 'continuing professional development policies and strategies should be explicitly incorporated in both initial employment contracts, job descriptions and performance review criteria.' It is also a good idea to enter into discussions about the funding available for training and conferences with a new/potential employer to ascertain at an early point in what ways one's CPD needs may be met within a job.

As part of Agenda for Change, the proposed new pay and grading system for the NHS, the new Knowledge and Skills Framework (KSF) should greatly assist with the process of both identifying and meeting CPD needs for individuals. On the basis of their job descriptions, all NHS staff, including clinical psychologists, will be expected to agree a personal development plan (PDP), in conjunction with their manager which will describe how their identified CPD needs will be supported each year. Having agreed a PDP, the proposed stages of assessment, referred to as the 'gateways' will then ensure that the individual's personal development needs are being met.

Appraisal/personal development plans   Once in employment the negotiation of need is most likely to come through appraisal. The role of appraisal is an essential tool, providing a forum through which a newly qualified clinical psychologist can discuss their developing CPD needs. The responsibilities within this fall to both the individual and the employer. An appraisal should take place at minimum on an annual basis. Due to contrasts between pre- and post-qualification already discussed and the particular needs unique to this time it may be necessary and good practice to have more frequent appraisals.

An appraisal is most likely to be done by one's line manager, however, for some this may not be a clinical psychologist. In these situations it may be necessary to gain the assistance of a more senior psychologist working either in the same or local department to enter into discussions around need. The possibility of the use of a mentor may also be of particular importance in this situation. Mentoring will be discussed in more detail later in the chapter.

It is not just the negotiation of need that makes the appraisal such an important process during the first few years post-qualification. Frequent feedback is essential at a time when the individual is likely to be feeling most vulnerable. Although the very nature of appraisals is anxiety provoking in itself, it is essential and can provide the framework for ongoing development through the identification of learning needs. The making explicit of learning needs once qualified should help the newly qualified clinical psychologist in the establishment of their identity. This should provide the opportunity for reassurance that they are not expected to be the 'super psychologist', thus working on some of the issues already discussed.

How to Meet the CPD Needs of Newly Qualified Clinical Psychologists?

Having identified one's CPD needs, careful thought and consideration then needs to be put into identifying appropriate methods of how to ensure these needs are met. Training courses and conferences are obvious methods available to improve and develop an individual's knowledge base. As has been previously discussed, however, it is not only the gaining of new knowledge that is important at this stage but other factors such as the development of support networks. Some areas have training schemes to support this career stage. The following description of a CPD scheme for newly qualified clinical psychologists in North West England is provided as an example of good practice.

The CONTACT Training Scheme – An Example of Good Practice

Wisely (2004) recently reported on 'CONTACT', a scheme operating within the NHS in the North West of England, which provides post-qualification training and support for newly qualified clinical psychologists. The scheme was initially set up in 1987 by a small group of newly qualified clinical psychologists who identified the need for increased peer support and CPD during the first few years following qualification. The scheme was originally known as the Basic Grade Training Scheme and was initially funded by Manchester Regional Health Authority.

Since 1987 the scheme has undergone a number of significant developments. As a result of the increase in training commissions on clinical psychology programmes for example, the scheme has experienced a significant increase in membership during recent years, from approximately 10–20 members in 1987, to approximately 80 registered members for the 2003–4 year. The scheme has also undergone significant changes in relation to its funding status. Although certain changes, including a more formal organizational structure of the scheme, have had to be made in response to the increase in membership, the basic structure of CONTACT has been retained since it began in 1987.

Clinical psychologists working in the North West, who are within their first three years of completing their clinical training are eligible to attend CONTACT for a period of two years. The scheme is currently funded by the Greater Manchester Strategic Health Authority as part of the North West Clinical Psychology CPD Scheme. It is run by a committee of members, who are elected on an annual basis. The CPD scheme's tutors facilitate the running of CONTACT in conjunction with the committee.

CONTACT organizes ten training days a year. Each training day consists of a business meeting, lasting approximately one hour, followed by a formal training session. There is also time allocated throughout the day for more informal peer support. The topics selected for the training sessions include an equal distribution of clinical and professional issues topics and are chosen on an annual basis by CONTACT members. The training sessions are facilitated by invited speakers, who are experienced clinicians from a range of disciplines working both locally and outside the North West.

The CONTACT scheme is formally reviewed on an annual basis by its members and changes are made in response to the feedback obtained. A recent survey of the scheme revealed that members rate it very highly and value it as part of their CPD. Specifically, the survey revealed that members found CONTACT an excellent means of both meeting other newly qualified clinical psychologists, in addition to providing information that can be applied to clinical practice and service development. Members who trained outside of the North West reported finding the scheme particularly helpful as it provided them with a forum for getting to know other newly qualified clinical psychologists in the area, thus building up their networks of support. A recent review carried out as part of the North West CPD Project (Golding, 2003a) revealed that service managers also generally view the scheme very positively. In the review by Wisely (2004) it was recommended that similar schemes be set up around the country.

In order to look more closely at CPD needs during the newly qualified phase, the South West Support network (Exeter, Plymouth, Southampton) organized a conference. They invited final year trainees and clinical psychologists in their first few years post-qualification. They focused on the following themes; issues around becoming a supervisor;

dispelling the myth of the 'super psychologist'; and held a workshop exploring the transitional issues to qualified status and how to manage them. The discussions from the day were around many of the themes outlined in this chapter, such as, autonomy, credibility and freedom from the demands of academia. The conclusions of the day were to organize two conferences per year, which took the format of structured speakers in the morning, and informal peer networking in the afternoon to continue to address these needs.

As well as accessing schemes such as those previously outlined, the use of a more senior clinical psychologist acting as a mentor may also be useful to assist with CPD-related issues during the first few years post-qualification. The opportunity to discuss the anxieties and discrepancies that can come with being newly qualified, in a safe setting which does not impact on working practice, may allow for a discourse in which the newly qualified clinical psychologist can work though their anxieties. The following describes an example of a mentor scheme, currently operating in North West England as part of the CONTACT training scheme.

The CONTACT Mentor Scheme – An Example of Good Practice

The mentor scheme for newly qualified clinical psychologists in the North West was established in 1992. It is currently open to all members of the CONTACT scheme (see above). The mentor scheme is funded by the Greater Manchester Strategic Health Authority. It aims to provide a named, experienced clinical psychologist (the mentor) to assist the newly qualified clinical psychologist (the mentee) in identifying their CPD needs and ways of meeting these. The scheme is co-ordinated by the CPD scheme's tutors, who assist newly qualified psychologists in identifying a suitable mentor from the database of clinical psychologists working within the North West who have indicated that they are willing to be mentors. A recent survey carried out as part of the Clinical Psychology CPD Project (Golding, 2003b) examined the uptake and satisfaction with the scheme. The survey revealed that although there was a relatively low uptake of the scheme among newly qualified clinical psychologists, those who had used the scheme to identify a mentor found the scheme very beneficial. As a result of the feedback from the survey, the existing scheme is currently under review and a number of developments are underway. These include the expansion of the scheme to all qualified clinical psychologists in the North West and the provision of a formal training programme for mentors.

The literature supports the importance of the employers' role at this stage. Corrie and Harmon (2001) propose that employers would do well to pay more attention to the ways in which they engage newly qualified members of the profession in terms of support, induction, supervision and CPD. Lavender and Thompson (2000) reported that newly qualified clinical psychologists view access to good/regular supervision as an important factor in the job selection process. Clare and Porter (2000) similarly highlighted that there is a responsibility for supervisors and managers in providing the environment to aid this transition. It is important, for example, for the employer to allow adequate time for the newly qualified clinical psychologist to not only engage in activities such as training and conferences, but at the time when new skill acquisition will be high, negotiating time for other less obvious CPD activities as previously described, is equally important.

Conclusions and Recommendations

The conclusions of the relatively limited number of available studies discussed here have generally been that the transition from trainee to qualified clinical psychologist is a significant period of change and adjustment. As newly qualified clinical psychologists form their new identity they will need support through the demands they face. Having to embrace their new working environment, while trying to establish themselves in their own working style, will be complex and challenging. During training they are likely to have modelled much of their working practice on their supervisors and lecturers. They now have the challenge of forming their own working identity. This identity needs not only to feel autonomous to themselves, but also needs to fit in with the working practices of the department within which they take up employment. Taking on the working values of a larger organization may pose as challenging for the individual who is still trying to establish their own working and therapeutic identity. This may be an ongoing challenge in the ever-changing world of the NHS, but the newly qualified clinical psychologist is likely to feel the most vulnerable. This vulnerable transition stage puts the individual at high risk of burnout as they continue to place high expectations on themselves.

The potentially detrimental impact on employers for failing to consider the CPD needs of newly qualified clinical psychologists has been outlined by several authors. Skovholt and Ronnestad (1992), for example, stated that without careful monitoring of needs during the first few years post-qualification, problems may develop which may then result 'in an increased risk that the profession will lose highly trained individuals due to an early re-evaluation of career choice'. Lavender (1993) similarly reported that the two most important factors found in a study of trainees when selecting jobs were the opportunity to work in the desired speciality and to receive good quality and regular supervision. In addition to these, three other factors were identified as important; geography (proximity to home), achieving the desired spine point, and the availability of post-qualification training. Of these five identified factors, three relate to CPD needs, which points to their importance for newly qualified clinical psychologists in their choice of jobs.

Clinical training programmes should be more explicit in training individuals to seek their own CPD needs, as they get relatively sheltered and nurtured during training. This can be through the provision of peer support together with space provided for reflecting on the process of transition. If these transition needs are made more explicit, it is likely that the ability of the newly qualified clinical psychologist to actively address them will improve. This has implications for both supervisors and managers in providing clarity about expectations and workloads, providing adequate supervision, and in attempting to create a supportive working environment where skills and confidence can be developed (Clare and Porter, 2000).

This chapter has spent a great deal of time focusing on the possible pitfalls that may be met at the newly qualified stage. However, the many positive aspects of qualification need mention too. The initial post-qualification period is an exciting time when knowledge and skills gained during training can be consolidated and developed. The newly qualified clinical psychologist brings with her, or him, a wealth of qualities and fresh ideas which can enrich services and should be harnessed.

The following checklist can be used as an aid for the employer and newly qualified clinical psychologist alike to monitor and develop CPD practices during the newly qualified phase:

- Ensure CPD policies and strategies are clearly stated in employment contracts and job descriptions (including allocation of supervision, time allocation for CPD activities and training budgets).
- Ensure attendance at regular supervision.
- Make CPD an explicit supervision agenda item.
- Make the potential anxieties of being newly qualified an explicit supervision agenda item.

- Reflect on the skills gained during training which can be used to facilitate the process of meeting CPD needs.
- Check out the availability of local training schemes – e.g., CONTACT.
- Develop peer support networks within psychology departments/ trusts.
- Obtaining a mentor early in one's career is a positive way of navigating the first few years post-qualification.
- The separation of line manager, supervisor and mentor can be an important early first step and a place where a number of newly qualified clinical psychologists face problems. These needs may need to be negotiated in the job negotiation phase.
- Ensure an awareness of the need to maintain a generic knowledge base through not only attending specialist training. This can also be done through reading general peer psychology journals as well as attending training days.
- Use annual appraisal to clearly identify developing CPD needs.

REFERENCES

Clare, P. and Porter, J. (2000). On becoming a qualified clinical psychologist. *Clinical Psychology Forum*, 136, 24–8.

Corrie, S. (1998). Beyond training: Reflections on a therapist's anxiety during the first year after qualifying. *Counsellor and Psychotherapist Dialogue*, 1, 10–13.

Corrie. S. and Harmon, G. (2001). Supporting the transition from trainee to newly qualified status: Some reflections from a workshop. *Clinical Psychology*, 4, 21–4.

Deeley, L., Donoghgue, K. and Taylor, D. (1998). From trainee to qualified – managing the transition: South-West support network for recently qualified psychologists. *Clinical Psychology Forum*, 121, 44–5.

Division of Clinical Psychology (2001). *Guidelines for CPD*. The British Psychological Society, Leicester.

Division of Clinical Psychology (2003). *Policy Guidelines on Supervision in the Practice of Clinical Psychology*. The British Psychological Society, Leicester.

Gelsthorpe, S. and Allen, C. (1989). Dead fish psychosis: The transition to Basic Grade. *Clinical Psychology Forum*, 19, 4–6.

Golding, L. (2003a). *Final Report of the Continuing Professional Development Survey of NHS Clinical Psychology Service Managers Working in the North West of England*. (Unpublished report.)

Golding, L. (2003b). *Mentor Scheme Survey Report*. (Unpublished report.)

Housten, J., Revell, J. and Woollett, S. (1989). Programme: Results of a survey of basic grade psychologists in the South West Thames Region. *Clinical Psychology Forum*, 19, 29–32.

Lavender, A. (1993). Factors determining trainees' choice of job. *Clinical Psychology Forum*, 60, 26–30.

Lavender, A. and Thompson, L. (2000). Attracting newly qualified clinical psychologists to NHS Trusts. *Clinical Psychology Forum*, 139, 35–40.

The Quality Assurance Agency for Higher Education (2003). *Handbook for Major Review of Healthcare Programmes*. QAA.

Rudkin, A. (2000). Trainee forum: Having the courage to lack conviction. *Clinical Psychology Forum*, 141, 47–8.

Skovholt, T. M. and Ronnestad, M. H. (1992). *The Evolving Professional Self: Stages and Themes in Therapist and Counsellor Development*. Chichester: Wiley.

Wisely, J. (2004). CONTACT: Meeting the professional development needs of recently qualified clinical psychologists in the North West of England. *Clinical Psychology*, 36, 23–34.

Chapter 6

Continuing Professional Development Mid-Career

Anna Daiches, Chrissie Verduyn and Annie Mercer

The aim of this chapter is to review the pertinent issues in relation to continuing professional development and the transition to B/Consultant Clinical Psychologist. This will include a discussion of the nature of CPD in clinical psychology and other public sector professions and a breakdown of the essential differences between 'A' grade and B/Consultant roles with reference to the *Agenda for Change*. Following this there will be a focus on the particular CPD issues mid-career. These include, individual versus service needs; the development of managerial versus clinical skills and resource issues. An example of good practice will be presented and a checklist for staff to follow covering the practical aspects of their CPD activity relating to this stage of the careers. As the authors practice within the child and family specialty many of the examples will be drawn from this field although the issues raised are applicable to all specialties.

Issues in CPD – The Individual, the Service and the Organization

Continuing professional development (CPD) has evolved formally as a concept over the past 15 years as employers and employees seek to redefine their relationship in the context of rapidly changing work demands. The practice and evaluation of CPD seeks to define and quantify the elusive concepts of skills, knowledge and ability. CPD aims to map out a professional's growth and change in the context of the extension and development of the roles and tasks they are being required to fulfil. CPD has come to the fore in a national climate where quantifiable targets are presented as the common language and form the basis of political might. Although some would argue that this common language is as useful as Esperanto, CPD is a feature of an age where transparency and public accountability, as well as equity, are paramount and where there are substantial challenges to professional power. In these times of accelerating change in communication, technology and expectations, where the shadow of the courtroom looms menacingly over many professions, especially those offering services to the public, CPD is central to the core notions of responsibility and professional regulation. Elsewhere in the public services, The Royal Town Planning Institute, for example, although emphasizing the benefits of CPD in terms of short- and longer-term individual ambitions and the development of personal qualities, makes clear that public satisfaction is central. 'The RTPI's chartered object is "to advance the science and art of town planning for the benefit of the public". It is in the public's interest that the Institute's members meet initial entry requirements and maintain and develop their professional knowledge and skills throughout the life of their membership. CPD helps to ensure this maintenance and improvement of competence' (RTPI, 2004). Although the organizations may appear disparate, the RTPI is wrestling with similar dilemmas as the British Psychological Society (BPS), not only in the often stormy relationship between the art and science of the profession, but in its possible move towards linking mandatory CPD to professional registration.

What Counts As CPD?

Meaningfully defining and recording CPD can be a tricky business. Most organizations have a broad definition of what constitutes CPD. The Scottish Executive, in their national framework for CPD in education, state that the 'range of experiences that contribute to teacher development is very wide and should be recognised as anything that enhances a teacher's professionalism' (Scottish Executive, 2004). This can include reading, reflection, action-based learning and home-based learning. Any CPD portfolio would be expected to reflect a range of activities but validating and quantifying the value and success of CPD activities is difficult if it consists solely of privately undertaken projects that produce no tangible outcome. Hence, although the Scottish Executive promotes this broad definition of CPD, if a qualified teacher wants to actually progress within their career, for example attaining Chartered Teacher Status, they must undertake the Chartered Teacher

Programme. This programme, run by universities, is an academically validated module based undertaking that prides itself on rigorous and consistent assessment procedures. Although it is possible for individuals to claim credit for prior learning, they have to provide evidence that this has been relevant and has impacted on professional practice. Obviously it is sound practice to credit only relevant prior learning, but some aspects of prior learning and attainment are easier to demonstrate than others, often those relating to quantifiable targets. Therefore, demonstrating better academic results for pupils is easier than demonstrating a more positive classroom culture, yet both could be an example of relevant prior learning and experience. The Chartered Teacher Programme also raises two fundamental questions that are central to CPD within psychology. The first is the thorny difficulty of resources for CPD, both in terms of funding and time. The second is the nagging worry that the reality of CPD is less about the developmental aspects of day to day working and more about increasing demands for formal qualification and an explosion in the industry of training where the range of quality is dramatic but the majority of training publicity still cries 'Get your CPD credits here'.

The *Agenda for Change*

The NHS *Agenda for Change* (DoH, 2003) is currently being implemented. In a comprehensive restructuring of NHS pay and conditions, the *Agenda for Change* covers all staff employed by the NHS except senior managers, doctors and dentists. The aims of the *Agenda for Change* are to deliver: equal pay for work of equal value; an objective way of grading jobs; greater scope to create new kinds of jobs and more flexible roles; harmonized terms and conditions and better links between career and pay progressions. A number of job profiles have already been developed and agreed in partnership with unions and this includes the Family of Psychological Job Profiles (AMICUS, 2004). These profiles have been developed using a 16 factor scale which considers the demands of the post in terms of: communication and relationship skills; knowledge, training and experience; analytical and judgemental skills; planning and organizational skills; physical skills; responsibilities for patient/client care; responsibilities for policy and service development implementation; responsibilities for financial and physical resources; responsibilities for information resources; responsibilities for research and development; freedom to act; physical effort; mental effort; emotional effort and working conditions.

It is anticipated that there will be six core job profiles, each with their associated pay band(s). These profiles are; Assistant Clinical (Applied) Psychologist; Trainee Clinical (Applied) Psychologist; Specialist (Newly Qualified) Psychologist; Highly Specialist (Applied) Psychologist; B/ Consultant, Head of Speciality/Consultant Lead Clinician and Head of Department. There are key areas that differentiate the Highly Specialist and B/Consultant, Head of Specialty/Consultant Lead Clinician roles, and which identify the relevant areas of CPD as: responsibility for long-term planning of specialist services; holding a budget; day to day management of staff of specialist service; allocation and placement of students on doctoral training programmes; lecturing, teaching in specialist field; co-ordination of research and development activities for specialist area and interpretation of policies. Not all these key areas are part of job descriptions but the transition to B/consultant involves further development of skills and competencies already acquired as well as the attainment of a broad range and depth of competence and knowledge around management and service area developments.

CPD and Career Progression

National Assessors' Guidelines

The transition to B/Consultant Clinical Psychologist is a nationally monitored and evaluated process overseen by the BPS Assessors, on behalf of the Department of Health (Division of Clinical Psychology, 2002). It is now accepted practice that an interview using National Assessors should always take place in the event of re-grading to a B/consultant grade post. In fact, it is advised that National Assessors should be involved in all aspects of the recruitment process, including short listing. No individual will automatically be awarded a 'promotion' to B/Consultant status as a reward for length of service or success within his or her current job description. The transition will only occur with a move to a new job description either within the same service or by moving to another service. This obviously raises retention issues as individuals find themselves unable to progress further, in pay terms, in a job that it may well be agreed they are undertaking to the highest standard. Promotion has been identified as the most frequent, and often appropriate, reason for clinicians leaving services (Golding, 2003b).

The National Assessors also provide a key set of guidelines outlining what would be necessary CPD preparation for transition to a B/Consultant post. They outline that the following kinds of experience, ability and achievement are likely to be useful:

- management training and experience – including knowledge of personnel issues such as recruitment, appraisal and discipline;
- knowledge and experience of the management of groups other than psychologists;
- highly specialist clinical skills and experience;
- skills and experience in service planning and development, and also in resource issues;
- knowledge of current policies and strategies;
- research achievement;
- skills in teaching; and
- evidence of supervision of clinical psychology trainees.

This list should form the template for planning and accessing CPD activities for those preparing for application for B/consultant posts. The placing of management training and experience at the top of the list is a key issue that will be explored further below.

Supervision

Supervision is a CPD key activity for all levels of clinical psychologists. It is not more pertinent to the aspiring B/Consultant than to other practitioners but it can hold the key to meeting many knowledge and skill objectives necessary to make the transition. Green and Youngson (2003) highlight this point when they state that 'with the opportunity that the supervisory relationship offers for systematic and considered reflection with a respected colleague comes the potential to improve practice in other realms of clinical psychologists' working lives such as management, research and teaching.' Carr (1996) found that supervision, in-house journal clubs or case presentations were prominently identified as CPD needs by clinical psychologists in Ireland. Conversely, formal courses were the least commonly desired CPD activities.

Cohen (1995) makes the critical point that although one purpose of CPD is acknowledged to be career development; CPD is also about maintaining confidence. Supervision, in its many forms, is an ideal means by which an individual can consider career development and maintain confidence as they delve into new professional roles and responsibilities. In a recent survey of new B Grade Clinical Psychologists working in the North West of England, one respondent, when asked what CPD they wish they had undertaken before gaining their B/Consultant post stated, 'I think it is helpful to take on particular duties under supervision to help prepare for the transition. However I think peer support and good supervision are invaluable once you are in post' (Daiches, in press).

It is important for supervision to be recognized as a key CPD activity and not secondary to workshops and courses which often appear to offer more demonstrable rewards. A narrow definition of supervision is not helpful and as Green and Youngson (2003) assert 'supervision need not be restricted to their traditional focus on psychotherapeutic exchanges'. They identify four potential main functions of supervision: managerial, educative, promotion of professional and personal development and support. Golding (2003b) discovered that supervision was indeed afforded a high status by respondents identifying their CPD needs: 101 individuals rated supervision as one of their top five CPD needs, while only 38 put attending courses/conferences in the same category.

As with many other aspects of CPD there is a call for specific and equitable positions on supervision for all services. Between, and within, services consistency is a key element as 'clear and detailed service or departmental policies and guidelines on all aspects of supervision lead to increased expressed satisfaction from both supervisor and supervisee' (Green and Youngson, 2003) In due course professional registration is likely to lead to more formal guidance. While training in supervision is provided in relation to trainees on placement, psychologists as a profession have paid scant regard to training in supervision, post-qualification.

Appraisals

In terms of government policy the appraisal system, or individual performance reviews (IPRs) are seen as essential in the planning and monitoring of CPD activity and are the main forum for negotiations of individual and service priorities (see below). The document *Continuing Professional Development: Quality in the New NHS* (DoH, 1999) describes appraisal as the 'corner stone for assessing the CPD needed for each individual'. Green (1995) explains that the NHS has attempted to develop a managerial culture in which 'organisational goals can be translated into operationally defined targets for individual workers using an IPR system'. Devonshire (1997), however, views IPRs as a 'technique to promote organizational issues rather than satisfy personal needs' and the status of the appraisal system among clinicians is ambiguous. Although no-one identified the appraisal system as a hindrance to the planning and undertaking of CPD activity, only 31 out of 224 clinicians surveyed, in a recent study of clinical psychologists' view of CPD, identified the appraisal process as one of the three main factors that encouraged them to participate in CPD activities (Golding, 2003b). While 79 per cent of respondents were involved in an appraisal process, only 17 per cent were finding that it was actually a corner stone in their CPD activity. This fact, combined with the 21 per cent of those surveyed who did not have an IPR in place, suggest that the government emphasis on appraisals has not yet permeated through the profession.

Although the system of individual appraisal has been identified as the most common way that service managers use to identify CPD needs, the support for the system is not necessarily strong (Golding, 2003c). In a focus group consisting of clinical psychology managers working in North West England, one manager reflected that 'I must own up and say that we have been even less structured around IPRs and CPD . . . over the last few years [I] have . . . resisted some aspects of some IPR on the basis that it is yet another system' (Golding, 2003a). Another manager, in the same focus group, stated that the IPR systems are 'very strict, paper led and absolutely useless' (Golding, 2003a). Although some managers identified the system as important, flexibility was identified as a key element to its success. One service manager, praising the use of informal systems of identifying CPD needs, stated that 'I nevertheless had to have that structure in my head, so it's important to have it there and then to break the rules ever so slightly, to conform to what the requirements of the department are', while another respondent made a related argument, 'I like having stuff on paper because you can refer back to it and you can audit it, but you mustn't get obsessional about that.'

The evidence suggests, therefore, that while IPR systems do have a role in career development, they are neither as ubiquitous a tool as supervision in the world of CPD for clinical psychologists nor as universally celebrated. Appraisal systems need to be developed that reflect the needs of services and the individuals within them in order that managers do not feel that IPRs are just another layer of bureaucracy that is being imposed upon them.

Leadership and Management Versus Clinical Skills

Pitting management and clinical skills against each other in a conflictual sub-heading is not an attempt to suggest that both areas are not integral to a lot of work undertaken at B/Consultant level. With scarce NHS resources for CPD however, and the need for aspiring B/Consultants to carefully plan their CPD activities, there is always a need to prioritize and the development of some skills does not occur. The huge majority of CPD activities that involve attendance on a course/workshop, (whether linked to a qualification or not) and related independent study, can be divided into five main categories:

1. *Practice centred* – for example post-qualification undertakings in Family Therapy, Cognitive Analytic Therapy, Solution Focused Brief Therapy and Narrative Therapy, Supervision.
2. *Issue centred* – for example training days on Diversity Issues, Involving Service Users.
3. *Population centred* – for example workshops focusing on the needs of people with eating disorders, asylum seekers, young offenders or those caring for people with dementia.
4. *Specialism centred* – for example special interest networks for Looked After Children, Neuropsychology.
5. *Service centred* – for example events discussing National Service Frameworks or the *Agenda for Change*.

Although many of these CPD activities may be an element in the development of a capable B/Consultant level practitioner, there is a dearth of opportunities for clinical psychologists to actually train in the art of management. This has been recognized by the BPS's Division of Clinical Psychology's Faculty for Children and Young People who recently produced a document recording the discussions between their committee and a group of National Assessors for B/Consultant grade posts around 'Competency models, workforce planning and *Agenda for Change*' (Fuggle and Rhee, 2004). They noted that there was significant difficulty recruiting to B/Consultant posts in some areas of the country, especially where the posts required significant leadership and management roles. They went on to state that 'It was considered that the difficulty in recruiting to B grade posts and Heads of Specialty posts might be linked to the lack of preparation for such posts. Whilst it is recognised that there is a responsibility upon individual services to provide opportunities and support to help staff develop these managerial and leadership skills it was also accepted that there has been relatively little CPD in this area' (Fuggle and Rhee, 2004). This lack of available CPD addressing managerial and leadership issues may not only be one reason for the 10 per cent vacancy rate for B/Consultant Clinical Psychologist posts nationally but is likely to mean that those in the other

90 per cent of posts may not be fully equipped to undertake all the requirements of the job.

Indeed when John and Smith (1994) described their experience of the White Hart DCP Management Development Course in Harrogate, which was attended primarily by NHS Clinical Psychology service managers and training course directors, they commented that this was the first formal management training that any of the participants had undertaken, even though many had been in managerial posts for a number of years. As with many areas of CPD they found that, 'Management training appears to provide no real answers about the right course of action within any situation', but they did go on to comment, 'it does provide a framework of indicators which should be considered, and some techniques for putting them into practice'.

As the profession moves towards core competencies, the *Agenda for Change* and statutory regulation, the need for more good quality management training, applicable to Clinical Psychologists in a variety of different settings, is paramount. In the *Agenda for Change* the 'day to day management of staff' is identified as one of the core features of a B/Consultant's role, be that as Head of Specialty or as a Consultant Lead Clinician. Other areas that the *Agenda for Change* identify as key are the responsibility for long-term planning of specialist services and the interpretation of policies, both very much management undertakings. Despite our variety of talents and multifaceted job profiles we cannot expect to learn management skills by osmosis.

Making CPD in management and leadership skills available is one matter but making it attractive for those who could benefit from it is another. For those clinicians currently in 'A' grade posts clinical skills are continuously identified as the priority in their decisions about their CPD. Although 71 out of 224 respondents identified management training as a CPD need in a survey of clinical psychologists in the North West of England, 96 identified general clinical training as their priority and 138 identified specific clinical gaps (Golding, 2003b). This may be due to issues around confidence and consolidation but also reflect the demand for specialized clinical services (see below). Not only is management training not identified by many clinicians as important, that is until they find themselves in a management position for which they feel they lack the relevant skills (John and Smith, 1994), it is not seen as intellectually stimulating in the same way as the development of clinical skills. As one respondent in a recent survey of the experiences of new B/Consultants stated when asked what CPD they wish they had received prior to starting their new job 'probably a bit more focus on management CPD, though I always assumed that it would have been very boring' (Daiches, in press). Another respondent to the same survey reflected the tendency for learning these skills 'on the job', with limited training, 'Being given more management responsibility in my new post was a very steep learning curve'. Steep learning curves can be challenging and invigorating but also have close relatives in those pesky little mites, stress and burnout. Service managers also report that their staff are undertaking CPD to increase clinical skills and knowledge rather than managerial skills or an improvement in policy development (Golding, 2003c).

The fact that the need for management training tends to be identified by those already in the job was illustrated by Harmon and Callanan's (1995) survey of CPD needs in the South West region. They found that management training was identified as the biggest CPD need by almost 20 per cent of respondents, putting it above all other CPD activities. They note that 'what does seem apparent is the emphasis on CPD management training and consultation skills within the group of psychologists surveyed. Whilst this figure may not be regarded as surprising given respondents' average time in the profession (17.1 years in this sample), it does confirm the informal belief that as psychologists become more senior in the profession, management and organisational issues become as prominent as clinical issues if not more prominent for some' (Harmon and Callanan, 1995).

Similarly, in Golding's (2003c) survey of NHS service managers in the North West management training was identified as the respondents' biggest training need. Only 63 per cent had received any management training with 9 finding it very useful, 9 finding it fairly useful and 1 finding it unhelpful. Quality, therefore, as well as availability is a key issue in trying to negotiate and prioritize CPD activities.

Knight and Devonshire (1996), in their survey of CPD needs and activities among 96 Clinical Psychologists in the South Thames region, recognized that a lack of coherent CPD in management had the potential to be detrimental to the profession as a whole, and its position within the NHS, and warned that we 'must remember that managerial skills are not confined to being utilised within the profession and that they are key to the development of Clinical Psychology within the NHS'. The importance of maintaining a wide definition of CPD, that includes management skills, is outlined in the DCP's CPD guidelines point 8, 'CPD should extend beyond purely clinical applications to include the development of skills and knowledge such as research and development, audit and evaluation, management and organisational issues' (DCP, 2001).

This mismatch between what 'A' grade clinicians personally identify as their CPD needs and that which is likely to help them fulfil the requirements of a B/Consultant post is likely to be associated with the lack of clarity in career progression across the profession. As Fuggle and Rhee (2004) state, 'In clinical child psychology we do not have any agreement about career pathways, or the required steps to B grade. This makes it hard for A grade staff to plan their CPD and prepare for B grade'. In their action points for addressing this lack of clarity it was agreed that, 'The BPS National Assessors would clarify competencies currently expected of clinical psychologists progressing to B/Consultant posts in child and adolescent services. Some of this work will develop in line with Agenda for Change profiles for senior psychologist posts'. There was also a recognition that there was a need to 'develop clear plans of action to help and support A grade clinical psychologists into B/Consultant posts; either managerial or specialist'.

Currently, therefore, the profession is beginning to realize the need for clear structures and support systems in the move to B/Consultant, especially with the move towards core competencies and the introduction of the *Agenda for Change*. Alongside this is a recognition that specific management-focused CPD needs to be available prior to, or during this transition. Although this training is hard to find, there have been examples of good practice in the UK.

CPD and Services

Individual Versus Service Needs

As highlighted above, as many as 75 per cent of new B/Consultants move to a new organization to gain their post (Daiches, in press). This has broad implications in terms of retention of staff but also brings sharply into focus the debate between the individual and the organization's needs (as well as other stakeholders such as service users) when planning and allocating resources to CPD. The individual, the service, the trust, the organization, the service users and the profession all have needs that they want to see met through CPD.

Historically, the individuals' perceived career needs and personal interests may well have taken the lead in choice of CPD activity, if not necessarily allocation of resources. In 1979 Patterson pondered the status of CPD and argued that 'Many psychologists see CPD only in terms of personal vocational growth and that such a focus ignores events that impinge on the "continuing development of the profession"'

(Patterson, 1979). Hayes (1992) found that, when asking respondents to rate the relative importance of their own CPD to various personal objectives and stakeholder issues, 'the needs of the individual were paramount'. Similarly Harmon and Callanan (1995) found that 'the CPD that people had engaged in was rated as very important for themselves but only moderately important for their managers and service'. The situation is definitely changing as we move towards the regulation of CPD and the profession as a whole.

Green (1995) states that CPD can be part of a structured framework of career development but that the emphasis is on the needs of the organization, 'the political passion of the current era is that professional education in the NHS should be driven by employers' priorities . . . just as the skills profile of the workforce as a whole needs to match the business requirements of the organisation, so the post-qualification training of the individual practitioner should be linked to the specific quality and quantity of healthcare contracts.'

Green (2000) continues to argue that the needs of individual practitioners will be subsumed under organizational priorities if we consider the government directive *Continuing Professional Development: Quality in the New NHS* (DoH, 1999), 'CPD: Quality in the New NHS is explicit that in future patient need and service priority will take even greater precedence over the career interest of individual clinicians when resources are allocated to future post-qualification training' (Green 2000). His argument seems solid when considering the bold statement that '*A First Class Service* (DoH, 1998) defines CPD as a process of lifelong learning for all individuals and teams which meets the needs of patients and delivers the health outcomes and healthcare priorities of the NHS and which enables professionals to expand and fulfil their potential.'

Currently, it seems that service managers are taking a less dismissive view of CPD and its link to the career goals of individual clinicians. In a recent focus group for service managers a typical comment was, 'I wouldn't pay for my staff to do something if I couldn't see the relevance for the service or the relevance for someone's long term career development' (Golding, 2003a). This also highlights the tricky issue of resource allocation which is the subject of the next section.

Resources

In 1995 Lindley and Bromley, in their consideration of the future directions of CPD in Clinical Psychology, recognized that it had to become seen as an essential part of people's jobs, built into contracts and performance reviews. They also highlighted, however, that mandatory CPD makes the question of 'Who pays for it?', both in terms of time and resources, even more pertinent. They state that 'the DECP recognise that budgets for CPD are low – if certification is contingent on CPD, the unions' hands would be strengthened in budgetary discussions.' Resources can also be considered in terms of what training is available and whether that training is what is needed for those moving towards B/consultant posts.

Continuing Professional Development: Quality in the New NHS (DoH, 1999) states that 'CPD should be a partnership between the individual and the organisation, its focus should be the delivery of high quality NHS services as well as meeting individual career aspirations and learning needs.' This need to balance individual and organizational needs is often used as an argument in the allocation of resources to CPD with many service managers and directorates expecting staff to financially contribute to their own CPD and/or undertake it in their own time (Golding, 2003b). It is postulated that as the CPD will, hopefully, forward the career prospects of the individual they have some responsibility to meet the cost. It is also argued that, if they leave the service, they would retain the benefits while they would be lost to the service they leave behind. This argument is powerful but seems not to recognize that most individuals would be leaving one NHS post for another NHS post therefore maintaining the benefits to the organization as a whole.

The question of resources is essential when considering all the important negotiations in CPD. Only with clear budgetary policies could we work towards equal opportunities in CPD for all clinical psychologists. Similarly, if there is a clear link between appraisal systems, accreditation and CPD, there needs to be an equitable system of funding and the relationship between individual and organizational needs to be formalized. That resources should be such an integral and contentious issue is no surprise for NHS employees. When Knight and Devonshire (1996) questioned clinical psychologists in the South Thames area about the aspects of CPD that they were dissatisfied it was not the quality of training or supervision that they identified. Dissatisfaction resulted from budget restrictions, lack of training opportunity and insufficient time allocated to CPD activity. Resources, resources, resources.

Service managers also identify resources as the biggest obstacle in meeting CPD needs identified through individual appraisals (Golding, 2003c). Out of 30 managers surveyed, 14 indicated limited CPD funds, three uncertain funds and one no funds whatsoever. Forty per cent of the respondents also identified time restraints due to waiting time targets to be a particular difficulty in maintaining appropriate levels of CPD.

Practitioners have also identified that there is not enough time to engage in CPD activities. Knight and Devonshire (1996) found that over half of respondents to their survey judged the time allocated to CPD activity as 'not adequate', with a quarter of those individuals limited to less than an hour per week for CPD by their organization. Clearly, less than an hour a week would not allow clinicians enough time in their normal working week to undertake a mandatory amount of CPD, which is a difficult conundrum as we move towards CPD activity being linked to professional registration. It is also clear that if sufficient time is devoted to individual and peer supervision and self-directed reading then, for many individuals, there would be no extra time to attend one day workshops, let alone any extended post-qualification training. The situation has clearly not improved as 75 per cent of North West Psychologists have cited 'lack of time' as the main barrier to undertaking CPD activity and 51 per cent identify 'lack of financial support from employer' as an additional concern (Golding, 2003b). As clinical psychologists are commonly responsible for managing their own time, this raises an issue of how individuals prioritize CPD within their own schedules.

As discussed above, the content of CPD activity needs to be negotiated so that it meets the needs of as many stakeholders as possible but, once this negotiation has taken place; sufficient resources need to be available to undertake the activities. In terms of CPD resources, the government's aim is for 'employers to align their existing training funds with local service objectives and clinical governance plans with an emphasis on work based learning' (DoH, 1999). It will be interesting to see whether these aims are met and, if so, what the quality and quantity of CPD available to Clinical Psychologists will be.

Individuals need to be aware of department and trust policies concerning resources for CPD and frequently take this into account when considering taking up a particular post. Lavender and Thompson (2000) found, however, that spine points, location, supervision and specialty all rated more highly than either CPD resources or career opportunities as priorities for clinical psychologists seeking a new job.

The Issue of Specialization

Within the *Agenda for Change* the delivery of specialist services are given a high priority. The move from band 7 to band 8a–b is characterized by the ability to plan and deliver highly specialist services. In addition to this, the current template for the creation of new posts is often in partnership with other agencies and accompanied by very specific job descriptions, roles and responsibilities (i.e., Sure Start, Looked after Children Services, Working with Asylum seekers etc). Generic posts, even within multidisciplinary settings are becoming less frequent. In the May 2004 BPS Appointments Memorandum there were 65 specialist 'A' grade posts versus only 50 generic 'A' grade posts. Similarly there were 23 B/Consultant posts advertised that were specialist and 15 that were generic. Specialist is defined here as a post where the majority, and usually all, of the responsibilities relate to a specific client group or an organization and/or initiative that offers services outside the remit of generic departments. Examples of these specialist posts included; plastic surgery team, pain management, palliative care, youth offending teams, looked after children, weight management teams, cardiac rehabilitation, Sure Start and personality disorders service. Interestingly, only one post was identified as a specific management rather than clinical role, with an emphasis on the development and promotion of psychology services across their Trust and the NHS as a whole. This drive towards increased targeting of services, and increasingly early specialization, in career terms, is partially driven by well-funded government initiatives that carry with them specific targets. For example, posts within Sure Start are becoming available that are directly linked to the government's target of eradicating child poverty, with numerous specific outcome measures being used to quantify success in the short and longer term. These targets include, greater use of nursery education, lower use of child protection services, an eventual improvement in property values for the local community to the ultimate goal of increased levels of taxation when the children that have, hopefully, benefited from the Sure Start scheme go on to be higher wage earners than the previous generation. The increasing evidence of the reduced life opportunities in terms of education, health, mental health and employment of looked after children has fuelled the allocation of considerable CAMHS funding (£50 million in 2003–4 rising to £92 million in 2005–6) to provide a comprehensive, effective and accessible service for this client group. This presents a challenge to clinical psychology training to respond to changes in workforce needs. The model of a 'child specialist' trainee undertaking a 'generic child' placement or two with some element of specialization in a later 'child' placement is changing. Increasing numbers of trainees, and the consequent demand for placements, has resulted in trainees receiving experience, while training, with targeted services rather than in the traditional stand-alone psychology department taking in referrals from a variety of referrers. Trainees are required to consider how core competencies can be attained and think about generalizable skills and a common knowledge base.

Equally, for qualified staff taking a first post in a targeted service need not involve, for instance, a career working 30 years with the under fives. CPD for recently qualified and mid-career posts needs to address a rapidly changing knowledge and skills base. Transferable skills, such as working with non-health agencies, involving users in service planning, and opportunities within posts to sample work with different target populations may need to be considered as part of career development in appraisal.

As a result of substantial investment, children's services are following the path of adult services many years ago which led to the wide range of 'adult specialist' services, in which clinical psychologists are now employed: for instance forensic, health, primary care, psychosis and so on. CPD for all current psychology specialisms needs to be reactive to the changing patterns of service delivery and national priorities. This is particularly evident as clinical psychologists take on wider management roles.

An Example of Good Practice: 'An Introduction to Clinical Leadership and Management for A/B Grade (Highly Specialist to B/Consultant) Child Clinical Psychologists'

Two of the chapter's authors (Chrissie Verduyn and Annie Mercer) Heads of Child Clinical Psychology Services in Manchester & Salford and Liverpool & South Sefton respectively, were aware of the difficulties in recruiting to B/Consultant posts. Furthermore, as National Assessors, they were also mindful of the issues addressed above, in relation to the lack of opportunity for training in leadership and management which had a particular focus on child settings. The demand for such a course was sampled across the North West England. There were a sufficient number of individuals within child clinical psychology requesting this training for the first course to run in 2002. The course was so successful that it ran again in 2003. Recruitment was by self nomination supported by the participant's line manager. All clinical psychologists throughout the North West were invited to apply via the two local DCP special interest groups. The application form requested applicants to identify the areas they wished the course to consider.

Aims of the Programme

The programme's aims were:

1. To introduce key concepts in management and leadership.
2. To provide a knowledge base of NHS structures and processes relevant to child clinical psychology.
3. To develop and integrate management of leadership skills in relation to a work-based project.
4. To explore the role of B/Consultant Clinical Psychologist from a professional and personal perspective.
5. To apply the above within a multi-agency perspective.

The course ran over six months with two full days at the beginning and end and three half days in between. The course used accessible venues at no cost and ran within a very small budget, trading heavily on goodwill from speakers.

Psychologists attended the course at no cost and were able to claim their travelling expenses and time away from their service base in the normal fashion. Well received courses may be achieved with a relatively limited budget, co-ordination and good will but this is rarely sustainable.

Format

Each of the sessions were topic led and began with a lecture and opportunities for discussion, followed by small group work either on a task related to the topic or on the participants' projects. There were small syndicate groups of up to five members, with the same membership throughout the course. Handouts, relevant background reports and references were provided. Lectures were delivered by health managers in significant leadership positions with experience of working with CAMHS and clinical psychologists, and by clinical psychologists in similar leadership positions. The emphasis was on operational and strategic issues in management and leadership with less attention being paid to purely professional issues. All the sessions were also facilitated by the course leaders.

Over the six months duration of the course, each of the participants was required to carry out a project. They were asked to identify a current problem, issue or area of development within their post which was within the scope of their current responsibilities. They then agreed this with their professional line manager, aiming for something they could realistically achieve in the time. The idea was that the project allowed people to apply what they were learning in the other aspects of the course to their day to day working practice and attempt to integrate their increasing knowledge, and develop their competencies and skills. A format was provided for presenting various stages of the project within the small syndicate groups and reflect upon barriers to success with a focus on action planning. A written résumé of the project was handed in by the participants on completion of the course. The projects included 'Developing a consultation service for mental health work for children with moderate learning disabilities', 'Assessing the feasibility of a psychological service for women leaving domestic violence in a Sure Start area' to 'Evaluation of a child psychology drop in service' and 'Establishing the role of the clinical psychologist in the developmental disorders mini-team'.

One of the themes that ran through the course was the psychological journey to B/Consultant Clinical Psychologist and opportunity was provided to reflect on one's own psychological preparedness to take up a leadership and management position. The small groups and the discussions around projects allowed participants to consider these issues and reflect on their personal journey and views of themselves as authority figures and leaders. Participants were invited to reflect on the psychological and emotional work they needed to undertake, in addition to the knowledge and competencies they would need to acquire for a successful transition to B/Consultant grade.

The programme was as follows:

Session 1: Roles and responsibilities in clinical psychology   A national assessor reviewed the core competencies required in the B/Consultant role and discussed the sort of selection that could be expected. This helped candidates consider their own personal needs in relation to aspiring to become a B/Consultant. In the afternoon, participants presented their project area to the group and used the group to help them develop the first stages of their action plan.

Session 2: Understanding finance   An NHS Director of Finance provided a lecture on financial aspects of management, consideration of budgets, financial control on the business planning cycle. In small groups the participants reviewed the progress of their projects and had opportunities to discuss further action plans.

Session 3: From national policy to local service delivery An NHS Director of Nursing who had been a Care Group Manager within CAMHS presented a lecture on the process whereby national policy affects service delivery, through the modernizing NHS agenda; strategic health authority, local modernization board, social care and primary care trusts. This was followed by presentations on the role of the Clinical Director within CAMHS and the role of the Psychology manager. In syndicate groups the participants then considered their contribution to quality assurance in their service having read a document on clinical governance between the two sessions.

Session 4: Managing staff A general manager in CAMHS introduced some themes concerning the management of staff including staff appraisal and performance management. The small group task then was to consider managing staff issues and a role play case scenario was presented. The syndicate groups had to work on applying some of what they had learnt to a situation they may potentially find themselves in.

Session 5: The national CAMHS picture A Head of Clinical Psychology Service who had been involved in developing the National Service Framework for Children and Young People gave an overview of the national picture and reflections on the implications for clinical psychology services and CAMHS services generally. A B/Consultant Psychologist lead for children with learning disabilities, who was also the Regional Development Worker, provided some updated information on strategic thinking concerning children with learning disabilities.

The syndicate groups then worked on the final review of their projects. The course ended with participants working in pairs to consider what they needed to do individually to continue with their professional development. A plenary and feedback session completed the course.

Evaluation

Participants evaluated each session and completed a questionnaire three months after the end of the course. Feedback was very positive indeed. Participants particularly valued gaining a wider perspective from their attendance on the course, being able to contextualize services and themselves within a national framework and apply this at a local level. In terms of how the course was organized and delivered, participants found the syndicate group discussions very helpful. They also cited applying what they had learnt through project development, the consideration of various leadership styles and managing staff as very helpful. Almost all reported that they had put what they had learnt into practice, which included; writing two successful bids for service development, changing procedure in receiving referrals to their service, successfully applying for and achieving B/Consultant posts and generally improving on their planning, evaluation and review of service development. All respondents would recommend the course to others in a similar position and generally found the course to be useful, relevant, supportive and informative.

This course can only be the beginning for many of the participants who, if successful in achieving a B/Consultant position, would be in their post for many years. It introduced the participants to various aspects of leadership and management. How this applied to their own specialist area and service required consideration in order to determine their personal CPD needs. There are always time constraints. Consideration for future courses would include building in the perspectives of senior managers from other agencies by inviting participation in training.

There are a variety of leadership programmes available within the NHS which clinical psychologists can avail themselves of, additionally there are management training programmes often in house, e.g., dealing with disciplinary and performance management issues. As well as courses such as that described above it is important that clinical psychologists make use of these broader opportunities to develop their skills and competencies alongside their multidisciplinary and multi-agency colleagues. Because of professional structures and client group specific service considerations there is an argument for setting off down this path alongside clinical psychology colleagues from the same speciality at the key point of transition from highly specialist to aspiring B/Consultant grade. The course described provides a well received format in beginning this journey.

Summary

This chapter considers the challenges faced by Clinical Psychology as it, alongside many other professions, comes to terms with the changing nature of continuing professional development. In this period of flux, awaiting the implementation of the *Agenda for Change* and possibly moving towards statutory registration, the transition to B/Consultant Psychologist can be difficult to plan for and negotiate. This chapter explores that transition to B/Consultant in detail and considers the CPD activities that are necessary to make the move meet the needs of the greatest number of stakeholders. The roles of supervision and appraisal have been discussed, alongside the need for accredited courses in management, leadership and clinical skills. The issues of priority, resources and quality lie at the heart of the debates around CPD and it has been repeatedly shown that clarity, transparency and equity in policy documentation are key to the profession meeting the challenges of tomorrow and attracting to B/Consultant posts clinical psychologists who are both competent and confident.

Checklist for CPD Activity for Transition to B/Consultant Clinical Psychologist

Based on the areas covered in this chapter, the following is a practical checklist for readers to use in the transition to B/Consultant Clinical Psychologist:

1. Awareness of the range of CPD activities which are applicable:
   * supervision and peer support;
   * private and structured reading;
   * ongoing research;
   * shared study and joint projects;
   * training events;
   * teaching, training and supervising others; and
   * attendance and participation in short courses, workshops and conferences.
2. Clear CPD plan set up in appraisal system.
3. Negotiation of individual, service and other stakeholders needs.
4. Consideration of the National Assessors' guidelines and the areas that need to be covered:
   * management training and experience – including knowledge of personnel issues such as recruitment, appraisal and discipline;
   * knowledge and experience of the management of groups other than psychologists;
   * highly specialist clinical skills and experience;
   * skills and experience in service planning and development, and also in resource issues;
   * knowledge of current policies and strategies;

- research achievement;
- skills in teaching; and
- evidence of supervision of clinical psychology trainees.

5. Accessing good quality individual and/or peer supervision.
6. Documenting activities in CPD log.
7. Participation in local CPD projects to influence what is available.
8. Participation in evaluation of CPD activities in order to monitor and maintain quality.
9. Consideration of CPD resources when looking for posts.

REFERENCES

AMICUS (2004). Family of Psychology Job Profiles. www.amicus-health.org

Carr, A. (1996). A survey of clinical psychologists in Ireland. Part two: Research, job satisfaction, continuing professional development and private practice. *Clinical Psychology Forum*, 96, 24–9.

Cohen, L. (1995). Continuing professional development for clinical psychologists: Carrot, stick or cattle prod? *Clinical Psychology Forum*, 76, 31.

Daiches, A. (in press). A survey of Continuing Professional Development activities undertaken by new B grades in the North West.

Devonshire, P. (1997). Continuing professional development. *Clinical Psychology Forum*, 99, 12–16.

Department of Health (July 1998). *A First Class Service: Quality in the New NHS*. HSC 1998/113. Department of Health, London.

Department of Health (1999) *Continuing Professional Development Quality in the New NHS*. Department of Health, London.

Department of Health (March 2003). *Agenda for Change: Proposed Agreement*. Department of Health, London.

Department of Health (2003) *Children's Social Services Funding, 2004–05*. Department of Health, London. www.children.doh.gov.uk

Division of Clinical Psychology (2001) *Guidelines for Continuing Professional Development*, British Psychological Society, Leicester.

Division of Clinical Psychology (2002) *Recruitment and Selection to Senior and Consultant Psychologist Posts in Health and Social Care*. British Psychological Society, Leicester.

Fuggle, P. and Rhee, K. (2004) Competency models, workforce planning and Agenda for Change: What does it all mean, how do these developments link together and what are the implications for child psychologists? *Faculty for Children and Young People, Service and Practice Update*, 3(1).

Golding, L. (2003a). *Exploring Clinical Psychology Service Managers' Ideas About Continuing Professional Development: Report of a Focus Group*. Unpublished Report: North West Clinical Psychology CPD Project.

Golding, L (2003b). The continuing professional development needs of clinical psychologists in the North West of England. *Clinical Psychology*, 26, 23–7.

Golding, L. (2003c). *Final Report of the Continuing Professional Development Survey of NHS Clinical Psychology Service Managers Working in the North West of England*. Unpublished Report: North West Clinical Psychology CPD Project.

Green, D. (1995). Carry on learning. *Clinical Psychology Forum*, 76, 37–40.

Green, D. (2000). *Who Pays for CPD in Clinical Psychology?* British Psychological Society, Leicester.

Green, D. and Youngson, S. (2003). *Discussion Paper Regarding DCP Policy on Continued Supervision*, www.leeds.ac.uk

Harmon, G. and Callanan, M. (1995). A survey of clinical psychologists: Part one. *Clinical Psychology Forum*, 76, 31–6.

Hayes, N. (1992). Continuing professional development: Keeping up to date. *The Psychologist*, 5(11), 507–9.

John, C. and Smith, J. (1994). Helping us to manage: A consumer's view of the DCP management development course. *Clinical Psychology Forum*, 66, 3–5.

Knight, T. and Devonshire, P. (1996). A survey of the needs for CPD in a group pf clinical psychologists in the South Thames (West) Region. *Clinical Psychology Forum*, 87, 40–2.

Lavender, A. and Thompson, L. (2000). Attracting newly qualified clinical psychologists to NHS Trusts. *Clinical Psychology Forum*, 139, 35–40.

Lindley, P and Bromley, D. (1995). Continuing professional development. *The Psychologist*, 8(3), 215–18.

National Evaluation of Sure Start (2001) Cost-effectiveness evaluation methodological report. September 2001. www.ness.bbk.ac.uk

Patterson, T. W. (1979). The status of continuing professional development. *Clinical Psychologist*, 33(1), 22–3.

Royal Town Planning Institute (2004). *CPD Frequently Asked Questions*. www.rtpi.org.uk

The Royal Statistical Society (2004) *Continuing Professional Development*. www.rss.org.uk

Scottish Executive (2004). *CPD Questions and Answers*. www.scotland.gov.uk

Verduyn, C. and Mercer, A. (in press). *Report for Clinical Psychology CPD Group: Introduction to Clinical Leadership Management for A/B Grades for Child Clinical Psychologists 2003.*

Chapter 7

CPD and Service Managers

Amanda Caine and Laura Golding

Introduction

Earlier chapters in this book highlighted that the process of identifying, monitoring and prioritizing the continuing professional development (CPD) activities of clinical psychologists has become more formal over the past few years. Chapter 3 described the policy context to this including the requirements of clinical governance in the NHS (DoH, 1998) and the move to make CPD activity mandatory for all applied psychologists (BPS, 2003). All this means that NHS psychology service managers have to ensure that CPD structures are in place in their services to identify, prioritize and meet the CPD needs of their staff. Managers also have to meet their own CPD needs both as clinicians and managers in a fast changing NHS.

Chapter Plan

This chapter begins by looking at recent changes within the NHS that have impacted upon the provision of psychological therapy services. These changes stem, primarily, from the modernization of the NHS under a Labour government leading to the establishment of new structures and a renewed emphasis on excellent clinical standards. The increase in training commissions onto pre-qualification doctoral clinical psychology training programmes, coupled with staff from a variety of professional backgrounds now providing psychological therapies, has meant that clinical psychology service managers currently manage services that are larger, more varied and complex than ever before. This chapter goes on to examine the CPD needs of clinical psychology service managers in the light of these changes drawing on relevant literature and research. The chapter then looks at the role of managers in identifying and developing the CPD needs of their staff and services. It explores the role of CPD in the recruitment and retention of staff, and ways of balancing individual CPD needs and interests with the needs of services. The chapter ends with an action plan for managers.

A Changing NHS – Implications for Service Managers

Chapter 3 gave a comprehensive overview of recent crucial developments in NHS policy in relation to CPD and lifelong learning. It highlighted the amount and rapidity of change in the NHS within a short space of time and the consequences of this for service provision, service users and staff. These changes, coupled with many others within the NHS, pose a challenge to managers in all areas of the NHS as they are now responsible for the delivery of high quality services within a rapidly changing context.

As described in Chapter 3, The NHS modernization developments, stemming from *The NHS Plan* (DoH, 2000a), have led to significant investment within the NHS over the past five years. *The NHS Plan* summary states 'The purpose and vision of this NHS Plan is to give the people of Britain a health service fit for the 21st century: a health service designed around the patient. The NHS has delivered major improvements in health but it falls short of the standards patients expect and staff want to provide. Public consultation for the Plan showed that the public wanted to see:

- more and better paid staff using new ways of working;
- reduced waiting times and high quality care centred on patients; and
- improvements in local hospitals and surgeries' (Department of Health, 2000a).

The Plan included the promise of a significant investment in staff in order to enable the government to deliver a modernized health service. It stated that the targets for investment in staff were: 7,500 more consultants, 2,000 more GPs, 20,000 extra nurses and 6,500 extra therapists.

 Since the publication of *The NHS Plan*, further changes are being implemented through *Agenda for Change* (DoH, 2004a) the Draft Mental Health Bill and groups looking at New Ways of Working (NHS Modernisation Agency, 2004) which include exploring new roles and responsibilities for clinical psychologists.

In order to ensure standards of service *A First Class Service: Quality in the New NHS* (DoH, 1998) introduced the concept of 'clinical governance' as 'a framework through which NHS organisations are accountable for continuously improving the quality of their services and safeguarding high standards of care by creating an environment in which excellence in clinical care will flourish'. It also gave clinical governance the same importance as financial governance suggesting that an emphasis on quality and the need for financial responsibility are not contradictory or incompatible aims. There are seven pillars of Governance one of which is Continuing Professional Development.

The above developments led to the establishment of the National Institute of Clinical Excellence (NICE). This sets standards for clinical practice. Various guidelines have been published that have direct relevance to the practice of Clinical Psychology e.g., on Eating Disorders (NICE, 2004a) and Diabetes (NICE, 2004b). Others are due for publication e.g., NICE clinical guidelines on Depression, and Generalized Anxiety and Panic Disorder. These guidelines are published in a number of forms – detailed guidelines, summaries, and information for patients and the public. They outline care pathways and provide the evidence for specific interventions – e.g., it is recommended that cognitive behaviour therapy provided by a suitably qualified and supervised therapist is the treatment of choice for Generalized Anxiety. Such guidelines have major CPD implications for clinical and other applied psychologists working in the NHS. These will be discussed later in this chapter.

A First Class Service (DoH, 1998) makes the role of life long learning, or CPD, within the framework of clinical governance, clear:

> setting standards is not enough. We need consistent action locally to ensure that national standards and guidance are reflected in the delivery of services. That action will be guided by a single, robust framework – a new system of clinical governance – to monitor health care quality at a local level. This will be backed up by lifelong learning by staff, through rigorous professional self-regulation and through a new system of external monitoring.

More specific guidance is provided through further Department of Health publications such as *Delivering Race Equality: A Framework for Action Mental Health Services Consultation Document* (DoH, 2003a). This document focuses on achieving improvements in three generic aspects of delivery (information, appropriate and responsive services and community engagement). These are termed the 'building blocks' as they are fundamental to delivering improvements in the outcomes and experiences of black and minority ethnic users and their carers and relatives. The three basic strategic objectives for mental health services are:

- to reduce and eliminate ethnic inequalities in mental health service experience and outcome;
- to develop a mental health work force that is capable of delivering effective mental health services to a multicultural population; and
- to enhance or build capacity within black and minority communities and the voluntary sector for dealing with mental health and mental ill health.

Again, such guidance highlights the clear CPD needs for psychology services to enable them to make the changes required to achieve such key strategic objectives.

A First Class Service also provided the basis for the formation of the Commission for Health Improvement (CHI): 'To ensure the drive for excellence is instilled throughout the NHS, the government will create a new Commission for Health Improvement. It will complement the introduction of clinical governance arrangements. . . . As a statutory body, at arms length from Government, the new commission will offer an independent guarantee that local systems to monitor, assure and improve clinical quality are in place.' (DoH, 1997) From April 2004, CHI took on greater powers and became the new Commission for Health Audit and Improvement (CHAI) with an inspection and monitoring role (Health & Social Care (Community Health and Standards) Act, 2003).

CHAI's inspections are carried out within the framework of the standards articulated within the NICE guidelines and National Service Frameworks (NSFs). The NSFs which are central to NHS Psychology Services include those covering Mental Health (DoH, 1999), Older People (DoH, 2001a) and for Children and Young People's Services (DoH, 2004b). The standards pertaining to Learning Disability Services are covered by the White Paper *Valuing People* (DoH, 2001b). The NSFs set out overall objectives for services, which are then more closely monitored by the Strategic Health Authorities and CHAI reviews. Service managers need to ensure that they provide services that meet the standards within the NICE guidelines and NSFs and ensure that their staff are competent to deliver these services in the ways described. Within this, they have, therefore, to ensure that they balance the individual CPD needs of their staff against those of their services.

The NHS Plan led to the emergence of new structures such as the NHS Modernization Agency and the NHS Leadership Centre. The NHS Leadership Centre was established in April 2001 to promote leadership development across the NHS. It includes in its aims to 'provide a national framework to support the development of leaders from clinical and non-clinical backgrounds, linking individual performance, appraisal, personal development planning, leadership development, career management and succession planning' (DoH, 2003b). It makes a clear link between the role of leadership and management in achieving a modernized NHS: 'Effective leadership is a key ingredient in modernising today's health service. Better leadership means better patient care and improved working practices for NHS staff' (DoH, 2003b). The Leadership Centre is responsible for providing training programmes for a range of NHS managers, and aspiring managers, working at different levels of seniority. Some clinical psychology managers in the UK have accessed the specific leadership programmes provided by the Leadership Centre for Allied Health Professionals (AHPs) and Healthcare Scientists (HCSs). The Centre provides training for these groups on clinical leadership, consultant development, middle managers and service directors. In particular, it has developed its LEO programme (Leading Empowered Organizations) (DoH, 2000b) to include AHPs and HCSs.

The Department of Health document, *Organizing and Delivering Psychological Therapies* (DoH, 2004c) highlights the importance of good leadership in the provision of psychology services – 'Good leadership is essential to the delivery of effective psychological therapy. Indeed, much development and innovation in the organisation of psychological therapy services in the past owes to the vision of individual leaders. However, psychological therapy services also need clear management' (DoH, 2004c).

Organizing and Delivering Psychological Therapies (DoH, 2004c) aims to translate national policy to improve standards of mental health treatment and care into local action. Recommendations for future action in this document include that training in psychological therapy should be on 'a training needs assessment that considers the gaps in service for clients and the development requirements of local professionals. On returning to work settings, trained professionals should be supported in order to practice and disseminate their skills' (DoH, 2004c). A further recommendation is that the NHS should ensure that managers can 'coordinate different parts of psychological therapy services and offer clear leadership, both professionally and managerially' (DoH, 2004c).

Psychology service managers, and aspiring managers, are able to access leadership training offered by the NHS Leadership Centre on a multiprofessional basis. Currently, however, there is only one known bespoke course for clinical psychology managers on management and leadership. The White Hart Management and Leadership Development Course (The White Hart Management and Leadership Development Course, 2004) was established in the early 1980s. It aims to improve the managerial and leadership effectiveness of participants and tends to be cited within the profession of clinical psychology in the UK as the only course of its type.

The Impact of Change on Psychology Services

The challenges for all managers within the modernized NHS described above are huge – and this includes the managers of clinical psychology services. As well as being directly affected by the changes within the NHS stemming from *The NHS Plan*, clinical psychology service managers are generally managing services that are larger and often growing faster than ever before. A recent Department of Health document illustrates this stating that 'therapists from all professional backgrounds can make a valuable contribution to the provision, teaching, research and development of effective psychological therapies . . . psychiatrists, psychologists, psychotherapists, nurses, social workers, occupational therapists, counsellors, arts and drama therapists, child psychotherapists and family therapists' (DoH, 2004c). Clinical psychology managers, therefore, manage services that are increasingly provided within a rich and varied context. Managing increasing diversity, across many different dimensions, presents new CPD needs for such managers.

This is illustrated by the increase in the number of commissioned places on UK doctoral clinical psychology training programmes over the past few years. Figure 7.1 shows the increase in training places through the Clearing House for Postgraduate Courses in Clinical Psychology from 1997 to 2004. This much-needed expansion of the profession has led to new challenges for clinical psychology service managers who now find themselves managing more complicated and diverse services covering a wide range of specialisms.

In addition to the aims of *The NHS Plan*, and the general trend towards increasing the number of clinical psychology training places over the past decade, the profession is also influenced by the guidance from various National Service Frameworks. The Department of Health's Workforce Action Team (2000) has highlighted the need for a significant

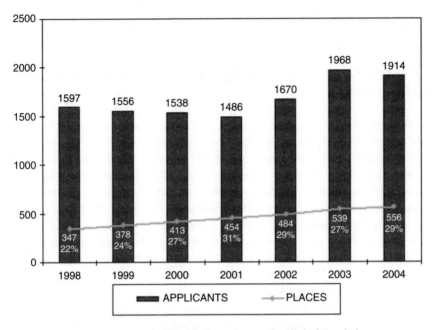

Source: The Clearing House for Postgraduate Courses in Clinical Psychology
Figure 7.1   The number of applicants for and places available on Doctoral Clinical Psychology Programmes

growth in the number of applied psychologists within the NHS in order to meet service demand.

A recent English survey of applied psychologists in health and social care and in the probation and prison service (BPS, 2005), found that there had been approximately an annual 9 per cent growth in the number of clinical psychologists on pre-qualification training courses over the past ten years. The report highlights the significant increase in demand for psychological care in recent years and predicts that this will only continue to increase with the implementation of NSFs. There has been an annual growth of posts of approximately 10 per cent and this is likely to increase too. The report estimates a demand–supply gap currently of minus 168 and suggests that this is likely to worsen to minus 412 by 2010 if there is no increase in the number of clinical psychologists being trained in the NHS. It recommends an increase in training commissions of 15 per cent. These figures highlight the rapid growth of psychological services within the NHS and the associated impact on managers. This in turn leads to new CPD needs for managers, as managers, and raises new challenges for managers in meeting the CPD needs of their individual staff and their services.

The CPD Needs of Clinical Psychology Service Managers as Managers

Like other NHS managers, clinical psychology managers have the task of ensuring that Clinical Governance is integral to their service and that they identify and meet their own CPD needs as managers as well as meet their CPD needs as clinicians. Crucially, they are also charged with the responsibility of ensuring that they identify and systematically meet the individual CPD needs of the staff they manage. These needs have to be balanced against the requirements of the services they deliver and be consistent with wider NHS agenda on life-long learning (DoH, 1998, 2001c). Managers use a variety of means to identify the CPD needs of their staff, most falling within a framework of appraisal or personal development plans combined with supervision.

As a small profession, it has not been until relatively recently that clinical psychology managers have started to attend to their needs as managers. The growth in the size of the profession, as described above, has meant that some psychology services have expanded considerably. In many areas, the reorganization of services within the NHS has resulted in psychology services merging within large mental health trusts. These developments mean that psychology managers now manage relatively large numbers of staff in increasingly complex service configurations. A recent survey of clinical psychology service managers by Gray (2004), for example, found that respondents manage services ranging from 1.8 wte (whole-time equivalent) to over 100 wte (average 30 wte). Psychology services usually also now include psychological therapists other than clinical psychologists such as, counsellors, counselling psychologists, cognitive-behaviour therapists, and of course Assistant Psychologists, trainees and administrative staff. Clinical Psychology managers are in the position of leading 'psychological services' within the NHS rather than only managing clinical psychologists, in order to meet the increasing demand for psychological assessment and intervention within the NHS. It is no longer the case, therefore, that simply being a qualified clinical psychologist necessarily provides managers with sufficient skills to manage their services.

There is little research exploring the CPD needs of clinical psychology service managers as managers. A recent survey (Golding, 2003b), carried out in the North West of England had as one of its aims to identify the CPD needs of clinical psychology service managers. A questionnaire was sent to 45 clinical psychology service managers working in the North West of England. Following recent reorganization of Trusts within the NHS, and the resulting changes in service structures, these managers consisted of the previous 'district' psychology managers as well as those managing the largest specialties in the North West. It asked questions about the nature of the managers' services, CPD structures, the managers' CPD needs as managers and data on recruitment and retention of their staff.

A total of 30 service managers completed and returned the questionnaires yielding a response rate of 66 per cent. Respondents managed services of varying sizes with the majority (10) managing between 40 and 100 staff. These included clinical psychologists, administrative staff, assistant psychologists, psychological therapists and counsellors.

Nineteen (63 per cent) respondents had received management training. Of those who had received this training, nine stated that they had found it very useful, nine found it fairly useful and one found it unhelpful. Respondents were invited to give open-ended answers to a question asking them to identify their training needs as managers. An analysis of their answers yielded the following main themes. The numbers in brackets denote the number of respondents who identified this training need. Only responses from two or more managers are reported here:

Service development issues:
Long-term strategic/service development   (5)
Resolving conflict/managing poor performance   (4)
Creating service level agreements   (2)
Advocating psychology in healthcare   (2)

Need to keep up to date with:
Government/NHS Department of Health policy   (9)
Organizational change   (2)
Professional issues – BPS etc   (2)

Increase knowledge and understanding of:
Take part in leadership/management training   (10)
Budgeting/financial control   (7)
Obtain regular support/peer supervision/mentor   (7)
Human resource issues   (4)
Information technology   (4)
Maintaining/improving clinical skills   (2)

Leadership and Clinical Governance

The need for good leadership and management skills within NHS organizations has been highlighted through the clinical governance structures. This is illustrated well by the main themes raised by CHI in its 20 clinical governance reviews (CGRs) of mental health trusts. The report (CHI, 2003) summarizes the key themes emerging from CHIs reviews in the seven technical components of clinical governance; together with a description of the service users' experience and the strategic capacity of trusts for improvement. It also highlights the good practice that CHI has found in its reviews. The report highlights the impact of reorganization change on the mental health trusts:

> Mental health trusts have experienced rapid organizational change. This has left many trusts, with multiple information systems for example, and the challenge in achieving coherence in this and the other areas of clinical governance. Mental health trusts are also generally large and diverse with a complex range of external relationships and the challenge of developing effective communication with staff operating from a multiplicity of sites. Many trusts lack the resources or infrastructure to support effective clinical governance while CHI review teams have commonly expressed concerns about trusts' capacity, managerial and clinical, to further develop this agenda.

CHI identifies the common characteristic of those Trusts performing well as including:

- Staffing – lower vacancy rates (particularly in psychiatry)/or active attempts to resolve vacancy problems, good progress with integration with social care, high staff morale, good progress with improving working lives.
- Leadership – cohesive, visible and well regarded by staff and partners.
- Strong relationships between clinicians and managers.
- Effective communication systems.

In contrast, Trusts that are performing less well also share common characteristics:

- Staffing – serious problems with recruitment generally in psychiatry and inpatient nursing, low morale and cultural and operational divide with social care staff.

- Leadership – seen as remote by staff, weaknesses in executive or non executive leadership.
- Disconnection between different parts of the trust.
- Lack of engagement of clinicians in management.
- Structures – limited structures below corporate level to support implementation and performance management of clinical governance, or structures to support clinical governance components.

The Relationship Between CPD and Good Practice

In addition to the above, a number of high profile NHS inquiries have highlighted the need for good management within the NHS and the role that CPD plays in this. This was one of the many issues highlighted in the Public Inquiry into Children's Heart Surgery at the Bristol Royal Infirmary 1984–1995 (The Report of the Public Inquiry into Children's Heart Surgery at the Bristol Royal Infirmary 1984–1995, 2001). The Department of Health's response to this report (DoH, 2002) noted the role of management and the training needs highlighted: 'managers should be subject to a code of behaviour and have the appropriate skills and competence to discharge their roles . . . more needs to be done to improve the quality of NHS management.' Further, the Department of Health noted the lack of training in management in the pre-qualification training programmes for NHS staff and recommended that 'All those preparing for a career in clinical care should receive some education in the management of healthcare, the health service and the skills required for management.' So where do clinical psychology service managers fit into this?

The Department of Health's recent report into the organization and delivery of psychological therapy services states that 'Psychological therapists report difficulties gaining access to further training and CPD'. – 'an effective program' of CPD is needed. This will 'ideally be integrated with routine staff appraisal and clinical supervision to ensure a high quality of practice and to ensure that any problems that arise in the interaction of patients are understood' (DoH, 2004c).

Despite the developments outlined above, there is little published research looking at the CPD needs of managers working in the NHS. A project that explored the CPD needs of the Allied Health Professionals' working in the North West of England (Taravandana, 2002) included work on the needs of AHP managers: 'The roles and responsibilities of AHP managers are continually changing and expanding and yet their CPD needs are often marginalized in order to support the requirements of clinical staff. To enable them to effectively embrace all the demands of modernization and the Health Professions Council (HPC), their learning and development needs in the following areas need to be addressed:

- management and leadership skills;
- managing learning;
- managing change;
- keeping up to date with NHS policy and modernization; and
- news ways of working' (Taravandana, 2002).

The project found that AHP's CPD priorities included training in leadership, management skills, change management, negotiating skills, influencing, thinking and working strategically. This suggests that NHS clinicians working as managers have CPD needs that are specific to their management role.

CPD Needs – Individual and Service

In addition to defining their own needs the survey of managers described above aimed to describe the current workforce, and the managers' views of CPD.

Clinical psychology service managers saw CPD as being vital to maintaining and improving the competence of their services independent of the size and type of service managed (Golding, 2003a). All but one of the managers had a system of appraisal in place in their service and saw this as vital to the identification of the CPD needs of their staff. The survey showed that the majority of managers managed a range of staff other than clinical psychologists. The most commonly cited groups included assistant psychologists, administrative staff, psychological therapists and counsellors. This shows the need for CPD structures in services to be flexible enough to encompass a range of related professionals. It also highlights the need for multiprofessional, as well as uniprofessional, CPD activities.

Respondents to this survey identified a number of factors that they perceived as outcomes in practice of their staff taking part in CPD activity. The most commonly cited outcomes were an increase in clinical knowledge and skills and an increase in motivation.

Respondents suggested that the amount of money available for meeting CPD needs and other resources was variable across the different services. This highlights a lack of uniformity of opportunity and a potential barrier to meeting the needs identified. Indeed, better access to information about CPD activities, the availability of funding for CPD activity and less pressure on time were cited most frequently as the factors that would increase and improve the CPD activity of their services.

The same survey examined data on staff in post in March 2001 compared to March 2002. This highlighted some interesting trends. The data indicate a fair degree of movement of staff in and out of clinical psychology services in the North West. It showed that overall, there was a net gain of 5.1 wte clinical psychologists which would be expected given the increase in training commissions. In the majority of cases, respondents indicated that when their staff left their services they changed posts within the NHS and within the North West. This shows an encouraging degree of commitment to both and shows overall a high level of retention of clinical psychologists within the NHS and the North West region.

The response rate from Golding's (2003a) survey is sufficient to be able to generalize some findings from these data to the wider pool of clinical psychology service managers. They show that this group has a high level of commitment to enabling their staff to take part in CPD activity in order to maintain and improve competence and thereby ensure that their staff are safe to practice.

Respondents were asked, at the end of the questionnaire, if they would be interested in taking part in a focus group to explore further some of the issues raised by the survey. A focus group took place in September 2002 (Golding, 2003b). The aim of the group was to explore further the themes generated by the survey and to enable some of the quantitative data gained from both surveys to be complemented by in-depth qualitative data and shed further light on some important issues.

The transcript from the focus group was analysed by two Assistant Psychologists in order to identify categories and key themes. Figure 7.2 presents the main theme categories schematically.

Participants generally felt that informal methods of identifying the CPD needs of their staff were helpful and some also felt that formal methods, such as appraisals, were useful too. They felt that there was a great need for them as managers to be flexible in identifying the CPD needs of their staff and achieving a balance between meeting the individual interests of staff and the needs of their services. Participants recognized the complex issues involved in identifying and meeting the CPD needs of their staff and in evaluating the outcome of CPD activity. They felt that the type of relationship they formed with their staff was

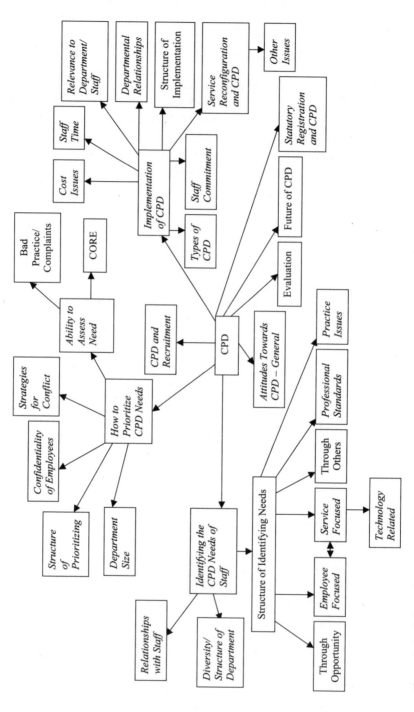

Figure 7.2 Schematic representation of the categories and themes generated by Golding's (2003) focus group

central to this process. Participants also highlighted the role that CPD has in enabling them to gain insight into the working practices of their staff and, therefore, in helping to maintain and improve competence. They also made a clear link between being able to offer good CPD experiences and recruiting and retaining staff. Participants' experiences of funding for CPD activity within their Trusts were mixed. Finally, participants anticipated that statutory regulation would bring about largely welcome changes in relation to CPD and had questions about how this would work and the impact of statutory regulation on practice.

Throughout the group, participants expressed some uncertainty about what CPD is in practice and how best to structure this within their services. The group process was such that the issues seemed more complex the more they were discussed. This is likely to have been, in part, a feature of the focus group methodology and was helpful in so far as it gave managers the opportunity to explore the issues thoroughly, beyond the point they were usually able to reach in more ordinary everyday discussions and settings. Participants expressed surprise at the length of their discussion within the group and viewed this positively.

The focus group allowed exploration of some of the themes from the survey enabling much richer information to emerge about some key issues. In particular, the importance managers place on informal, as well as formal, methods for identifying CPD needs, the role that CPD plays in recruitment and retention and the challenges of finding a balance between individual staff interests and service needs were highlighted through the group and help to make sense of information already gained through the surveys and through other aspects of the group.

Poor Performance

A First Class Service (DoH, 1998) proposes as one of the main components of Clinical Governance that procedures are in place for all professional groups to identify and remedy poor performance, for example:

- Critical incident reporting ensures that adverse events are identified, openly investigated, lessons are learned and promptly applied.
- Complaints procedures, accessible to patients and their families and fair to staff. Lessons are learned and recurrence of similar problems avoided.

- Professional performance procedures which take effect at an early stage before patients are harmed and which help the individual to improve their performance wherever possible, are in place and understood by all staff.
- Staff supported in their duty to report any concerns about colleagues' professional conduct and performance with clear statements from the Board on what is expected of all staff. Clear procedures for reporting concerns so that early action can be taken to support the individual to remedy the situation.

As NHS Psychology Service managers have responsibility for larger and more diverse services, it is essential that they acquire the skills and knowledge to respond to poor work performance in their work place from the staff they manage. There is evidence that managers see this as an important need (Golding, 2003a).

Managing Diversity

The Department of Health's (2003a) report *Delivering Race Equality* suggests that some basic changes, which have implications for CPD, need to be made to practice. It may be that more recently qualified clinical psychologists will have been better prepared to provide a culturally competent service. However, it can be argued that most therapies have been derived from a white ethnocentric base. This would suggest that we do have some work to do in this area if we are to deliver race equality. Table 7.1 illustrates pointers for improvement from this document with associated outcomes.

Clinical psychology service managers, along with other NHS managers, need to ensure that their services address issues of diversity and equality. A number of resources exist to enable managers to do this. These include the Department of Health's *Positively Diverse* programme (DoH, 2001d) which supports NHS Trusts in developing the capability and capacity for managing equality and diversity as mainstream issues through integration into core policy and practice. Details of the programme, and other Department of Health initiatives in this important area, can be found on the DoH's website following the 'Equality and Diversity' link. The programme offers a wide range of initiatives including a programme of learning and development. Clinical psychologists can link into these programmes as part of their CPD.

The BPS's DCP Race & Culture Special Interest Group provides another significant forum for clinical psychologists and others to

Table 7.1   Pointers for improvement and outcomes from The Department of Health's (2003a) report *Delivering Race Equality*

Pointers for improvement	Outcomes
Record information about beliefs and practices in patients' notes	Staff have the knowledge, skills and tools to enable them to deliver services to and in partnership with all groups in their community with confidence and sensitivity.
Build up knowledge of links with local religious organizations/ support network	
Provide access to appropriately trained interpreters so that consultations may take place in the language that patients are most comfortable with – do not use family members	Communities feel more confident in those services and readier to engage with them voluntarily.
Strive to ensure that patients have a choice regarding gender of practitioner where possible	
Require Board level reports on appropriateness and responsiveness of services to Black and minority ethnic communities as part of the Clinical Governance process	

address issues around diversity, seek advice and meet CPD needs through involvement with the SIG and/or attending national and local events organized by the SIG. Such events include the road shows that the SIG has recently been putting on to increase awareness of race and culture issues within the profession and beyond. Information about the SIG can be obtained from the BPS office in Leicester.

NICE Guidelines

NICE guidelines cover a variety of psychological disorders and suggest particular pathways and protocols for assessment and treatment. Clinical psychology is a small profession and has developed in a fairly individualistic, eclectic and ad hoc way. Such guidelines, however, mean that we will have to develop our practice in more standardized ways and be clearer about our relationships with other professionals providing psychological treatments. This has significant implications for CPD as clinical psychologists will have to be up to date and competent to practice in the ways demonstrated by NICE to be the most effective. For example the NICE Guidelines for Generalized Anxiety and Panic Disorder suggest that there are key priorities for implementation:

- The treatment option of choice should be available promptly.
- The treatment option of choice should be available without the need for referral to specialist mental health services.
- In the longer-term care of individuals with either panic disorder or generalized anxiety disorder, any of the following types of intervention may be offered and individual patient preferences should be taken into account. In descending order of long-term effectiveness, they are:
  - psychological therapy;
  - medication;
  - self help.
- If a psychological intervention is to be offered, then:
  - cognitive behavioural therapy (CBT) should be used.
  - CBT should be delivered only by suitably trained and supervised people who can demonstrate that they adhere closely to empirically grounded treatment protocols.
- Shared decision making between the individual and healthcare professionals should take place during the process of diagnosis and in all phases of care.
- Patients should be offered appropriate written information about their disorder and also about sources of support including local and national voluntary and self-help groups.
- All healthcare professionals involved in diagnosis and management should have consultation skills to demonstrably high standard (for example, those required of the MRCGP video assessment), so that a structured approach can be taken to the diagnosis and subsequent management plan of generalized anxiety disorder and panic disorder.
- If a patient presents in A&E, or other settings, with a panic attack, they should be referred to primary care for subsequent care, even if assessment has been undertaken.
- In most instances, if there have been two interventions provided (any combinations of medication, psychological intervention or

bibliotherapy) and the person still has significant symptoms, then offer referral to specialist mental health services.

Such recommendations have clear implications for the practice of clinical psychology and therefore inevitably for CPD.

User/Carer Involvement

A final example of NHS development which impact upon managers' own CPD needs and the CPD needs of their services is the area of user involvement. As a profession, our usual mode of practice is to provide individual formulations and treatment plans in collaboration with our service users. Clinical psychologists, therefore, are broadly supportive of involving users meaningfully in the delivery of services. However it may be too easy for us to rely on this as sufficient effort towards genuine user involvement. One recommendation in from a recent Department of Health (2004c) report is to involve service user groups in the planning and evaluation of psychological therapy services and develop a checklist of features against which performance can be measured. User involvement in services also helps to ensure that appropriate information about the service is available in a meaningful format and from a service user's perspective. There is a clear need, therefore, to develop systems for multiple routes for user involvement. Such changes in our practice have numerous implications in terms of CPD. These cut across recruitment and selection practices, through record keeping and report writing to involvement of users in service development and NHS Trust structures.

Action Plan

This chapter has covered a wide range of issues relevant to psychology service managers and CPD. We did not intend to provide readers with an exhaustive list, but wanted to stimulate thought and discussion around the link between NHS policy and service development and the CPD implications for services and individual staff. Within this, we have addressed the role of the service manager in meeting the CPD needs of their staff as well as themselves as managers. The action plan shown in Table 7.2 summarizes the main issue raised and suggests areas of action for managers in addressing these.

Table 7.2 An action plan for service managers

Service issue	Areas for action
New Ways of Working Issues raised, for example, in *The NHS Plan* and various National Service Frameworks	Be familiar with NHS targets and their implications, explore ways of reducing waiting times and review relevant research.
NICE guidance e.g., Eating Disorders, Generalized Anxiety and Panic Disorders – (a) 'stepped care' and use of protocols (b)routine measures of clinical outcome	Consult users and carers, undertake local research and audit
Delivering Race Equality: A Framework for Action	
To reduce and eliminate inequalities in experience and outcome	Acquire knowledge of local ethnic mix, undertake local research and audit
Management and Leadership Skills	
Creating and fostering an environment in which excellence in clinical care will flourish	Seek own supervision/mentoring at a level appropriate for a service manager. Explore multiprofessional NHS mentoring schemes
Resolving conflict/managing poor performance	Attend available courses e.g., LEO (Leadership in Empowered Organizations, the White Hart management and leadership development course, set up/pursue local training developments in this area etc.)
Actively address long-term strategic/service development	Join the BPS's DCP Managers' Faculty – to keep in touch with, and contribute to discussions about, policy and service development issues relevant to psychology services, and to give you a source of peer support and guidance Visit the NHS Leadership Centre website and make use of its resources www.leadershipdevelopment.nhs.uk

Continued

Table 7.2 *Continued*

Service issue	Areas for action
	Complete 360 degree assessment available at www.leadershipdevelopment.nhs.uk Apply to become a CHI reviewer – www.healthcarecommission.org.uk

Managing Change

For example (and there are many): • New roles and lead to role responsibilities e.g.,reform, prescribing • New grade of NHS psychologist i.e. Psychology Associates	Address the impact of change in your service through management supervision/mentoring Keep abreast of developments that will change such as Mental Health Act introduction of Psychology Associates

Managing Learning

• Developing the workforce • Delivering Race Equality • Working Together, Learning Together • More varied workforce • Psychological services • Greater degree of specialism • Supervision of trainees	Gain familiarity with the work of others through 'shadowing' Conduct regular appraisals (self and others) Encourage/facilitate maintenance of CPD logs in line with the BPS's most recent guidance. Visit the BPS's website(www.bps.org.uk) regularly to track developments regarding recording of CPD and progress with statutory regulation. Visit the HPC's website (www.hpc-uk.org) regularly to track development regarding the possible regulation of applied psychology and developments regarding the HPC's policy re CPD.

Keeping Up To Date with NHS Policy and Modernization

NSFs Valuing People, Older People. Mental Health, Children and Young People's Services.	Join the BPS's DCP Managers' faculty. Visit the Department of Health's website (www.dh.gov.uk) regularly Visit the NHS Modernization Agency's website (www.nhs.uk/modernnhs) regularly

Summary and Conclusion

This chapter has discussed some of the major changes within the NHS in recent years that impact upon the delivery of psychological therapy services. It highlights the many CPD needs that arise from these developments and how psychology service managers have to attend to their needs as managers as well as ensure that the staff they manage have their CPD needs identified and met within a systematic and effective framework of appraisal. The chapter has also highlighted the many issues that arise for managers when seeking to ensure that they meet the ends of their individual staff, accommodating personal and career needs, balanced against ensuring that they meet the CPD needs of their services so that they can provide a competent psychological therapy service to meet the needs of the NHS in the twenty-first century. These issues raise a number of dilemmas for managers leading to an increased need for psychology service managers to take up the many leadership and management courses currently offered within the NHS to ensure that they can meet this challenge.

REFERENCES

British Psychological Society (2003). Statutory regulation: Your questions answered. *The Psychologist*, 16(5), 264–5.

British Psychological Society (2005). *English Survey of Applied Psychologists in Health & Social Care and in the Probation and Prison Service*. The British Psychological Society: Leicester.

Commission for Health Improvement (2003). *Emerging Themes from Mental Health Trust Reviews*. Commission for Health Improvement, London.

Department of Health (1997). *The New NHS Modern Dependable*. Department of Health, London.

Department of Health (1998). *A First Class Service: Quality in the New NHS*. (HSC. 1998/13). Department of Health, London.

Department of Health (1999). *National Service Framework for Mental Health: Modern Standards and Service Models*. Department of Health, London.

Department of Health (2000a). *The NHS Plan: A Plan for Investment, a Plan for Reform*. Department of Health, London.

Department of Health (2000b). *Comprehensive Leadership Programme Announced for Nurses, Midwives and Health Visitors*. Press Release, 200/0690. Department of Health: London.

Department of Health (2001a). *National Service Framework for Older People*. Department of Health, London.

Department of Health (2001b). *Valuing People: A New Strategy for Learning Disability for the 21st Century. A White Paper.* Department of Health: London.

Department of Health (2001c). *Working Together – Learning Together: A Framework for Lifelong Learning for the NHS.* London: Department of Health.

Department of Health (2001d). *Positively Diverse: The Field Book: A Practical Guide to Managing Diversity in the NHS.* London: Department of Health.

Department of Health (2002). *Learning from Bristol: The Department of Health's Response to the Report of the Public Inquiry into Children's Heart Surgery at the Bristol Royal Infirmary 1984–1995.* Department of Health: London.

Department of Health (2003a). *Delivering Race Equality: A Framework for Action: Mental Health Service: Consultation Document.* Department of Health, London.

Department of Health (2003b). *An Introduction to the NHS Leadership Centre.* Department of Health, London.

Department of Health (2004a). *Agenda for Change: Proposed Agreement: Final Draft.* Department of Health, London.

Department of Health (2004b). *National Service Framework for Children, Young People and Maternity Services.* Department of Health, London.

Department of Health (2004c). *Organising and Delivering Psychological Therapies.* Department of Health, London.

Golding, L. (2003a). *Final Report of the Continuing Professional Development Survey of NHS Clinical Psychology Service Managers Working in the North West of England.* Unpublished project report.

Golding, L. (2003b). *Exploring Clinical Psychology Service Managers' Ideas about Continuing Professional Development: Report of a Focus Group.* Unpublished report.

Gray, I. (2004). *Managers' Faculty CPD Funding Survey.* Unpublished report.

Health & Social Care (Community Health and Standards) Act (2003). HMSO. London.

NHS Modernization Agency (2004). *New Ways of Working: Update.* NHS Modernization Agency.

National Institute for Clinical Excellence (2004a). *CG9 Eating Disorders: Core Interventions in the Treatment and Management of Anorexia Nervosa, Bulimia Nervosa and Related Eating Disorders – NICE Guideline.* NICE: London.

National Institute for Clinical Excellence (2004b). *CG15 Type 1 Diabetes: Diagnosis and Management of Type 1 Diabetes in Adults: Full Guideline Development Section.* NICE: London.

The Report of the Public Inquiry into Children's Heart Surgery at the Bristol Royal infirmary 1984–1995: Learning from Bristol (Cm 5207) July 2001. The Stationery Office.

Taravandana (2002). *CPD Strategy for the AHPs in the North West.* Unpublished Report. Cumbria & Lancashire WDC.

The White Hart Clinical Psychology Management and Leadership Development Course (2004). *Course Handbook.* The White Hart Clinical Psychology Management and Leadership Development Course: Harrogate.

Workforce Action Team (2000). *Mental Health National Service Framework Workforce Planning Education and Training Underpinning Programme: Interim Report by the Workforce Action Team.* Department of Health, London.

WEBSITES

British Psychological Society: www.bps.org.uk
CHI: www.healthcarecommission.org.uk
Department of Health: www.dh.gov.uk
Health Professions Council: www.hpc-uk.org
NHS Modernization Agency: www.nhs.uk/modernnhs
National Institute of Clinical Excellence (NICE): www.nice.org.uk
North West Clinical Psychology CPD Scheme: www.gmsha.nhs.uk/core/psychology

Chapter 8

Evaluating CPD: A Practical Framework, Illustrated with Clinical Supervision

Derek Milne, Ian James and Alia Sheikh

Introduction

The definition of CPD provided in Chapters 1 and 2 implies a key role for careful evaluation, but despite the growing importance of CPD, an agreed framework for its evaluation has yet to emerge. This is in contrast to the 'performance framework', which has been specified within the NHS for the evaluation of clinical services (DoH, 1998). The performance framework addresses six aspects of performance for a service, including fair access, clinical outcomes and the effective delivery of appropriate healthcare. In the latter category we find that the Department expects that appropriate healthcare is 'delivered by appropriately trained and educated staff' (p. 63). The same policy document (*A First Class Service: Quality in the New NHS*) notes that the effective delivery of healthcare requires a continuing process of updating and maintaining expertise. The NHS's Mental Health Frameworks (DoH, 1999) extended this emphasis by noting the need to 'develop lifelong learning and reflective practice' (p. 111).

It is, therefore, timely to ask: how might one best evaluate the effective delivery of 'appropriate' CPD? In the absence of a clearly prescribed approach within the NHS, one may either import evaluation methods from related areas (for example, from the psychotherapy process evaluation literature), or one can transfer a relevant framework from elsewhere within the NHS, as in the research and development initiative (R&D). We prefer the latter course of action, partly because such a framework is likely to be highly congruent with other forms of evaluation that will affect psychologists within the NHS. A further reason is that the framework we outline below is a simple yet powerful way to evaluate CPD, one that is unlikely to trigger debates about theoretical orientation. Our 'integrative' or general framework is also based on one of the most effective ways of fostering CPD, namely to promote reflection through careful questioning. For these reasons, we believe that this simple framework is appropriate for the task of evaluating CPD, whether as a participant, a provider, or as a purchaser. We will therefore use it to summarize relevant methods and ideas from the CPD and wider literature.

If we now import this framework from the R&D initiative, we can set out an approach to the evaluation of CPD, as in Table 8.1. Although there are alternative frameworks for evaluating CPD activities, we believe that Table 8.1 provides a coherent and practical approach, highlighting the main evaluation options.

Chapter Plan

Within the remainder of this chapter, we will go on to articulate how we believe these questions can best be answered, in relation to CPD. In order to keep our illustrations of evaluation suitably focused, we will refer primarily to clinical supervision as our example of CPD. There are several reasons for so doing. One of these is that supervision appears to be the most common form of CPD (Milne, Keegan et al., 2000). Also, within the profession (and within allied professions) supervision has become a mandatory part of career-long clinical practice. In addition, supervision is the area in which we believe we have greatest expertise, and therefore it provides us with our best source of evaluation illustrations. Lastly, being one of the most widely practised forms of CPD, with perhaps one of the longest histories, the evaluation literature in the supervision field is among the most extensive. Perhaps its closest competitor is the staff training and development literature, and where appropriate this field (and others that contribute additional ideas) will be introduced into our illustrations.

In the next section, following the headings in our framework (Table 8.1) we introduce our own thinking about what is the 'right' thing to do in the name of supervision (and related CPD). We continue the emphasis on reflection as a major ingredient, embedding it within an experiential learning cycle. We then show how guidelines and manuals can support such a theoretical model. In addressing the next question – 'has the right thing been done?' – we next show how process evaluations contribute to CPD, again providing an example from our own experience of work within the clinical supervision field.

Table 8.1 A framework for evaluating the effectiveness of CPD

Query	Approach
What is the right thing to do?	The 'right' form of CPD will be guided by our theoretical models, and by clinical guidelines, treatment manuals and professional consensus.
Has the right thing been done?	It is important to show adherence to the 'right' CPD method or approach, as in following a treatment manual faithfully or in providing supervision appropriately. Audit is one major way to evaluate CPD in terms of whether the 'right' thing has been done.
Has it been done right?	This relates to the points above, but moves us on to issues about whether a CPD activity has been provided with the necessary skill and interpersonal effectiveness. These are complementary and necessary aspects of competent activity, alongside adherence to a given approach.
Did it result in the right outcomes?	Psychologists will be especially familiar with this part of the framework, which concerns different kinds of results or outputs. Most common in CPD are reaction or satisfaction evaluations, but we should also assess learning outcomes and the transfer of these to our routine work.
Was the CPD context right?	This is one that we have added to the standard R&D list of key 'performance' questions. It is a question that most psychologists would also presumably regard as necessary, in that we tend to view behaviours as fundamentally linked to their context. In this sense, we need to evaluate whether CPD has the 'right' kind of facilitating environment (for example peer and manager support).

Having addressed the questions of what to do and whether it has been done correctly, we go on to ask whether in other respects it has been done well. This brings in other aspects of process, particularly those of skill (competence) and interpersonal effectiveness. Here we will try to show how CPD can be evaluated by outlining a way of evaluating supervision that has been developed locally. We then proceed to focus on whether a good model, one that has been adopted and followed faithfully, results in the intended outcomes. There are a number of options for making sense of outcome evaluation, and we adopt one of the best known, that of Kirkpatrick (1967), with appropriate modifications. In this penultimate section we will set out the four levels of outcome that CPD can achieve, and again illustrate it from supervision research. In the final section we will concentrate on the 'right' organizational climate for CPD activity.

What is the Right Thing to Do?

The cycle in Figure 8.1 summarizes the essential steps that need to be addressed when designing and delivering a CPD programme. Because of our emphasis on supervision, we refer to it as the 'supervision cycle', but it is taken from the teaching cycle (Goldstein, 1993) and would appear to apply to most CPD activities. Thus, the 'right thing to do' in designing and delivering CPD seems to us to entail four inter-linked steps. The provider, such as a supervisor, starts by identifying the participant's development needs and then sets appropriate learning goals. The content that is addressed and the methods used should then address these goals (see Table 8.2 for an example), leading on to an evaluation of the effectiveness of these steps in achieving the agreed goals.

Turning to the 'activity' part of the cycle, providers such as supervisors have a number of options through which to pursue the identified goals (see column 1 of Table 8.2). For example, they can give new information, or assign a task, or encourage the supervisee to experience how it feels to deliver or undertake a specified task. It is also customary to encourage reflection and the integration of the information learned from the four previous modes into a revised conceptual understanding. The themes described in column 1 are based on Kolb's (1984) experiential learning cycle of 'experimenting, experiencing, reflecting, and conceptualizing'.

It is relevant to note that, while the themes outlined in the columns of Table 8.2 may seem to suggest that the modes of experiential learn-

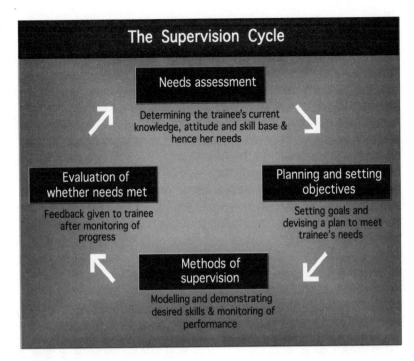

Figure 8.1 The supervision cycle
Source: Goldstein (1993)

ing are independent, this is far from the case. Consistent with Kolb's perspective, effective learning would normally involve the supervisor taking the supervisee through all of the different modes of learning as part of an integrated, multimodal encounter with something new or different. The four modes also interact in interesting ways, tempting the supervisor to deviate from the completion of the cycle. For example, a new and challenging conceptual understanding may only be attained through a supervisor's challenging of (or even disagreement over) the existing understanding held by the supervisee. This represents a deviation from the normal cycle, as here the supervisor is moving from 'conceptualizing' straight to the emotional/affective accompaniments to the 'activity' phase.

Improved competence will typically entail experimenting with an approach under conditions of anxiety (such as a role play), and it is therefore not surprising if a CPD participant seeks alternatives, such as a more comfortable conversation about the same competence. Direct

Table 8.2 The 'right' model, illustrated with reference to supervision

Key steps in supervision, following the experiential model	Related techniques used by the supervisor, designed to 'mediate' learning in the supervisee	Mini-outcomes and processes of learning, the 'mechanisms' of change
1. *'Conceptualizing'*: Give new information (e.g., giving the supervisee instructions – 'When undertaking a systematic desensitization programme, you do X, Y and Z.')	Informing; instructing; providing written material; managing the learning environment.	Add new information to existing knowledge-base; be clear about what needs to be done.
2. *'Doing'*: Give supervisee a task to do (e.g., 'Show me how you would introduce the idea of systematic desensitization to a client suffering from panic disorder.')	Behavioural experiment; role play; demonstrating / modelling; imagery work; simulation.	Develop new skills; identify areas of weakness; have experience of doing a task in a safe setting; develop confidence.
3. *'Reflecting'*: Get the supervisee to reflect (e.g., 'Are there any occasions when it may be inappropriate to use this approach?')	Socratic questioning; cognitive dissonance or awareness raising techniques; circular questioning; listing pros / cons; thinking time; self-disclosure; feedback.	Time and mental space to reflect; examine inconsistencies in current thinking; re-appraise situations; recognize alternatives.

Continued

Table 8.2 *Continued*

4. *'Experiencing'*: Get the supervisee to experience emotions/ sensations (e.g., 'How comfortable would you feel if I asked you to demonstrate the task in a role-play scenario right now?'; or: ' I will demonstrate the method, and I'd like you to focus on your emotional reactions to my questions.')	Focus on emotions (own and supervisees); legitimate and raise awareness of accompanying affective reactions to learning; explore and label physiological reactions.	Become more aware of impact of emotions; better empathize with clients; feel more contained in supervision session; be able to develop greater level of trust with supervisor; enhance 'here and now' and spontaneity experiences.
5. *'Re-conceptualizing'*: Get the supervisee to integrate more information and re-conceptualize (e.g., 'How might that relate to what happened/to theory/to your prior experience?').	Problem solve; brainstorm; formulate case jointly in session, stressing link to theory; summarize and 'chunk' relevant information; check grasp and clarity; self-disclose, to input own experience.	Be able to see the situation in a more coherent manner; have more clarity about client; be able to develop better conceptualizations; to recognize how others view something; to make related plans or set relevant objectives.

observation or recordings of our competence are likely to evoke related reactions, serving to make the smooth execution of the experiential cycle rare. When learning from experience there is a tension between holding on to what is currently known and developing a new, potentially better understanding. Nevertheless, there are occasions when supervisors may produce change purely by imparting new information to the supervisee (e.g., by simply outlining a fact and hence what the supervisee should do). The occasions when a supervisor may use such a directive approach tend to be when the learner has a concrete learning style, when the timing exquisitely addresses a development need (as when the supervisee is perplexed and anxious to resolve an understanding), or when there is insufficient time. For these kinds of reasons, therefore, moving smoothly around the experiential learning cycle is likely to be the exception rather than the rule. Note, however, that the learning impact of adopting a full, cyclical approach usually ensures improved outcomes and enjoyment.

In column 2 of Table 8.2 there are details of methods that might be used by the supervisor to bring about changes in the supervisee. These are described in observable terms (e.g., use of written material, role play, feedback). Omitted from Table 8.2 (to simplify matters) are items that we view as fundamental to effective learning (such as interpersonal effectiveness, collaboration) but which may be harder to pinpoint. Within our model of the 'right thing to do' (i.e., Figure 8.1) these items should be viewed as part of the surrounding context or development environment, influencing 'activity' and the other steps in the supervision cycle. In this sense, our methods may be thought of as 'mediators' of change, while the contextual factors are 'moderators', to borrow from the psychotherapy literature.

The impact of the supervisor's mediators and moderators are outlined in column 3 of Table 8.2, in terms of experiential learning impacts or outcomes. To continue the psychotherapy analogy, these are the 'mechanisms of change', the learning processes that result in development. Although from the evaluation perspective some of these outcomes and processes are rather subjective and even elusive in nature, it is possible to quantify them via the use of qualitative questionnaires and/or semi-structured interviews. For instance, the 'Helpful Aspects of Supervision Questionnaire' (HASQ) allows the supervisee to reflect on and note anything that might have been particularly helpful during an individual session. This has been adapted by the first author from Llewellyn et al.'s (1988) 'Helpful Aspects of Therapy Questionnaire', and has also been modified for use as a way to evaluate workshops (Helpful Aspects of Workshop Questionnaire' (HAWQ) – see Figure 8.2).

Helpful Aspects of Workshop Questionnaire (HAWQ)

Your Name (optional): _____

Date of Workshop: _____

1   Please rate how helpful this workshop was overall:

Very helpful	Fairly helpful	Neither helpful/unhelpful	Fairly helpful	Very helpful
1	2	3	4	5

2   Of the events which occurred in this workshop, which one do you feel was the most helpful for you personally? It might be something you said or did, or something the facilitators said or did. Can you say why it was helpful?

3   How helpful was this particular event? Rate this on the scale:

Neither helpful/unhelpful	Fairly helpful	Very helpful
3	4	5

4   Did anything else of particular importance happen during this workshop? Include anything else which may have been helpful or anything which may have been unhelpful.

Figure 8.2   The 'Helpful Aspects of Workshop Questionnaire' (HAWQ)

The HAWQ is appended, to facilitate evaluation of these forms of CPD (simply replace 'workshop' with 'supervision', as necessary).

One could argue that there should be a fourth column in Table 8.2, concerning the impact of the supervision on the client. This dimension has not been addressed above in order not to further complicate the model. However, this is clearly an important dimension, which is addressed more fully in Milne, James et al. (2002).

Having outlined a model of 'the right thing to do', one can next determine whether an example of supervision (or of another form of CPD) is consistent with it.

Has the Right Thing Been Done?

Prior to assessing the degree of adherence to a given model of CPD, one must identify the key features and define them clearly. This is akin to specifying standards within an audit. In the present example, the simplest test of adherence would be to determine whether the given sample of supervision (as per Table 8.2) contained those techniques described in column 2. These items are observable and thus are easily defined and reliably scored within a quantitative evaluation (an illustration, 'Teacher's PETS' follows shortly). But a qualitative approach to this form of CPD is also possible. Recent work by Milne et al. (2003) used a grounded theory analysis of a sample of CBT supervision to identify 14 such supervision methods and techniques. These were then defined and examples provided (see Table 8.3 for an illustration). The items identified were: agenda-setting and managing; behavioural tasks; re-evaluation of thoughts; collaboration; conceptualization; feedback; gathering information; goal setting; informing/educating; modelling; reflection; socialization to the model; summarizing and clarifying; supporting and understanding.

It is noteworthy that many of these items were reflected in previous work, which led to the development of a scale for evaluating training and supervision, called 'Teachers' PETS' (Process Evaluation of Training and Supervision: Milne, James et al., 2002). This scale, based on the above model of supervision, also had 14 well-defined items covering the activities of the supervisor, related (through alternating the coding focus, from supervisor to supervisee) to their impact on the supervisee's experiential learning (i.e., 'reflecting',

Table 8.3   Example of a qualitative approach: Two themes extracted from a grounded theory analysis of supervision

Theme	Definition	Examples of supervisor statements
Gathering information	Asking for information and facts; defining the client's problem	'Tell me about the panic.'
Conceptualization	Providing a model of coping/problem formulation/guiding learners to conceptualize	'One way of understanding this situation would be . . .' 'Some people make sense of things this way . . .'

'planning', etc.). In PETS, a supervisor typically submits a video recording of his or her supervision, which is coded using a 'momentary time sampling' technique, to determine the presence of these theoretically important items within the sample of supervision. The results of this assessment provide a profile of the methods used by the supervisor, which can be used to determine whether or not the supervisor was adhering to accepted standards of supervisory practice (sometimes called a 'structural' or 'content' evaluation). By virtue of concurrently recording the impact of these strategies on the learner, PETS allows one to also assess the effectiveness of the supervision (an 'outcome' or 'functional' evaluation). This evaluation criterion will be addressed soon, but next we turn to the third of our CPD evaluation framework questions.

Has it Been Done Right?

To know that some CPD, such as supervision, was provided in a theoretically sound way does not necessarily mean that it has been done 'right'. One only has to think of one's own efforts to develop competence to come up with examples to support this reasoning, such as trying to follow a guideline or a manual. A feeling of being 'de-skilled' may also occur, further diminishing competence. The more we try to follow the guidelines, the more we will tend to make a mess of the actual delivery, at least until we develop a good level of competence. Therefore, in addition to adherence to the 'right' approach to CPD, there should also be an evaluation of the supervision or CPD in relation to the competence with which it is delivered. Competence is the accurate and skilful provision of a validated model or approach in such a way that it is likely to result in significant change for the learner (Waltz et al., 1993). Hence, an evaluation of competence requires an assessment of the supervisor's level of skill in applying the model of supervision. Ideally, the evaluation would examine the delivery of supervision and a succession of its impacts (its generalization). This might include the impact on the trainee's learning (knowledge, skills and attitudes), transfer to that supervisee's routine work (including benefits for the client) and ultimately an evaluation of the system-wide impacts (Kirkpatrick, 1967). The latter could include the way that a good CPD programme within a service unit or department affects staff morale generally, perhaps measured by archival absenteeism/sickness data. This 'stepwise evaluation' logic (Milne, 2005) is picked up again in the next section.

If one conducted such an assessment in relation to the material in Table 8.2, one could rate the competence with respect to the supervisor's methods and techniques, and then gauge the impact on the trainee. In terms of the latter, one could invite supervisees to complete a post-supervision questionnaire regarding their experience of the supervision, such as HASQ, or perhaps employ a post-supervision interview.

There are other scales for examining competence. For example, together with colleagues, the authors are currently working on STARS (the Supervision Training and Assessment Rating Scale). STARS is designed to foster effective CBT supervision through pinpointing competent supervisory practices and by corrective feedback. In addition, prior to the evaluation aspect, STARS provides a series of guidelines on competent practice, one per item, representing a supervision manual.

The scale is composed of 15 items and a combination of checklist and rating scale response formats are used for the evaluation of supervision. The individual items are set out as discrete statements of the main supervisory activities (e.g., 'agenda setting'), each of which is then defined in terms of observable behaviours. These behaviours are assessed as either present (circle 'Y' for yes), absent (circle 'N' for no) or not applicable (circle 'NA'). As all STARS items are phrased as desirable supervisory behaviours, 'yes' replies are taken to indicate adherence to the supervision standards, 'no' replies to indicate non-adherence (i.e., the behaviour would normally be expected to occur); and 'not applicable' to indicate that the item was not relevant within the observed sample. In this way, higher scores on the checklist part of STARS indicate 'better' supervision. That is, supervision that adheres closely to the expected CBT standards, at least in the view of this group of experienced supervisors. We plan next to seek the consensus of others nationally, in addition to other psychometric work (contact the second author for details). For each STARS item there is an activity-specific rating scale. This is intended to capture the effectiveness or outcome of each supervision skill, and to furnish feedback to the supervisor ('formative' evaluation). Finally, there is an overall rating of competence, which might be used for accreditation or research purposes ('summative' evaluation).

Such aspects provide important foundations for the evaluation of CPD. They allow standards to be defined and agreed consensually, appropriate methods and their delivery to be justified and specified, and clarify how participants, providers and purchasers alike can benefit.

Did it Result in the Right Outcomes?

An especially important dimension of evaluation is whether the outcomes of CPD resulted in changes in the 'right' areas. This equates to the question: 'were the goals of CPD achieved?' It is these changes that justify the implementation of CPD in the first place, making the outcomes a necessary part of CPD evaluation.

While various models of outcome evaluation have been proposed in the literature, Kirkpatrick's (1967) taxonomy for the evaluation of training is 'the most popular' (Arthur et al., 2003, p. 235) and provides a clear framework with which to evaluate change resulting from a CPD activity. As outlined earlier, according to Kirkpatrick there are four levels of outcome: 'reactions' to the CPD, 'learning', 'results', and 'impacts'. Specifically, 'reactions' include affective and motivational responses, such as the delegates' liking of, and feelings towards, a training programme (e.g., 'satisfaction' with the inter-personal effectiveness of the CPD provider and opinions about the 'acceptability' of the content/material). The second level of outcome, learning, is normally defined cognitively (for example, an increase in declarative and/or procedural knowledge), behaviourally (i.e., improved proficiency), or affectively (e.g., attitude change). The next level, 'results', is represented by the use of what has been learned in a CPD context (such as a workshop) to the workplace, so providing evidence that this produced a result across settings and time ('transfer' or generalization). Finally, the fourth level of outcome – impact – occurs when CPD creates system-level changes, such as cost reductions, decreased absenteeism and turnover, increased staff morale, or higher quality of care in services. Based on this model, therefore, change can be conceptualized on four interdependent levels, allowing for a thorough examination of the outcomes of CPD. It is a taxonomy because these levels are increasingly complex and hence exacting to procure or evaluate. As we will all have experienced, measuring 'reactions' to CPD can be done very simply, as in a simple workshop 'satisfaction' rating out of 10. However, judging the extent to which CPD contributes to improved psychology services is much more difficult. On the other hand, 'reactions' are of minimal value (formatively, summatively, or in any other respect). To illustrate, Warr et al. (1999) obtained the familiar positive reactions to a training programme, but found that these 'were generally unrelated to subsequent job behaviour' (p. 351). By contrast, to establish that something like supervision makes a service more effective is highly useful information. A major meta-analytic review, summarizing nearly 400 staff training studies (Arthur et al., 2003), also showed that these progressively more exacting levels of evaluation were associated with substantial decreases in the obtained effect sizes. The authors speculated that this progressive decrease in the obtained effectiveness of training, from 'reactions' to 'impact', was due to such factors as a lack of opportunity for the trainees to perform new skills, and adverse post-training environments (such as a lack of support from managers or supervisors for the trainees newly acquired competences).

As a way of illustrating Kirkpatrick's (1967) model, and the kinds of measures that can be used to evaluate CPD outcomes, we will now apply this taxonomy to our theme of supervision. For convenience, we have chosen a sample of papers from the review of supervision provided by Milne and James (2000). Table 8.4 displays a summary of each study, highlighting the measure that was used to evaluate the impact of supervision, as well as the outcomes that were obtained.

For example, in Clark et al.'s (1986) study, the impact of supervision was assessed via ratings of observed skills, and it was shown that changes in performance level and skills were the primary outcome of a training programme. Thus, change in this study occurred at Kirkpatrick's level of 'learning effects'. This outcome seems consistent with the goals and methods of the programme, which comprised a lecture, demonstration, practice, and feedback components. More impressively, Dyer et al. (1984), found that a supervision programme led trainees to transfer specific behavioural changes to their work with their clients. These learning and transfer outcomes were also found as a result of an in-service programme for supervisors by Ivancic et al. (1981). Observations showed that trained staff modified their interactions with clients, illustrating changes at both the behavioural (skill transfer) as well as the organizational (quality of care) levels. A training programme by Fleming et al. (1996) added a 'reaction' evaluation. They reported that their training resulted in high satisfaction among supervisees, knowledge improvement and the transfer of skills from a simulated training situation to their clinical interactions (generalization). Finally, Frisch's (1989) study demonstrated how evaluation of the 'impact' level in Kirkpatrick's (1967) taxonomy can be accomplished. In this study, supervision was evaluated by means of structured interview, survey questionnaire, and a self-report measure. The findings showed that supervision resulted in changes at the affective, cognitive, behavioural, and organizational levels. Affective change was represented by increased job satisfaction, while cognitive change included increased knowledge of supervision practice. Organizational change ('impact') was demonstrated through increased job productivity.

Table 8.4 A mini-review of the literature, indicating methods and measures for evaluating the 'right' outcomes in clinical supervision

Study	Method of evaluation	Outcomes
Clark et al. (1986)	Behavioural assessment (observing and rating supervisor's skills)	Changes in performance/skills.
Dyer et al. (1984)	Random observational procedures. Ratings according to established instrument.	Students spent more time engaged in activities that were functional and age-appropriate. These results were maintained for a 5-month period.
		Increased the amount of time students engaged in activities in age-appropriate curricular domains. Therefore, more well-rounded schedule of activities provided. Quality of planned activities improved.
Ivancic et al. (1981)	Observations.	Staff interactions with clients: increased language interactions. Supervision procedures effective in increasing and maintaining (4–5 months) staff behaviours.
Fleming et al. (1996)	Observational procedures via videotape. Scored by means of recording frequency of use of each of nine skills used by supervisor.	Improvement in skill and performance from baseline to post-training phase.
		Supervisors generalized use of skills from simulated training situation to actual interactions with supervisees (skill transfer). General improvement of teaching performance.

Continued

Table 8.4 *Continued*

		Supervisees reported satisfaction (received praise, other positive feedback).
Frisch (1989)	Structured needs assessment interview (job responsibilities, difficulties)	Increased knowledge (of sound supervisory practices).
	Survey questionnaire (potential topic areas to be covered in supervisory training, rated by supervisors as 'needed', 'interesting but not essential', and 'not needed').	Increased job satisfaction and productivity. Change in interpersonal behavior as a result of application of skills in problem solving, time management, conflict resolution, social skills training.
	Self-report measure assessing job satisfaction and productivity.	

This study, therefore, illustrates how supervision can be evaluated across all four 'outcome' levels.

The above studies are cited as an illustration to highlight the utility of Kirkpatrick's (1967) framework, as applied to supervision or more generally to CPD. While this selection of papers is not meant to be exhaustive, it is hoped that this brief review provides a practical example of how levels of change may be conceptualized, measured, evaluated, and specifically targeted in CPD. It is also hoped that the above review sheds light on how these same evaluations, based on the proposed framework, can be applied to CPD in general. For example, training workshops may also be assessed for the impact on participants' effect, knowledge, skill transfer and organizational change.

Because of the fundamental importance of generalization (it is the main reason for having CPD, after all), we will now examine how it has been evaluated in a bit more detail. To do this, we will draw on the staff training literature, as this is more sophisticated about generalization than the comparable supervision field. It also affords a different and popular example of CPD, the workshop.

In general, workshops are effective in promoting CPD. Arthur et al.'s (2003) review yielded effect sizes of 0.60 for reaction evaluations, 0.63 for learning criteria, 0.62 for transfer and 0.62 for impact criteria. While government policy recognizes the value of workshops, there is also a keen awareness that training needs to be complemented by supportive work environments and good management practices: 'What matters is that staff are trained, organised and managed properly' (DoH, 1998, p. 45). The international and UK literature agree with this conclusion. In 1988 Baldwin and Ford drew attention to what they termed the 'transfer problem' (p. 63), and a review of training throughout the twentieth century recognized that this problem was still far from solved (Haccoun and Saks, 1998). Similar conclusions have been reached in the UK. Brooker (2001), summarizing the 'phenomenal success story' of psychosocial interventions training (PSI) in terms of expansion, also noted more soberly that 'there are very real problems with the implementation of PSI in routine clinical services' (p. 28). In fact, some of the studies included in Brooker's review had hugely disappointing transfer outcomes (e.g., Fadden, 1997).

What do we need to do to minimize the transfer problem? Fadden herself drew attention to no less than 33 'difficulties' experienced by her cohort of therapists, who had received CPD in the family interventions aspect of PSI. These ranged from the unavailability of appropriate clients to illnesses and holidays. The most common general factor concerned problems with the workplace, such as integrating family work with other responsibilities. One problem-solving option is to analyse the transfer environment, in order to try and counter-balance such difficulties with at least as many transfer-reinforcing factors. Milne, Gorenski et al. (2000) reported a 'case study' of this kind, finding from staff interviews (post-PSI workshop), that the reported 'boosters' outweighed the 'barriers', resulting in a good degree of transfer (shown by audit as well as self-report). A 'see-saw' was used to depict this tension between pro- and anti-transfer factors, with peer support for the use of the newly developed PSI skills the single most important booster. They went on to summarize 20 such factors from the international PSI literature. These ranged from selecting training sites carefully to providing regular supervision. Interestingly, several other CPD approaches were noted, including studying and co-working with a buddy, and the use of a manual, suggesting the value of a 'package' of methods.

An alternative approach is what might be termed the 'self-control' approach. Instead of trying to maximize the CPD intervention (e.g., more or better workshops) or the transfer environment, this approach relies on developing transfer skills as part of the CPD method. In Milne, Gorenski et al.'s (2000) summary this was termed 'preparing staff for the tribulations of innovation' (p. 277). Marx (1986), in a welcome piece of reflexivity, saw that this kind of preparation could follow the way that we think of therapy. Specifically, he proposed an imaginative 'relapse-prevention' approach to the transfer problem, arguing that those receiving CPD should work explicitly to anticipate 'slips'. In his example this included making a commitment to retain a skill, thinking carefully about the support needed to avoid a slip, and considering various 'remedies' for any such slip. An evaluation of a standard PSI workshop versus one with a Marx-inspired relapse-prevention module at its close favoured this self-control approach (Milne, Westerman et al., 2002). The group of NHS professionals receiving the relapse-prevention module reported significantly greater generalization of the PSI methods to their routine work.

These evaluations of the transfer of staff training illustrate the considerable difficulty in procuring lasting change in the professional's workplace, but also show how careful evaluation can help to formulate and reduce the 'transfer problem'. If nothing else, they should encourage CPD purchasers, providers and participants to recognize the vital necessity of going beyond the 'grateful testimonial' of the reaction evaluation. This is equally true of the other forms of CPD, though perhaps best captured in this training literature. We next resume our focus on supervision, but continue to emphasize the work environment as a necessary condition for successful CPD.

Was the CPD Context Right?

Like any other human activity, CPD (and its evaluation) requires a facilitating environment to prosper. This makes the CPD environment an important dimension to evaluate, since any problems in improving psychological care (etc.) may not be due to the CPD experiences (e.g., supervision) but to the 'right' opportunities to use those experiences. This might be thought of as the 'motivational' dimension within the workplace.

Psychologists will be particularly aware of the importance of a variety of environmental factors in influencing how we behave at work. In relation to CPD, our local survey of psychological therapists (Milne, Gorenski et. al, 2000) gave a typical example of how several environmental factors can impinge on CPD. The 30 therapists within this illustration were interviewed about the conditions that they thought influenced their CPD activity. They suggested that sufficient time and practical help were crucial. In relation to research activity, the group indicated that adequate library facilities, a supportive research culture within the psychology department (for example collaboration with colleagues over projects), and obtaining favourable outcomes were also influential. A meta-analysis of the effectiveness of training reached similar conclusions, highlighting the role played by the organizational climate and by the support provided by peers and managers (Colquitt et al., 2000). Theoretical accounts concur. For instance, in Eraut's (1994) analysis the lack of 'an encouraging work context' is one of the 'formidable problems' (p. 56) in the way of CPD.

The number of variables that can influence our CPD activities is great, as illustrated in the West and Farr (1989) model, which identified four broad aspects of the organizational context. The first of these were 'factors intrinsic to the job', such as the degree of discretion we have in pursuing one form of CPD over another. Second, there are 'group factors', such as how much specific support exists from peers or the prevalent norms regarding CPD (e.g., amount of available funding). Third, there are 'relationship factors', such as the service leaders support for CPD. And lastly, West and Farr identified ten different 'organizational factors' that can have a bearing, such as the opportunities that exist for CPD.

A briefer but equally useful framework for thinking about the right CPD environment is that of 'measurement, monitoring and management' (Cape and Barkham, 2002).

The 'Right' Form of Measurement

The right environment would feature agreement on the most appropriate instruments with which to assess CPD, and their ready availability. Although psychologists have not yet reached a consensus on the appropriateness of any given instruments in relation to CPD (or for that matter in relation to common mental health problems, such as depression) there are signs that certain broad criteria are gaining acceptance (Barkham et al., 1998). The exemplary work these authors undertook on achieving consensus over instruments is a relevant model for measurement in relation to the evaluation of CPD. Their 'DIY' criteria ('design', 'implementation' and 'yield') are clearly relevant to CPD.

Design issues include appropriate psychometric status for the instruments used to measure CPD. On the implementation side we need to ensure that the instruments we use are feasible, in the sense of not requiring extensive training or time to administer. To illustrate, one reason that we have been developing STARS is because 'Teacher's PETS' takes too long to administer within routine service arrangements.

It is also important that instruments have sufficient yield to make their use worthwhile. This includes the ability of an instrument to provide monitoring data that guide the management of an effective CPD system. The right CPD environment will, therefore, include the use of instruments for which there is a consensus, quite possibly based around the DIY criteria.

The right environment will also include support for the use of the selected measurement tools. To illustrate, Townend et al.'s (2002) survey of clinical supervision within the UK highlighted the need for access to tapes and video cameras. Good quality video recordings provide an excellent basis for the measurement, monitoring and management of CPD activities, such as supervision. 'Teachers PETS' is used in relation to video recordings and furnishes a rich profile of supervision and its initial impacts (see earlier in chapter).

The right environment can also be facilitated by adopting approaches to measurement that are attractive to participants, purchasers and providers alike. A good example is the use of tapes for relatively informal processes of review between supervisor and supervisee, such as 'interpersonal process recall'. Another local example is the adoption of the 'HASQ' within the clinical training programme at Newcastle University. This simple, brief and non-threatening instrument is made readily available to supervisors and supervisees, through its publication within the course's Placement Handbook. These parties are then encouraged to use the instrument from time to time.

Monitoring the CPD Environment

One of the important uses for instruments is to provide monitoring data, thereby allowing managers and others to adjust CPD as indicated. A number of systems exist in order to monitor and feedback information to clinicians, including those designed to monitor a service users' response to treatment. To illustrate, Lambert et al. (2002) divided 1,020 users into groups, to determine if feedback to the therapist on client progress had any impact on either the outcome for the service user or on the number of the sessions attended. Lambert et al. (2002) found that this feedback increased the duration of treatment and improved the outcomes for the service users. Almost twice as many of those users in the feedback group achieved clinically significant change. The authors contrasted this systematic approach with the traditional reliance on arbitrary or personal reasons for defining either progress or the duration of treatment.

In relation to creating the right CPD environment, the above example of providing feedback needs to include a loop taking the information back through the management system. In our experience, it has been useful to assess regularly how staff are progressing with their treatment programmes in order to feedback key data to managers and others with an important role to play in creating the right environment. Specifically, as touched on earlier, we have interviewed staff who have received CPD training and supervision in psycho-social interventions (PSI) for enduring mental health difficulties in order to clarify the 'barriers and boosters' to their use of the approach (Milne, Gorenski et al., 2000). The simple 'seesaw' diagram was then used to provide an effective means for feeding back to key stakeholders and facilitating discussion of any indicated problems.

Managing the Right Environment

Part of the essential management function is surely to ensure that staff receive the necessary training and supervision in relation to their duties. Again, what constitutes sufficient training and supervision requires careful measurement and monitoring. However, the general picture appears to be that higher supervisor support contributes to improved clinical outcomes. For instance, Tharenou (2001) surveyed a sample of 1,705 staff members and conducted multiple regression analyses of their comments on the training that they had received. She found that greater involvement in training and higher supervisor support both contributed to greater use of the training within the workplace. She also found evidence that employer support contributed to the use of training. However, it was concluded that 'the behaviour of the supervisor . . . is the most important aspect of the work environment for their participation in training and development in the next twelve months' (p. 618). The study also noted the importance of employer support, through approval, funding and the creation of a positive learning climate. By contrast, Tharenou (2001) did not find that workloads, job challenge or barriers at work predicted participation in training and development.

Another example of using a survey method to pinpoint management implications is the work of Townend et al. (2002). Their survey of clinical supervisors within the British Association of Behavioural and Cognitive Psychotherapists (BABCP: N = 280) led to several recommendations directed at managers. In addition to the need to access video recording equipment (noted earlier), they identified a lack of suitable supervisors (especially in relation to specialized problems), a need to set standards regarding adequate supervision (they found a lack of adherence to supervision models), greater supervisor training and monitoring, and the need to establish benchmarks and audit systems to contribute to improved practice.

In a well-managed CPD environment, such modifications to the system will themselves be part of a systemic approach to the promotion of CPD. Various such systems exist, such as organizational development (OD) and continuous quality improvement (CQI). An illustration of an OD approach has been provided by Fleming et al. (1996). They developed a competency-based supervisory training programme, which was evaluated in two group homes for individuals with learning disabilities. Staff from both homes received training in supervision and were required to return to the group homes to in turn supervise the client-related activities of the paraprofessional staff whom they supervised within the homes. This system was overseen by a consultant, therefore providing a good example of an 'educational pyramid' (consultant > supervisor > supervisee > service user). They found that this pyramid approach to OD led to increases in appropriate supervision, which in turn led to improved work performance by the paraprofessionals receiving the supervision.

CQI was one of the eight practice improvement methods reviewed by Cape and Barkham (2002). CQI consists of cycles of analysing current practice, consideration of possible improvements, testing out these changes, and monitoring the results. Although providing a coherent structure for enhancing service environments, these authors found little evidence in support of the CQI approach. In particular, the three randomized controlled trials of CQI that they located showed no advantages. However, they did acknowledge that the CQI approach explicitly takes account of organizational factors and the way that these relate to staff performance.

In practice, most psychologists will have had some experience of CQI or OD systems, as in the arrangements that are in place throughout the UK in relation to clinical supervision. We refer here to the way that Clinical Tutors within clinical training courses will take responsibility for ensuring that the relevant physical resources are available to supervisors for the measurement of their work, and that they receive appropriate training and support in order to deliver high quality supervision. CPD is then further promoted by the creation of networks of supervisors, routine '3-way' reviews of particular placements, and other arrangements (for example peer reviews of local good practice).

Summary and Conclusions

CPD is concerned with maintaining, enhancing and guaranteeing the quality of our work. This implies a major role for evaluation, whether one is focusing on the delivery or effectiveness of CPD. In order to get the provision and evaluation of CPD right, we have set out an expanded R&D framework that poses five fundamental questions of any method of CPD, though our theme has been that most popular form of CPD, clinical supervision. We believe that evaluation firstly needs a firm rationale, a conceptual model that guides everything that follows. For us, the right thing to do in CPD is to foster experiential learning, which then implies the need to evaluate such critical features as the techniques used and their impact on learning. Next, the framework indicates the need to consider whether these right things have indeed been done, an audit matter. A couple of measurement options were presented, to show how this might be achieved. If CPD is provided in conformity to some given standards, we next want to know if the way in which that was done was appropriate, in terms of the competence/proficiency of the CPD facilitator and in such terms as interpersonal effectiveness. Only if these questions are addressed can we reasonably attribute the 'right' outcomes to the CPD. Lastly, we stressed that the management and evaluation of CPD requires the 'right' environment, which is a final dimension for the evaluation of CPD.

We are keenly aware that this account is strongly coloured by our own work, and that we have focused fairly exclusively on supervision. However, at every point there seems to be a clear parallel for other forms of CPD, and we also think that our research work is a useful device for articulating the many evaluation issues and options. To illustrate, the five basic questions we pose apply equally to brief workshops or lengthy part-time courses of CPD, and our examples indicate possible foci for their evaluation (e.g. see Table 8.2). Indeed, our framework itself indicates some major quality criteria for all forms of CPD, which we hope will help to enhance and guarantee the CPD that we all receive.

Acknowledgements

We are indebted to our colleagues for their stimulating collaboration over the STARS instrument: Ivy-Marie Blackburn, Mark Freeston, Peter Armstrong and Kirstine Postma.

REFERENCES

Arthur, W., Bennett, W., Edens, P. S. and Bell, S. T. (2003). Effectiveness of training in organizations: A meta-analysis of design and evaluation features. *Journal of Applied Psychology*, 88, 234–45.

Baldwin, T. T. and Ford, J. K. (1988). Transfer of training: A review and directions for future research. *Personnel Psychology*, 41, 63–105.

Barkham, M., Evans, C., Margison, F., McGrath, G., Mellor-Clark, J., Milne, D. and Connell, J. (1998). The rationale for developing and implementing core batteries for routine use in service settings and psychotherapy outcome research. *Journal of Mental Health*, 7, 35–47.

Brooker, C. (2001). A decade of evidence-based training for work with people with serious mental health problems: Progress in the development of psychosocial interventions. *Journal of Mental Health*, 10, 17–31.

Cape, J. and Barkham, M. (2002). Practice improvement methods: Conceptual base, evidence-based research, and practice-based recommendations. *British Journal of Clinical Psychology*, 41, 285–308.

Clark, H. B., Wood, R., Kuehnel, T., Flanagan, S., Mosk, M. and Northrup, J. T. (1986). Preliminary validation and training of supervisory interactional skills. *Journal of Organizational Behavior Management*, 7(1/2), 95–115.

Colquitt, J. A., LePine, J. A. and Noe, R. A. (2000). Toward an integrative theory of training motivation: A meta-analytic path analysis of 20 years of research. *Journal of Applied Psychology*, 85, 678–707.

Department of Health (1998). *A First Class Service: Quality in the New NHS*. Department of Health, London.

Department of Health (1999). *National Service Frameworks for Mental Health*. Department of Health, London.

Dyer, K., Schwartz, I. S. and Luce, S. C. (1984). A supervision program for increasing functional activities for severely handicapped students in a residential setting. *Journal of Applied Behavior Analysis*, 17, 249–59.

Eraut, M. (1994). *Developing Professional Knowledge and Competence*. London: Falmer.

Fadden, G. (1997). Implementation of family interventions in routine clinical practice following staff training programmes: A major cause for concern. *Journal of Mental Health*, 6, 599–612.

Fleming., R. K., Oliver, J. R. and Bolton, D. M. (1996). Training supervisors to train staff: A case study in a human service organization. *Journal of Organizational Behavior Management*, 16(1), 3–25.

Frisch, M. B. (1989). An integrative model of supervisory training for medical center personnel. *Psychological Reports*, 64, 1035–42.

Goldstein, I. L. (1993). *Training in Organizations*. Pacific Grove: Brooks/Cole.

Haccoun, R. R. and Saks, A. M. (1998). Training in the 21st century: Some lessons from the last one. *Canadian Psychology*, 39, 33–51.

Ivancic, M. T., Reid, D. H., Iwata, B. A., Faw, G. D. and Page, T. J. (1981). Evaluating a supervision program for developing and maintaining therapeutic staff-resident interactions during institutional care routines. *Journal of Applied Behavior Analysis*, 14, 95–107.

Kolb, D. A. (1984). *Experiential Learning*. New Jersey: Prentice-Hall.

Kirkpatrick, D. L. (1967). Evaluation of training. In R. L. Craig and L. R. Bettel (eds.), *Training and Development Handbook*. New York: McGraw-Hill.

Lambert, M. J., Whipple, J. L., Vermeersch, D. W., Smart, E. J., Nielsen, S. L. and Goates, M. (2002). Enhancing psychotherapy outcomes via providing feedback on client progress: A replication. *Clinical Psychology and Psychotherapy*, 9, 91–103.

Llewellyn, S. P., Elliott, R., Shapiro, D., Hardy, G. and Firth-Cozens, J. (1988). Client perceptions of significant events in prescriptive and exploratory periods of individual therapy. *British Journal of Clinical Psychology*, 27, 105–14.

Marx, R. D. (1986). Improving management development through relapse-prevention strategies. *Journal of Management Development*, 5, 27–40.

Milne, D. and James, I. (2000). A systematic review of effective cognitive-behavioral supervision. *British Journal of Clinical Psychology*, 39, 111–27.

Milne, D. and James, I. (2002). The observed impact of training on competence in clinical supervision. *British Journal of Clinical Psychology*, 41, 55–72.

Milne, D. and Westerman, C. (2001). Evidence-based clinical supervision: Rationale and illustration. *Clinical Psychology and Psychotherapy*, 8, 444–57.

Milne, D., Carpenter, J. and Lombardo, C. (2005). A stepwise approach to evaluation of staff training: Rationale and illustration. (In preparation: available from the first author.)

Milne, D., Gorenski, O., Westerman, C., Leck, C. and Keegan, D. (2000). What does it take to transfer training? *Psychiatric Rehabilitation Skills*, 4, 259–81.

Milne, D., James, I., Keegan, D. and Dudley, M. (2002). Teacher's PETS: A new observational measure of experiential training interactions. *Clinical Psychology and Psychotherapy*, 9, 187–99.

Milne, D., Keegan, D., Paxton, R. and Seth, K. (2000). Is the practice of psychological therapists evidence-based? *International Journal of Healthcare Quality Assurance*, 13, 8–14.

Milne, D., Pilkington, J., Gracie, J. and James, I. (2003). Transferring skills from supervision to therapy. *Behavioural and Cognitive Psychotherapy*, 31, 193–202.

Milne, D., Westerman, C. and Hanner, S. (2002). Can a relapse-prevention module facilitate the transfer of training? *Behavioural and Cognitive Psychotherapy*, 30, 361–4.

Townend, M., Ianetta, L. and Freeston, M. (2002). Clinical supervision in practice: A survey of UK cognitive behavioural psychotherapists accredited by the BABCP. *Behavioural and Cognitive Psychotherapy*, 30, 485–500.

Tharenou, P. (2001).The relationship of training motivation to participation in training and development. *Journal of Occupational and Organizational Psychology*, 74, 599–621.

Waltz, J., Addis, M. E., Koerner, K. and Jacobson, N. S. (1993). Testing the integrity of a psychotherapy protocol: Assessment of adherence and competence. *Journal of Consulting and Clinical Psychology*, 61, 620–30.

Warr, P., Allan, C. and Birdi, K. (1999). Predicting three levels of training outcome. *Journal of Occupational and Organizational Psychology*, 72, 351–75.

West, M. and Farr J. L. (1989). Innovation at work: Psychological perspectives. *Social Behaviour*, 4, 15–30.

Chapter 9

The British Psychological Society and CPD

Zenobia Nadirshaw, Ian Gray and Laura Golding

Introduction

The British Psychological Society (BPS) is the learned and professional body incorporated by Royal Charter for psychologists in the United Kingdom (BPS 2004a). The Society has a membership of over 40,000 and is a registered charity.

The key charter object of the Society is 'to promote the advancement and diffusion of the knowledge of psychology pure and applied and especially to promote the efficiency and usefulness of members by setting up a high standard of professional education and knowledge'. The Society is authorized under its Royal Charter to maintain the Register of Chartered Psychologists. It has a Code of Conduct (BPS, 2000), and investigatory and disciplinary systems in place to consider complaints of professional misconduct relating to its members. The BPS is also an examining body granting certificates and diplomas in specialist areas of professional applied psychology and has a quality assurance programme for accrediting both undergraduate and postgraduate university degree courses.

Chapter Plan

This chapter describes the responsibility of the BPS for CPD and links these responsibilities to major contextual issues including the Health Professions Council (HPC, 2003), the development of the NHS Knowledge and Skills Framework (NHS KSF) (DoH, March 2003, October 2004) and the National Occupational Standards for Applied

Psychology (Generic) (BPS and STMC, 2004). With the Society voting to make CPD mandatory for members holding Practising Certificates, the chapter goes on to discuss the mechanisms for implementing this decision including the role and responsibility of the Society's Standing Committee for CPD (scCPD). A detailed account of specific CPD requirements is presented. The final section of the chapter reviews the contribution of and guidance provided by the Division of Clinical Psychology (DCP).

The Role of the Society

In line with all other healthcare professional bodies, the BPS was charged with the responsibility to take account of the guidance provided in the Health Service Circular 154, *CPD: Quality in the New NHS* (DoH, 1999a). This stated that, 'By April 2000, training and development plans should be in place for the majority of health professional staff in the NHS'. It went on to say that continuing professional development was an important element 'in the delivery of a range of Government objectives focusing on the needs of patients by delivering the health outcomes and healthcare priorities of the NHS as set out in NHS Service Frameworks and local Health Improvement programmes'. An article in the Society's publication, *The Psychologist* (BPS, 1999), in response to this, reminded all chartered psychologists to abide by the Society's Code of Conduct (BPS, 2000). This stated that psychologists should endeavour to maintain and develop their professional competence, to recognize and work within its limits and to identify and ameliorate factors that restrict it. A key role of the Society is to reassure the public that chartered psychologists practice at an appropriate level of competence. The Society's CPD policy provides the means to offer such an assurance and to monitor psychologists' ongoing learning and development.

All psychologists have a responsibility to ensure that their professional knowledge, skills and performance are of a high quality, up to date and relevant to their field of practice. They maintain their fitness to practice via their CPD activity. It is the responsibility of applied psychologists offering services to the public, to keep themselves up to date through life-long learning throughout their careers. They need to ensure that their work reflects changes in practice so that they contribute to high quality service user care in the context of a changing and complex work environment and changing attitudes, expectations and needs of contemporary British society.

The Health Professions Council (HPC)

The HPC is an independent Healthcare Regulator. Since 2002, it has had a UK-wide remit to protect the public, uphold professional standards and set standards of proficiency, conduct, performance and ethics and standards of education and training. Applied psychologists *may* be registered through the HPC. The Society's rejection (BPS, 2005b) of the current proposals (DoH, 2005), for statutory regulation by the HPC creates uncertainty concerning future arrangements for statutory regulation for applied psychologists. The HPC works on the guiding principles of:

- protection of the public;
- transparency;
- communication and responsiveness;
- working collaboratively;
- providing a high quality service; and
- value for money and audit.

The HPC has set several objectives. One of the three objectives they still have to meet is the proper and appropriate establishment of standards on CPD (HPC, 2003). At the time of writing, the HPC has been undertaking a UK-wide consultation on CPD in preparation for this.

The HPC defines CPD as 'a range of learning activities through which professionals maintain and develop throughout their career to ensure they retain their capacity to practice safely, effectively and legally within their evolving scope of practice' (Allied Health Professions Project, 2003).

The HPC has endorsed a range of CPD activities including:

- work-based learning: e.g., reflective practice, clinical audit, significant event analysis, user feedback, membership of committees, journal club;
- professional activity: e.g., membership of Faculty/Special Interest group, mentoring, teaching, expert witness, presentation at conferences;
- formal/educational: e.g., courses, undertaking research, distance learning, planning or running a course;
- self-directed learning: e.g., reading journals, articles, reviewing books/articles, updating knowledge via Internet, television and press; and
- other activities: e.g., public service.

Mandatory CPD

Members of the BPS voted to make CPD mandatory in 2000 for all psychologists holding a practising certificate. The Society's statutes (BPS, 2004a) were amended to include this requirement. Statute 13(2) states that 'chartered psychologists holding Practising Certificates will be required to engage in CPD and to maintain their professional competence to provide the psychological services they are offering or agreeing to offer.' This statute applies to all chartered psychologists holding a practising certificate irrespective of the number of hours worked or degree of experience or time taken out of the profession for specific reasons such as maternity leave or long-term sick leave. In addition, the consultation of the new Code of Conduct document with the BPS Ethics Committee (BPS, 2005a) includes in Section 2, Competent Conduct, the expectation that all chartered psychologists will comply with the Society's CPD policies and that psychologists will maintain their own records of their CPD activities and submit them to the Society when required and requested. Those who do not comply with the Society's CPD policy and requirements will be removed from the Register.

Members who hold practising certificates will be expected to submit their CPD records from 2005, with the possibility of sanctions being applied, by the Society, for non-compliance, from October 2006. These members will be required to:

- maintain a continuous, up-to-date accurate record of their CPD activities;
- demonstrate that their CPD activities are a mixture of learning activities relevant to current or future practice;
- seek to ensure that their CPD has contributed to the quality of their practice and service delivery;
- seek to ensure that their CPD benefits the service user; and
- record and present a written portfolio containing evidence of their CPD upon request.

It is expected that members who do not hold a practising certificate will still have an ethical obligation to undertake and maintain a record of CPD but they will not be required to submit their CPD records to the Society on an annual basis.

In addition, in line with the Society's Equal Opportunities Statement and Policy (BPS, 1994) all psychologists need to ensure that they maintain an up-to-date knowledge of equal opportunities issues and how these can impact on their day-to-day work as a member of the psychology profession.

The Standing Committee for CPD (scCPD)

The scCPD was set up in 1998 with a view to developing and sharing information on CPD in a way that all applied psychologists would find helpful. This was in the context of the planned move to statutory regulation (DoH, 2005) and the need to link CPD records to the issuing of practising certificates (BPS, 1999).

The scCPD membership consists, among others, of nominated representatives from the Society's sub-systems including Divisions and Branches. The reporting structure of this committee to the Membership and Professional Training Board (MPTB) is via the Chair and Deputy Chair. The scCPD's terms of reference stipulate that it should meet at least six times a year and drive forward a clear policy and a planned approach to implementing CPD on behalf of the Society. A CPD Officer came into post in 2001 to support the scCPD's work.

The scCPD is responsible for:

- advising MPTB on the Society's policy on CPD for applied psychologists;
- providing an opportunity for the coordination of and exchange of information about the work of the different Divisions of the Society and other relevant systems on CPD;
- approving the different Divisional CPD requirements in order to ensure compatibility with those of the Society as a whole; and
- taking other steps and initiatives the committee considers appropriate to further the CPD agenda for psychologists in the United Kingdom.

The scCPD, requires all psychologists holding a practising certificate to demonstrate fulfilment of core outcomes on their annual CPD records. These core outcomes are based on the six key roles of the National Occupation Standards (NOS) for Applied Psychologists (generic) (BPS and STMC, 2002). They are:

1. *Ethics*: develop, implement and maintain personal and professional standards and ethical practice.

2. *Practice*: apply psychological and related methods, concepts, models, theories and knowledge derived from reproducible research findings.
3. *Research and evaluation*: research and develop new and existing psychological methods, concepts, models, theories and instruments in psychology.
4. *Communication*: communicate psychological knowledge, principles, methods, needs and policy requirements.
5. *Training*: develop and train the application of psychological skills, knowledge, practices and procedures.
6. *Management*: management of the provision of psychological systems, services and resources.

It is expected that the first four key roles are common to all chartered psychologists. Individuals must be able to relate their CPD to cover at least some aspect of each of these. Items 5 and 6 above will apply where relevant to an individual's role as a practising psychologist e.g., a clinical psychologist. Further information about the numbers, key roles and the units, which comprise them, are available in a leaflet entitled *National Occupational Standards in Applied Psychology (Generic) – Quick Reference Summary*, available on the Society website www.bps.org.uk/cpd

Policy Statement: The Requirements of the Society

The BPS's scCPD defines CPD as 'any process or activity that provides added value to the capability of the profession through the increase in knowledge, skills and personal qualities necessary for the appropriate execution of professional and technical duties, often termed competence' (Phillips et al., 2002).

Planning and Recording Format

The format for planning and recording CPD is common across the Society for all chartered psychologists. It consists of the following documents:

- A plan, which identifies development needs and any activities, planned to meet those needs.
- A record of activity, which provides a record of each separate CPD activity undertaken (including unplanned activities as well as

those planned for). This includes space for description of the activity, reflective practice/evaluation and future development needs identified as a result of the review and reflection.

- A summary log, which brings together the activities undertaken against each development need showing the relationship to the relevant NOS key role. The summary log will be the only document that will be required to be submitted in the early stages of monitoring – although the first two documents will have to be provided as further reference if those records are selected as part of the qualitative monitoring exercise undertaken by the scCPD as well as the different Divisional assessors/representatives of the Society. It is expected that all the Divisions of the Society will provide specific advice and greater details of the CPD policy and guidelines within the context of the Society-wide CPD framework.

The Society's policy statements make explicit the following general expectations of all its applied psychologists. They will:

1. Undertake CPD in accordance with the above.
2. Take part in CPD and the range of CPD activities dependent on:
   - experiences and opportunities for CPD in their work;
   - personal learning needs;
   - preferred learning style;
   - the relevance of CPD activities to their practice;
   - the diverse roles and different contexts of practice (for example clinical practice, education, management, teaching and training, research);
   - the complexities of their professional practice;
   - the changing nature of personal professional practice and that of the profession as a whole;
   - striving for excellence and maintaining awareness of the limitations and scope of practice;
   - understanding and working within and responding appropriately to the limits of professional practice;
   - practising within the individual professional's moral, ethical and equal opportunity framework;
   - thinking critically about personal practice and its context;
   - communicating and collaborating effectively across other professional groups and across multi-agency contexts;
   - managing unfamiliar practice and experience effectively; and
   - providing evidence of specific CPD activity relating to Education, Practice, Management and Research and Training.

Evidence Framework

Examples of the evidence that the scCPD members and the correspond-ing Divisional representatives/assessors will look for in submitted CPD records are likely to be along the following lines:

Education

- Undertaking further study to top up existing knowledge and skills via formal teaching awards, day courses and conferences;
- being a reviewer for a professional journal;
- writing an article for a professional journal; and
- being involved in a learning or teaching committee, becoming a member of a specific sub-group or clinical issues, which has impact on patient care.

Practice

- Ensuring safety and efficacy of practice by attendance on courses relating to new legislation (e.g., Disability Discrimination Act, Race Relations Amendment Act, etc.);
- learning new techniques/models that have clinical applications of effectiveness on patient/service-user care;
- working and learning through multiprofessional learning and train-ing opportunities via in-service presentations, peer review, journal club to name but a few examples; and
- other examples that provide evidence of ability to deal with the new, non-routine challenges.

Management

- Undertaking study of management modules as part of the individ-ual's seniority level and career progression;
- working with other senior managers (for example, in the NHS on specific strategic business plans);
- working on supporting redevelopment and implementation of national and other local policies; and
- being a member of a senior managers group/forum (e.g., senior supervisors group, Faculty, Division or its sub-committees).

Research and Training

- Being a member of a committee for postgraduate training of other psychologists;

- undertaking teaching and training via formal lectures to graduate and postgraduate students of psychology;
- offering conference presentations;
- writing up research proposals/protocols and getting approval from the local ethics and research committee;
- being a member of the local ethics research committee;
- submitting articles to peer-reviewed professional journals;
- being a referee for scientific journals; and
- becoming a supervisor for the profession and updating one's knowledge and skills as a supervisor.

An online CPD records system has been introduced, and is available on the Society's website, in response to feedback from a pilot study. The results of the usability trial of the online system were encouraging with over 75 per cent of the participants giving positive feedback and offering suggestions for improvement. Consequently revisions were made and the online system is now fully active and available, to members, on the Society's website (www.bps.org.uk/cpd/index/cfm).

Proposals for Applied Psychologists Returning to Practice

Current proposals from the Society suggest that applied psychologists returning to clinical practice (i.e., after maternity leave, long-term sick leave, career break etc.) will be required to submit a CPD plan to the Society for approval. It is suggested that such plans, and subsequent supporting CPD activity records, will be scrutinized by CPD assessors during the first year of the psychologists' return to practice. It is envisaged that, where applicable, the returning psychologists will discuss and agree a CPD plan with their employers that meets the needs of the individual psychologist who is returning to clinical practice as well as the needs of the service in which he or she will be working. These procedures, however, have yet to be formally agreed by the Society.

Newly qualified psychologists will automatically receive their first Practising Certificate once they have gained chartered status and joined the Register of Psychologists.

The DCP–CPD Sub Committee

Following the first edition of the DCP's guidelines for Continuing Professional Development (CPD) in 1998, the CPD Sub Committee published revised guidelines, (DCP, 2001). These guidelines are set against key Department of Health policies such as clinical governance, as outlined in detail in Chapter 3.

It was important to move the thinking from the way the profession of clinical psychology viewed CPD, which tended to be in the form of attending training courses. The aim was to widen this, in line with wider NHS developments, to include other types of activity including those that enabled psychologists to maintain and improve their competence within the workplace through, for example, shadowing a more experienced colleague, using the Internet etc. These guidelines also introduced the idea of maintaining CPD records to ensure that DCP members had formal evidence of what they had been doing and reflections on how their clinical practice had changed due to the CPD activity. More recently, there has been a move away from thinking of CPD in terms of number of hours spent doing relevant activities and towards the notion of competency-based defined outcomes. CPD activity should be based upon ongoing learning and development with a focus on individual practitioner's learning achievements and how these enhance service delivery – impacting directly or indirectly on patient/service-user care.

The DCP guidelines include the policy and conditions for CPD, the form and content of CPD and quality assurance, monitoring and evaluation of CPD. The thinking behind the guidelines was to offer guidance to clinical psychologists to keep pace with the latest professional standards and practice in line with wider NHS developments around life-long learning. The guidelines also make explicit the link between professional development and career progression. The guidelines also make explicit the individual clinical psychologist's responsibility to limit their practice to those areas where they have specialized, to maintain an awareness of the scope of their practice, to monitor how their practice has changed or might change in response to different legislative and service settings.

The DCP's CPD guidelines provide an example of a model of CPD and an explanation of their purpose. They also give guidance on demonstrating achievement of the outcomes of CPD activity and a list of suggested activities to generate learning objectives and to assist reflection on practice, learning outcomes and future needs. The guidelines emphasize the fact that learning through CPD is life-long, irrelevant of the number of years in practice and whether the individual practitioner was in full-time or part-time employment. Implicit in the guidelines is the fact that clinical psychologists are governed by the concept of professional competence encompassing the following elements:

- a responsibility to ensure safety and efficacy of practice;
- an ability to think critically about current practice, learn from this and apply the learning to new work arrangements;
- a recognition that clinical psychologists' competence does not exist in a vacuum but is affected by their interactions with other professionals from statutory and non-statutory service sectors and in the context in which they work;
- ensuring the competence and scope of practice develops over time; and
- an ability to deal with new, non-routine, challenges.

A four-step model

The four-step model shown in Figure 9.1 identifies a common framework, which offers:

- an explanation of the model and its purpose;
- guidance on identifying learning needs using different techniques;
- an increase from 'input' to 'output' measures through the submission of an appropriate CPD record and demonstration of evaluative practice;
- increased recognition of the importance of learning through work-related exercises;
- CPD activity to be planned and evaluated in line with identified learning needs and personal development plans; and
- greater responsibility on clinical psychologists for their own CPD in relation to:
  - understanding, working within and responding appropriately to the limits of their professional practice;
  - demonstrating effectiveness in their practice;
  - working within the profession's moral, ethical and equal opportunity framework;
  - thinking critically about personal practice and its context; and
  - communicating and collaborating effectively across other professional groups in multiagency contexts.

Figure 9.1 indicates clearly that CPD should be seen as a continuous learning process that guides clinical psychologists through the different stages of their careers and throughout their working life.

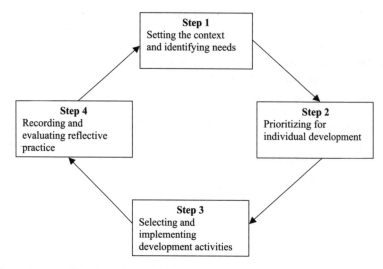

Figure 9.1   Cyclical four step model of CPD
Source: Division of Clinical Psychology (2001) *Guidelines for CPD*. BPS, Leicester

As a starting point it is important to:

- evaluate current knowledge skills and experience;
- assess current capabilities, strengths and weaknesses;
- explore ways to overcome limitations and improve performance;
- identify sources of information and different strategies and techniques to identify learning and development needs;
- undertake and appreciate the varied sources of learning, which goes beyond attendance of courses and conferences;
- be open to new ideas and find new ways of becoming efficient and more effective;
- learn through good and bad, planned and unplanned experiences and be open to various learning opportunities; and
- develop one's own development and match it with the overall service context in which the individual practitioner practices.

Core Competencies in CPD

The DCP's CPD Sub Committee consulted with the various special interest groups within the DCP to identify core competences in the form of knowledge and skills that would be expected of pre Agenda for Change A Grade and B/Consultant Grade Clinical Psychologists in the following areas:

- assessment;
- therapeutic interventions;
- consultancy and management;
- research;
- service evaluation and quality assurance;.
- teaching and supervision; and
- knowledge of social and cultural issues and the impact of social inequalities relative to the rights of vulnerable, disadvantaged section of society.

The competencies are further divided into knowledge and skills components that would be expected of A Grade and B/Consultant Grade clinical psychologists in relation to the depth, breadth and fullness of the knowledge, skills and attitudes that would be expected of clinical psychologists at different levels of seniority and practice and training. This is in line with the Society's current *Criteria for the Accreditation of Postgraduate Training Programmes in Clinical Psychology* (CTCP) (BPS, 2002). It is expected that managers of psychology services and university-based teaching faculty staff members offer a working context that is particularly suited to enable trainee clinical psychologists to develop learning outcomes specified in the accreditation criteria. Clinical psychology training programmes must ensure that they provide their trainees with the knowledge and skills needed to develop the competencies for fitness for purpose and practice through a mixture of academic teaching, research and clinical placement experience that covers the core competencies across a range of client groups presenting with a variety of psychological problems in a wide range of service settings and demonstrating the use of more than one psychological model.

The CPD Sub Committee has a range of roles and responsibilities relating to supporting the clinical psychology profession in its CPD requirements, offering advice and training via DCP branch events, assisting the scCPD's work in relation to the recent Society pilot study, informing the DCP Executive Committee regarding statutory regulation and the CPD agenda and ensuring that quality of professional practice is maintained through the effective use of the DCP Guidelines on CPD. The Sub Committee contributed to the scCPD's pilot project, which invited psychologists to tender their CPD logbooks for assessment. The exercise resulted in a range of findings relating to how clinical psychologists defined CPD activity and the type and level of activity undertaken in the name of CPD work. A lack of reflective practice on the part of some psychologists was apparent. There were also indications that some psychologists were not demonstrating the impact of CPD activity on their personal and professional development and how the selected development plan was linked to the service objectives and needs of the service user. The CPD Sub Committee is currently developing a network of interested NHS- and university-based clinical psychologists who have CPD as a major work responsibility.

In Conclusion

The Society has placed, and is placing, great importance on the development of its CPD strategy from a position of having established CPD as a mandatory requirement. In the context of the Health Professions Council and future statutory regulation, the NHS KSF, and the development of National Occupational Standards for Applied Psychology, the Society has developed a detailed implementation plan specifying both the content and process of CPD. The role of the DCP in augmenting the work of the Society's standing committee is discussed.

REFERENCES

Allied Health Professions (2003). *Allied Health Professions Project (AHP) Demonstrating Competence through CPD*. Final Report, AHP Project, London.

British Psychological Society (1994). *Equal Opportunity Statement and Policy* BPS, Leicester.

British Psychological Society (1999). Statement on continuing professional development (CPD). *The Psychologist*, 12, 309–10.

British Psychological Society (2000). *Code of Conduct, Ethical Principles and Guidelines*. BPS, Leicester.

British Psychological Society Committee on Training in Clinical Psychology (2002) *Criteria for the Accreditation of Postgraduate Training Programmes in Clinical Psychology*. Membership and Qualifications Board, BPS, Leicester.

British Psychological Society (2004a). *Royal Charter, Statutes and Rules*, BPS, Leicester.

British Psychological Society (2004b). *Continuing Professional Development (CPD) – New Society Requirements'*. BPS, Leicester.

British Psychological Society (2005a). *Code of Ethics and Conduct: Consultation Draft*. BPS, Leicester.

British Psychological Society (2005b). *Response of the British Psychological Society to 'Applied Psychology: Enhancing Public Protection: Proposals for the Statutory Regulation of Applied Psychologists'*. BPS, Leicester.

British Psychological Society and STMC (2002). *National Occupational Standards in Applied Psychology (Generic)*. BPS and the Science, Technology and Mathematics Council, Leicester.

CPD Helpline available on email: cpd@bps.org.uk. Telephone 0116 252 9916.

DCP (2001). Division of Clinical Psychology. *Guidelines for CPD*. Available from BPS, Leicester, online at: http://www.bps.org.uk

Department of Health (1999a). *Continuing Professional Development: Quality in the New NHS*. HSC 1999/154. Department of Health, London.

Department of Health (1999b). *Clinical Governance in the New NHS*. HSC 1999/065. Department of Health, London.

Department of Health (March 2003). *The NHS Knowledge and Skill Framework and Related Development Review: Working Draft*. Department of Health, London.

Department of Health (October 2004). *The NHS Knowledge and Skills Framework (NHS KSF) and the Development Review Process (October 2004)*. Department of Health, London.

Department of Health (2005). *Enhancing Public Protection: Proposals for the Statutory Regulation of Applied Psychologists*. Department of Health, London.

Green, D. (2000). *Who Pays for CPD in Clinical Psychology?* DCP Information Leaflet no. 3. Available from BPS, Leicester.

Health Professions Council (April 2003). *Continuing Professional Development*. 031/TR/A5.

HPC Consultation on CPD (2004). *Presentations and Lectures (September–December 2004)*. HPC, Park House, 184 Kennington Park Road, London, SE11 4BU.

Phillips, M., Cruikshank, I. and Friedman, A. (2002). *Continuing Professional Development: Evaluation of Good Practice*. Professional Associations Research Network, online at: www.parn.org.uk

Chapter 10

CPD – The Multiprofessional Context

Claire Grout

Introduction

Earlier chapters have described the 'what, why and how' of CPD for clinical psychologists and other applied psychologists. This is, of course, an appropriate focus for the profession, particularly considering the probable forthcoming mandatory CPD requirements linked to the statutory regulation of applied psychologists. It is, however, important to remember that CPD has a much wider role across the whole of the healthcare system. This chapter explores the multiprofessional context of CPD within the NHS.

The first section describes the importance of multiprofessional working in today's NHS, and how learning together supports improved patient care and enhances the working lives of healthcare professionals. There is much variation in the terminology used to describe multiprofessional CPD; so the second section of the chapter attempts to clarify this. This is followed by a discussion of the effectiveness of multiprofessional CPD which is another area of debate. This includes an overview of the evidence, demonstrating in which situations the outcomes are likely to be most positive.

Much shared learning is based on the assumption that collaboration is good. However there will inevitably be tensions between uniprofessional and multiprofessional CPD. The fourth section of the chapter identifies why this may happen and how potential difficulties can be addressed. The fifth section explores how the CPD needs of clinical psychologists may be met on a multiprofessional basis. Finally, the

CPD requirements of other healthcare professions are explored for comparison in the last section of the chapter.

The Importance of Multiprofessional Working and Learning

Teamwork is required to meet the increasingly complex needs of service users in healthcare. As the need for teamwork has been recognized, so the pressure to change the way in which healthcare professionals are educated has arisen. Unidisciplinary training will still play an important role in CPD but there is equally a need to build a culture of shared values and understanding between different staff groups (DoH, 1999). Government policy, with its central emphasis on the effective use of resources to meet needs, has spearheaded interprofessional developments in practice.

The Department of Health (DoH, 1999) stated that CPD must focus on the needs of patients and deliver the health outcomes and healthcare priorities of the NHS. A key area for action was that more opportunities should be created for multidisciplinary and team-based learning that cross primary, community and acute sectors of care. Work-based learning was actively encouraged, for example reflection within a team following an untoward incident, and identifying lessons to be learned.

In *Working Together, Learning Together* (DoH, 2001), the Government followed up this theme, reinforcing the need to make application of learning systematic, and using investment effectively. A core value identified was working effectively in teams to ensure a seamless service for patients, and appreciating the roles of other staff and agencies involved in the care of patients. This document proposed that, wherever practical, learning should be shared by different staff groups and professions. Core skills such as communication, undertaken on a shared basis with other professions, should be included from the earliest stages in professional preparation in both theory and practice settings, centred on the needs of patients. CPD should be increasingly focused on the development needs of clinical teams, across traditional professional and service boundaries. The Department of Health (2001) also described the establishment of the NHS University to support the achievement of these goals.

Organizations are very important in determining how learning is implemented, and can foster or inhibit the process. Davies and Nutley (2000) describe the key features of a learning organization.

Team learning is vital for the organization, because it is through teams that organizations achieve their objectives. This also helps with the shared understanding of, and commitment to, the organizational vision. Davies and Nutley suggest that learning that is limited to individual professions and traditional approaches to education may be insufficient to bring about substantial changes in the learning capacity in an organization.

It has also been recognized that risk management is an important factor in multiprofessional CPD. Local arrangements for CPD should be very closely linked to clinical governance plans, and be supported by a clear infrastructure, with explicit lines of accountability (DoH, 1999). The Association for the Study of Medical Education (ASME) (2003) identified the Clinical Negligence Scheme for Trusts (CNST) as a potential driver in postgraduate interprofessional education.

There are other reasons which have been proposed for multiprofessional CPD. Pirrie et al. (1998) note that the integration of workforce planning shifting from occupation-based to service-based is best supported by multiprofessional education and training from the commissioners' point of view.

The end goal of multiprofessional CPD is not only to improve patient care but also to enhance the working lives of healthcare professionals. Kennard (2002) showed that students who undertook a module focusing on collaborative practice had more positive perceptions about their work and were less likely to emphasize work demands in terms of shift patterns, fatigue and/or stress.

Mental health professionals are particularly vulnerable to severe emotional exhaustion and psychological tension; the intrinsic components of mental health practice are a source of stress for practitioners (Sharkey and Sharples, 2003). Managing risk has been particularly associated with stress, and this is dependent on team communications; therefore Sharkey and Sharples developed a team-based learning pack on risk management. They showed that developing knowledge and skills while developing the team can lead to lower levels of stress.

The Government has shown its intent in further progressing the multiprofessional CPD agenda. As mentioned in Chapter 3, in August 2003 the Government announced the award of contract for a project to support the way healthcare professionals learn after their first registration (DoH, 2003). The framework will support and encourage creative and innovative learning and development for healthcare staff, based on the skills and competences needed to meet the needs of patients. It will particularly encourage shared learning across professions and at different levels of practice.

What is Multiprofessional Learning?

'Shared learning' has been advocated as the way forward. However there are many discrepancies in the terminology used: 'interprofessional', 'multiprofessional', 'shared' and 'collaborative learning', among others, have been used interchangeably. Headrick et al. (1998) suggest that 'interprofessional' better reflects the need for dynamic interaction among professionals to ensure that learning goes beyond merely having members of different professions sharing the same classroom together. The United Kingdom Centre for the Advancement of Interprofessional Education (CAIPE) (www.caipe.org.uk) describes interprofessional learning as the opportunity for professions to 'learn with, from and about one another to facilitate collaboration in practice'.

Harden (1998) goes into greater detail on the subject and describes eleven steps in a continuum, with uniprofessional education at one end of the spectrum and transprofessional education at the other. Transprofessional learning is described as interprofessional learning (exploring the subject from one's own and other professional angles), based on experience of the real world. Harden suggests that the place and format of the teaching will define where it is on the continuum.

More important than the terminology is to consider the goals of the multiprofessional learning experience. CAIPE describes effective interprofessional education as having the following components:

- works to improve the quality of care;
- focuses on the needs of service users and carers;
- involves service users and carers;
- promotes interprofessional collaboration;
- encourages professions to learn with, from, and about one another;
- enhances practice within professions;
- respects the integrity and contribution of each profession; and
- increases professional satisfaction.

Effectiveness of Multiprofessional Learning

What evidence do we have that multiprofessional learning is effective? Campbell and Johnson (1999) suggested that multiprofessional education was a 'fashion' based primarily on social influences rather than on established principles and theories or results of valid research. They suggested that the lack of evidence means that it is not necessarily true that health professionals learning together will develop into more effective teams.

The major study to date has been that performed by Zwarenstein et al. (2004). Their Cochrane review assessed the usefulness of interprofessional education interventions compared with education in which the same professions were learning separately from one another. Their premise was that objective measures of improved professional practices, or improved patient/client morbidity, survival, or user satisfaction, are the criteria against which claims for interprofessional education should be judged. There was a large body of literature; a yield of 1,042 papers, of which 89 were retained for further consideration. However none of these studies met the inclusion criteria for methodological quality. Zwaranstein et al. point out that this does not imply there is evidence of ineffectiveness, and indeed they have subsequently performed further work with amended criteria.

Cooper et al. (2001) performed a systematic review of evidence for interdisciplinary education of undergraduate healthcare professionals. Again, they found large amounts of evaluation data compared to small amounts of research data. The number of professional groups ranged from 2 to 13, with a variety of healthcare professionals being involved both at student and faculty level, including psychology. Students were found to benefit from interdisciplinary education with outcome effects primarily relating to changes in knowledge, skills, attitudes and beliefs, in particular on understanding of professional roles and team working. Effects upon transfer of learning into professional practice were not discernible, but there was a lack of follow-up outcome measures.

The situation for learning is important, with a clinical environment proposed as more effective than the classroom (Finch, 2000). Ker et al. (2003) developed a simulated ward environment for medical and nursing students, centred around patients with common medical conditions. Students were allocated to interprofessional teams and after a briefing in the form of a ward report took responsibility for the ward for a shift. Observers charted progress in relation to collaborative team working, leadership, prioritization and clinical competence. The exercise was perceived positively by all participating groups. This is a good example of a learning opportunity reflecting real healthcare practice, in a 'safe' environment. This can potentially be repeated and developed at different stages of training.

Horsburgh et al. (2001) suggest that shared learning for first-year students should focus on teamwork skills, working towards relevant and common educational goals, before they have a chance to develop a true professional identity. As they progress, other outcomes such as understanding of each other's roles will be incorporated. Early inter-disciplinary learning has been found to be most beneficial so that it benefits later participation in interdisciplinary activities (Cooper et al., 2001). At a later stage, attitudes towards other professionals may be entrenched and act as barriers to successful teamwork. However this is disputed by Pirrie et al. (1998) who suggest there is greater impact later in training and at postgraduate level when they have had a chance to reflect upon their practice.

Multiprofessional CPD has been less well studied than learning at undergraduate level, despite its importance. The use of Practice Profes-sional Development Plans, which are development plans for the whole team in the primary care practice, play a key role in monitoring quality improvement. The way in which interprofessional education is app-roached within this is important to success; Dr Charles Campion-Smith (ASME, 2003) suggests it should be 'effective, patient-centred, fun, inclusive and democratic'. An important feature to remember is that participants do not need to all learn the same thing, as each will bring to and take away something different from the situation.

The Department of Health (DoH, 2001) proposes the use of clinical networks to support inter-professional education. An example is a Masters programme in public health medicine in the South West which allows development of specialists from a range of professions.

Programmes such as the New Generation Project (see website) are seen to be the mainstay of future healthcare education. The New Generation Project was established in 1999 to take forward inter-professional education at Southampton and Portsmouth Universities, and was identified by the Department of Health in 2002 as a leading-edge site. They are developing and delivering an integrated common learning programme across 11 professional programmes. The curricu-lum includes both 'learning in common' which are topics common to the programme but taught and assessed within profession specific programmes; and 'interprofessional learning' where students come together in multiprofessional learning groups to learn from and about each other and are assessed on their achievement of interprofessional learning outcomes. The outcomes of the common learning curriculum are interesting to note; students will learn and be assessed on their ability to:

- respect, understand and support the roles of other professionals involved in health and social care delivery;

- make an effective contribution as an equal member of an interprofessional team;
- understand the changing nature of health and social care roles and boundaries;
- demonstrate a set of knowledge, skills, competencies and attitudes that are common to all professions, and which underpin the delivery of quality patient/client focused services;
- learn from others in the interprofessional team;
- deal with complexity and uncertainty;
- collaborate with other professionals in practice;
- understand stereotyping and professional prejudices and the impact of these on interprofessional working; and
- practice in a patient-centred manner.

Although there has been little evidence shown to date on the effectiveness of multiprofessional education, the current focus on evidence-based education should improve outcomes of future research. Certainly there appears to be a positive future in encouraging multi-professional learning at an earlier stage with clear outcomes for the benefit of the individual, the team, the service, and most importantly the patient.

Tensions Between Uniprofessional and Multiprofessional CPD

As professions come together so rivalries and misconceptions about respective roles and responsibilities may become evident. Interprofessional learning may in fact erode professional values or entrench negative stereotypes that professions hold about one another (Campbell and Johnson, 1999).

Barriers to effective multiprofessional learning have been well documented (Atkins and Walsh, 1997; Headrick et al., 1998; Pirrie et al., 1998). These include:

- differences in history and culture;
- historical interprofessional and intraprofessional rivalries;
- differences in language and jargon;
- differences in schedules and professional routines;
- varying levels of preparation, qualifications and status;
- differences in requirements, regulations and norms of professional education;

- unequal numbers;
- fears of diluted professional identity;
- differences in accountability, payment and rewards;
- differences in management structures, styles of decision making and committee cycles; and
- concerns regarding clinical responsibility.

A common barrier to CPD within any profession is resources, and this can cause tension when different staff groups have access to different funding opportunities. Multiprofessional groups have overcome this by pooling CPD funding to create partnerships and concentrating resources to deliver on healthcare priorities. Atkins and Walsh (1997) suggest that programmes of this type mostly benefit health service managers and administrators by cost containment. However, Headrick et al. (1998) suggest that effective multiprofessional learning requires a different use of resources: teachers who can coach rather than lecture; professional time as a team together; and support from the leadership of each profession.

Kennard's study (2002) of 57 post-qualified health professionals undertaking a part time top up degree in health studies showed that most interest in collaborative practice came from those already actively engaged in multidisciplinary work and with a clear sense of role within that context. No evidence was found to associate this form of shared learning with new or enhanced collaborative activity. Poor perceptions between disciplines were associated with low levels of contact in the workplace.

A clear shared objective is crucial (Headrick et al., 1998). A place to start is that most health professionals have at least one characteristic in common: a personal desire to learn, and one shared value, to meet the needs of their patients or clients.

Finch (2000) describes the role of education providers. To deliver on the aspirations of multiprofessional learning the NHS depends wholly on the ability of education providers to comprehend, embrace and provide interprofessional training. They need a clear definition of what this actually means in terms of working practices.

CAIPE, founded in 1987, promotes and develops interprofessional learning as a way of improving collaboration between practitioners working with patients, clients and carers. CAIPE has been involved in extensive and continuing research into the evidence base for interprofessional education. Its work, informed by research, is to develop interprofessional learning in universities and in the workplace. Its focus is on the ways professions learn with and about each other, foster mutual respect and respect for the views of service users, overcome obstacles to collaboration and facilitate change.

Harden (1998) describes a three dimensional model: the extent to which the approach to multiprofessional education adopted matches the context for learning (stage of learning, type of students, learning situation) and the curriculum goals, provides an indication of the success. Harden defined a formula to predict success of a multiprofessional programme:

$$S = (B - D) \times E$$

where:

S = likelihood of success of the multiprofessional programme
B = benefits to be gained from the multiprofessional programme
D = disadvantages to be encountered in implementing the programme
E = ease of process of implementing the multiprofessional activity

This will help to define whether the programme is worth the effort to implement at a particular time.

Parsell and Bligh (1998) define six principles in planning a multiprofessional programme:

1. Detailed planning and organization involving all stakeholders.
2. Integration of theory with practice and relevance to work.
3. Interactive student-centred learning activities.
4. Teachers as role models for multiprofessional working.
5. Establishment of a comfortable learning climate.
6. Rigorous evaluation for research and further development.

Learners need to be 'ready' to learn together. Horsburgh et al. (2001) sought to identify attitudes of first-year medical, nursing and pharmacy students towards shared learning. The majority of students responded with positive attitudes. The perceived benefits, including the acquisition of teamworking skills, were seen to be beneficial to patient care and likely to enhance professional working relationships. However there was some difference between the groups; nursing and pharmacy students indicated more strongly that an outcome would be more effective teamworking; medical students were the least sure of their professional role and considered that they needed more knowledge and skills.

Evidence from a study of course organizers, students and health professionals (Pirrie et al., 1998) suggests that multidisciplinary education is neither an easy nor a cheap option. It needs to be adequately resourced, the rationale needs to be explicit to teachers and students, and clear and achievable objectives set. This is reinforced by Atkins and Walsh (1997) who demonstrated that collective ownership of the agenda, process and outcomes is an effective catalyst.

Much shared learning is planned on the assumption that collaboration is good, but less attention is paid to identification of the true beneficiaries (Atkins and Walsh, 1997).

How the Needs of Clinical Psychologists May Be Met on a Multiprofessional Basis

As with all professions, there is a need for certain CPD to be undertaken for clinical psychologists as a distinct group. However, there are many situations where it may be constructive and beneficial to pursue multiprofessional learning. Indeed, many clinical psychologists already take these opportunities; in a survey performed in the North West of England, 66 per cent of respondents cited examples of good practice in terms of multiprofessional activity they had taken part in during the previous year (Golding, 2003).

The most effective learning is in practice; solving patient problems and service issues through multiprofessional forums. Clinical seminars and 'action learning sets' are common methods used to achieve this. Shadowing other professions can be valuable for understanding their roles, responsibilities and approaches to patient care. There are also a number of subject areas, besides clinical or service-focused activities, which are ideal for multiprofessional learning. These include: management and leadership; teaching and training; information technology; and research and publication skills.

The practice of CPD is in itself an ideal forum for multiprofessional activity. Use of portfolios and reflective practice are areas that all professions are tackling. Successful mentoring can underpin the lifelong learning process, and cross-professional mentoring relationships are encouraged.

CPD Requirements of Other Healthcare Professions

The advent of compulsory CPD in order to maintain statutory registration has been the turning point in CPD activity for many professions.

Until this time, most professional bodies had merely recommended participation in continuing education as a means of keeping up to date with practice. It is likely that the Council for the Regulation of Health-care Professionals, which is going to oversee the practices of each regulatory body, will eventually stipulate the CPD system to be used by all professions. This is likely to standardize requirements, so it will be interesting to see which, if any, of the current professional formats it follows. Further information on professional requirements can be found on the relevant websites.

Doctors

The principle of good medical practice is stated as being to keep knowledge and skills up to date and regularly to take part in 'educational activities which maintain and develop competence and performance'. There is no set target and no format for keeping records, although most post-graduate colleges require their members to perform a certain amount of continuing education per year and provide recording formats for this purpose.

NHS appraisal for doctors will incorporate a review of documentation, including learning events and a personal development plan, but other doctors rather than a professional body will undertake this review. The GMC website gives thorough guidance on what constitutes CPD, and sets out aspects of knowledge, skills, attitudes and behaviours that should be addressed through CPD.

Dentists

Legislation in November 2001 made CPD compulsory for dentists. They are required to complete 250 hours of CPD (www.gdc-uk.org) every five years, of which at least 75 hours should be 'verifiable CPD' that meets specific educational criteria and for which participation can be proved by certification. Each dentist must submit an annual statement of hours, and there is random sampling of complete records.

Forms for keeping records are available but not compulsory. The recording sheet is very simple, just recording educational events. It is thought that the recording alone will allow for reflection, and that it is professional judgement which ensures the learning is relevant (Wang, 2002).

Nurses

Since April 2001, the United Kingdom Central Council (UKCC) has audited how registered nurses, midwives and health visitors are meeting the post-registration education and practice (PREP) standard. This means they must have undertaken a minimum of 35 hours' learning activity during the three-year period leading up to renewal of registration. Learning activity needs to be recorded in a personal professional profile and must include an explanation of how it developed practice. Each month up to 10 per cent of individuals are selected for audit and asked to submit CPD summary forms, showing how their learning has helped to improve care for patients and clients. Plenty of guidance is provided.

Pharmacists

Pharmacists have been provided with forms to record their CPD, in both paper and the Royal Pharmaceutical Society's preferred electronic format. Considerable information is provided on how to undertake and record CPD, demonstrating why the learning was needed, how they went about it, and what the outcome was for their practice (in the format of reflection, planning, action, and evaluation). No targets have been set at the time of writing, prior to formal legislation, but pharmacists are currently advised to complete one CPD form per month. Submission of records every 3–5 years will be a component of revalidation. Currently, pharmacy is the only profession where feedback is provided to individuals on their CPD submissions.

Allied Health Professionals and Healthcare Scientists

As discussed in earlier chapters, applied psychologists including clinical psychologists are due to be registered with the Health Professions Council (HPC) in 2005. They will join 12 other professions regulated by the HPC (arts therapists, biomedical scientists, chiropodists and podiatrists, clinical scientists, dieticians, occupational therapists, orthoptists, prosthetists and orthotists, paramedics, physiotherapists, radiographers, and speech and language therapists). Members of other professions, and support workers, may register with the HPC in the future.

The HPC has decided that CPD will be linked to registration, but has yet to set out details. It is planned to launch the system in 2006. It will be linked to national standards and avoid monitoring compliance based simply on number of hours undertaken each year.

The system will take account of the AHP project on demonstrating competence through CPD (see Department of Health website). This project developed a common framework as well as profession-specific models, the approach reflecting the reality of the workplace. However the resulting document is very in-depth and rather cumbersome. The HPC programme will also build on the work of others, for example, the radiography CD-ROM system that is going web-based.

Conclusions

This chapter has reviewed the literature on multidisciplinary learning in CPD within healthcare and discussed some of the pros and cons of multi- vs. uniprofessional approaches. Although there is currently a lack of robust data on the effectiveness of interprofessional education, the most beneficial team learning seems to be in the workplace, based around common service-related needs. What is clear, however, is that development of a clinical team, focused around patient needs, is essential for the provision of high quality care and this is the direction in which the NHS is developing. For the future, *all* NHS professions will need to undertake CPD as part of their professional revalidation. It will be valuable to share learning on aspects of this, such as recording methods and mentoring skills and, where appropriate, to pool learning resources while also ensuring that uniprofessional needs are met separately.

REFERENCES

Association for the Study of Medical Education. (ASME) (2003). Lifelong learning: Building the continuum of professional and interprofessional learning for health and social care. *ASME and CAIPE Joint Conference.*

Atkins, J. M. and Walsh, R. S. (1997). Developing shared learning in multiprofessional healthcare education: For whose benefit? *Nurse Education Today,* 17, 319–24.

Campbell, J. K. and Johnson, C. (1999). Trend spotting: Fashions in medical education. *British Medical Journal,* 318, 1272–5.

Cooper, H., Carlisle, C., Gibbs, T. and Watkins, C. (2001). Developing an evidence base for interdisciplinary learning: A systematic review. *Journal of Advanced Nursing,* 35, 228–37.

Davies, H. T. O. and Nutley S. M. (2000). Developing learning organisations in the new NHS. *British Medical Journal*, 320, 998–1001.

Department of Health (1999). *Continuing Professional Development: Quality in the New NHS.* HSC 1999/154. Department of Health, London.

Department of Health (2001). *Working Together – Learning Together: A Framework for Lifelong Learning for the NHS.* Department of Health, London.

Department of Health (2003). *Developing a Shared Framework for Health Professional Learning Beyond Registration. Briefing.* Department of Health, London.

Finch, J. (2000). Interprofessional education and team working: A view from the education providers. *British Medical Journal*, 321, 1138–40.

Golding, L (2003). The continuing professional development needs of clinical psychologists in the North West of England. *Clinical Psychology*, 26, 23–7.

Harden, R. M. (1998). Effective multiprofessional education: A three-dimensional perspective. *Medical Teacher*, 20, 402–8.

Headrick, L. A., Wilcock, P. M. and Batalden, P. B. (1998). Interprofessional working and continuing medical education. *British Medical Journal*, 316, 771–4.

Horsburgh, M., Lamdin, R, and Williamson, E. (2001). Multiprofessional learning: The attitudes of medical, nursing and pharmacy students to shared learning. *Medical Education*, 35, 876–83.

Kennard, J. (2002). Illuminating the relationship between shared learning and the workplace. *Medical Teacher*, 24, 379–84.

Ker, J., Mole, L, and Bradley, P. (2003). Early introduction to interprofessional learning: A simulated ward environment. *Medical Education*, 37, 248–55.

Parsell, G, and Bligh, J. (1998). Educational principles underpinning successful shared learning. *Medical Teacher*, 20, 522–9.

Pirrie, A., Wilson, V., Harden, R. M. and Elsegood, J. (1998). Promoting cohesive practice in healthcare. *Medical Teacher*, 20, 409–16.

Sharkey, S. B, and Sharples, A. (2003). The impact on work-related stress of mental health teams following team-based learning on clinical risk management. *Journal of Psychiatric and Mental Health Nursing*, 10, 73–81.

Wang, L. N. (2002). Are health professions comparable in requirements for CPD and revalidation? *Pharmaceutical Journal*, 269, 707–8.

Zwarenstein, M., Reeves, S., Barr, H., Hammick, M., Koppel, I. and Atkins, J. (2004). Interprofessional education: Effects on professional practice and healthcare outcomes (Cochrane Review). In: *The Cochrane Library*, Issue 1. Chichester UK: John Wiley and Sons Ltd.

WEBSITES

Centre for Advancement of Interprofessional Education: http://www.caipe.org.uk

Department of Health: http://www.dh.gov.uk

General Medical Council: http://www.gmc-uk.org

General Dental Council: http://www.gdc-uk.org

Health Professions Council: http://www.hpc-uk.org
New Generation Project: http://www.mhbs.soton.ac.uk/newgeneration/newngp/
   about.htm
Nursing and Midwifery Council: http://www.nmc-uk.org
Royal Pharmaceutical Society: http://www.rpsgb.org.uk

Chapter 11

The NHS Knowledge and Skills Framework

Richard Toogood

Background

The Department of Health published the NHS Knowledge and Skills Framework (NHS KSF) and the associated developmental review process in October 2004 (DoH, 2004). This forms part of the Agenda for Change (AfC) initiative on pay and conditions (DoH, 2003). In response to this, the British Psychological Society (BPS) set up a working group to enable it to advise their members and the wider psychology workforce within the NHS of the implications and processes involved in implementing KSF. The joint Amicus/Family of Psychology (representing the BPS's Divisions of Clinical, Counselling, Health and Occupational Psychology (DCP, DCoP, DHP and DOP)) working group produced guidance to the membership in June 2005 based on several months' intensive work on the KSF. There is now a comprehensive guidance document available for NHS psychologists, which needs to be read in conjunction with the October 2004 Department of Health KSF document as well as the BPS's CPD guidance (BPS, 2004) and CPD guidance issued by the Society's divisions such as the DCP (2001).

Chapter Plan

This chapter describes the KSF and its position within the overall AfC process. It explains the structure of the KSF, including the core dimensions and the profession-specific dimensions. It goes on to describe how post outlines will be produced and how these will be directly linked to progression through the pay scale and the developmental review process. The chapter then discusses the proposed post outlines for the Family of Psychology and ends with reflections on the likely implications of the KSF and AfC for individual applied psychologists, their employers, professional bodies and unions. Throughout, the chapter links the KSF process to the wider NHS CPD context and makes explicit where these are interwoven. This chapter's description of the KSF and its implementation are taken from the DoH (October 2004) KSF publication referred to above.

What is the NHS KSF?

The NHS KSF is a single framework on which to base the process of review and development for all staff who come under the Agenda for Change National Agreement. It is one of the three underpinning strands within the AfC Agreement. The first strand, job evaluation and assimilation to the new pay spines, should be completed by December 2005. The second strand is harmonization of terms and conditions for all staff, including annual leave, maternity leave and other HR benefits, and, finally, the third strand is the development and implementation of the KSF with its associated developmental review process. Post outlines for all NHS staff should be in place by the end of 2005/early 2006.

The KSF supports active learning and development to advance individuals and teams. It is designed to support the development of individuals in the posts in which they are employed. For the first time in the NHS's history, the KSF provides a workforce-wide 'toolkit', which will be used in the developmental review process, including the provision of CPD. As it is a workforce-wide application, it is specifically designed to promote equality and diversity for all staff and is structured to be of use to all professions within the national AfC agreement, including applied psychologists. The KSF is based on a partnership approach between post holders, their managers and union representatives, and, as with the other elements of AfC, the Trusts have clear targets for its implementation throughout their workforce.

The Structure of the NHS KSF

The KSF is a broad generic framework that describes the application of knowledge and skills to any particular post in the NHS. It is made up to 30 dimensions. These capture those broad functions within the NHS that are deemed necessary to provide good quality services to the population. There are six core dimensions that are applicable to every single job within the NHS. These are:

1. Communication.
2. Personal and people development.
3. Health, safety and security.
4. Service improvement.
5. Quality.
6. Equality and diversity.

These are described as *core* dimensions as they underpin and reinforce any specific functions that need to be performed. These are the foundation of all roles within the NHS and are as applicable to large volume ancillary workers as they are to highly specialist and highly qualified clinical delivery staff.

In addition to the six core dimensions, there are 24 other dimensions that apply to some, but not all, jobs throughout the NHS. The specific dimensions are grouped into four themes, which are:

1. Health and well-being (HWB 1–10): There are 10 dimensions within this theme, for example, promoting health and well-being or providing interventions and treatments.
2. Estates and facilities (EF 1–3): There are 3 dimensions within this theme, for example, dealing with supplies systems and logistics, vehicles and equipment, etc.
3. Information and knowledge (IK 1–3): There are 3 dimensions within this theme which deal with information capture, processing and systems management.
4. General dimensions (G 1–8): There are 8 dimensions grouped together and include areas such as people management and development and innovation.

There is no hierarchy in respect of the above themes or dimensions, with no one dimension better than another. All are essential to provide good quality services within the NHS. Each of the dimensions has 4 levels ranging from level 1, as the minimum level expected of all workers, to level 4 where workers employ expert knowledge and skills or deal with more complex areas. For example, within the communication dimension, at level 1 post holders would be expected to 'communicate with a limited range of people on day-to-day matters', whereas at level 4 post holders would be expected to 'develop and maintain communication with people on complex matters, issues and ideas and/or in complex situations'. An overview of the NHS KSF core dimensions and level descriptors is presented in Table 11.1.

Table 11.1 An overview of the NHS Knowledge and Skills Framework: The core dimensions

Core dimensions	Level descriptors			
	1	2	3	4
1 Communication	Communicate with a limited range of people on day-to-day matters	Communicate with a range of people on a range of matters	Develop and maintain communication with people about difficult matters and/or in difficult situations	Develop and maintain communication with people on complex matters, issues and ideas and/or in complex situations
2 Personal and people development	Contribute to own personal development	Develop own skills and knowledge and provide information to others to help their development	Develop oneself and contribute to the development of others	Develop oneself and others in areas of practice
3 Health, safety and security	Assist in maintaining own and	Monitor and maintain health, safety and	Promote, monitor and maintain best practice in	Maintain and develop an environment

Continued

Table 11.1 *Continued*

	others' health, safety and security	security of self and others	health, safety and security	and culture that improves health, safety and security
4 Service improvement	Make changes in own practice and offer suggestions for improving services	Contribute to the improvement of services	Appraise, interpret and apply suggestions, recommendations and directives to improve services	Work in partnership with others to develop, take forward and evaluate direction, policies and strategies
5 Quality	Maintain the quality of own work	Maintain quality in own work and encourage others to do so	Contribute to improving quality	Develop a culture that improves quality
6 Equality and diversity	Act in ways that support equality and value diversity	Support equality and value diversity	Promote equality and value diversity	Develop a culture that promotes equality and values diversity

Every NHS post, and therefore every post holder, will be required to aspire to level 1 on each of the 6 core dimensions with many professionally qualified staff achieving levels 2 and 3 and expert/consultant clinicians achieving level 4. In some respects the 4 point scale does limit professions such as psychologists with newly qualified staff, because of their knowledge and skills, often achieving level 3 and above on these core dimensions. The same limiting factor applies to the specific dimensions for applied psychologists.

Developing Post Outlines

Every post within the NHS will have a KSF post outline. Outlines are intended to reflect the requirements (in terms of the knowledge and skills) of the post and are seen as reinforcing both the job description and person specification. Every outline must include an appropriate level from each of the 6 core dimensions. In addition, post outlines will have an unlimited number of specific dimensions which are meant to reflect critical aspects of the post. The national guidance advises that it is unusual to need more than 7 specific dimensions for a particular post, giving no more than 13 dimensions in total. Each dimension must be described in terms of levels and, more specifically, indicators which describe which knowledge and skills need to be applied at that level. Table 11.2 describes the indicators for the core dimension 1 (communication) level 3 – 'develop and maintain communication with people about difficult matters or in difficult situations'.

For the individual to meet a defined level they will have to show that they can apply knowledge and skills to meet all of the indicators in that level. Alongside each of the indicators are some examples of application which show how the KSF may be applied in different posts (see Table 11.2). However, these are very useful in enabling both managers and post holders to judge whether that particular level is appropriate and whether the indicators are being met.

The KSF and the Family of Psychology

The joint Amicus/Family of Psychology working party met from October 2004 to June 2005. Its role was to recommend levels for each of the grades of psychologists (excluding trainees up to now) for

Table 11.2 Indicators and examples of application for level 3 of the core communication dimension

Core 1/level 3
Develop and maintain communication with people about difficult matters and/or in difficult situations

Indicators	Examples of application
a) identifies the range of people likely to be involved in the communication, any potential communication differences and relevant contextual factors	The people with whom the individual is communicating might be: – users of the services (such as patients and clients) – carers
b) communicates with people in a form and manner that: – is consistent with their level of understanding, culture, background and preferred ways of communicating – is appropriate to the purpose of the communication and the context in which it is taking place – encourages the effective participation of all involved	– groups (including families) – colleagues and co-workers – managers – workers from other agencies – visitors Communication differences might be in relation to: – contexts and cultures of the different parties – degree of confusion or clarity
c) recognizes and reflects on barriers to effective communication and modifies communication in response	– first/preferred language – levels of familiarity with the subject of the communication/ context in which the communication is taking place
d) provides feedback to other workers on their communication at appropriate times	– level of knowledge and skills – sense of reality
e) keeps accurate and complete records of activities and communications consistent with legislation, policies and procedures	Communication might take a number of forms including: – oral communication – signing
f) communicates in a manner that is consistent with relevant legislation, policies and procedures	– written communication – electronic communication (e.g., email, databases) Purpose of communication might include: – asserting a particular position or view – breaking bad news – encouraging and supporting people

Continued

Table 11.2 *Continued*

- explaining issues in formal situations (such as courts)
- explaining outcomes of activities/interventions
- exploring difficult issues
- facilitating meetings
- helping people make difficult decisions
- making scripted presentations
- presenting and discussing ideas
- providing technical advice to non-technical specialists
- representing views
- seeking consent
- sharing decision making with others including users of services
- sharing information
- supporting people in difficult circumstances

Barriers to communication
- environmental
- personal
- social

Modifies communication through, for example:
- deciding what information/ advice to give/not give as the communication proceeds
- modifying the content and structure of communication
- modifying the environment
- modifying the methods of communicating
- using another language
- using different communication aids

Legislation, policies and procedures may be international, national or local and my relate to:
- confidentiality
- data protection (including the specific provisions relating to access to health records)
- disability
- diversity

each of the 6 core dimensions. In addition, the working party agreed which specific dimensions were applicable for psychology professions within the NHS and then followed the same process with the specific dimensions. The specific dimensions recommended are:

- HWB1 Promotion of health/well-being
- HWB2 Assessment and care planning
- HWB3 Protection of health/well-being
- HWB6 Assessment and treatment planning
- HWB7 Interventions and treatments

The working party judged the specific dimensions to have sufficient content for some or most psychologists' jobs. Dependent upon the core qualification, knowledge and skills and the specific specialty, at least one, and often two or three, of the above dimensions within the health and well-being theme were considered to be applicable. Applied psychology is a broad church and the task of the working party was to be inclusive rather than limit the range and application which the dimensions would represent. For example, a Health Psychologist would have HWB1 as a key area whereas a Clinical Psychologist would be more involved with HWB6 and HWB7. In addition to the health and well-being dimensions, the following dimensions were considered to be applicable to research, teaching, development and management skills which psychologists have, either as a qualification or would seek to develop throughout their careers:

- IK2 Information collection and analysis
- G1 Learning and development
- G2 Development and innovation
- G4 Financial management
- G5 Service and practice management
- G6 People management

The working party acknowledged that 11 specific dimensions exceed the general expectation for only 7. However, in constructing KSF outlines for each post, the working party considered that clusters of up to 7 specific dimensions could be constructed dependent upon the stage and key targets for individuals as their career progresses. For example, a newly qualified psychologist may be far more involved with the health and well-being dimensions, whereas more senior staff may have key development areas in service and project management.

The Amicus/Family of Psychology Guidance

The guidance that has been produced by the Amicus/Family of Psychology working party (BPS, 2005) comprises of four sections. There is a Table of Family of Psychology KSF dimensions and levels, which recommends dimensions and levels for each pay banding from Assistant band 4 to B/Consultant band 9. There is as yet no KSF level for the Trainee grade as essentially the curriculum in training forms the KSF for this grade of psychologist. However, the working group will consult with the Group of Trainers in Clinical Psychology and hopes to publish this in due course. Second, the working group has constructed overviews of knowledge and skills for each of the Assistant and qualified posts. The overview is referenced by the post title and banding with each of the level descriptors that are applicable to each of the dimensions for that post highlighted. These give the KSF levels expected for that post at the second gateway. This is one of two points (the other being the foundation gateway) which is set at a fixed point towards the top of each pay band and confirms that individuals are applying their knowledge and skills to meet the full demands of their post. In a sense this is a target for post holders to work towards within the developmental review process (see below).

Twelve months after assimilation, the foundation gateway discussion will take place. This is based on a subset of full KSF outline for that post. It checks that individuals can apply the basic knowledge and skills required from the outset in a post coupled with that needed after 12 months of development and support. Like the full KSF outline, subsets should be developed using a partnership approach and should be a fair and consistent way of reviewing everyone who fills that post at that point in time.

Using the KSF in the Developmental Review Process

All staff in the NHS that come under AfC will have annual NHS KSF developmental reviews. Chapter 4 of this book described the developmental review process which has four stages:

1. A review between the post holder and their reviewer, usually their line manager, of the individual's work against the demands of their post.
2. Production of a Personal Development Plan (PDP).

3. Planned learning and development to achieve the learning and development targets.
4. Evaluation some 12 months later with particular emphasis upon outcomes and how the individual has applied the learning.

Clearly for psychologists the review process needs to be undertaken in conjunction with guidance around CPD expectations and requirements and may be informed by the National Occupational Standards for Psychology and BPS Division guidance. Essential messages of partnership, clarity and agreement must be maintained with a developmental review process being live and active and not 'a paper chase'. There is a normal expectation of progression for every individual through the pay band. An essential element of the KSF process is that there should be no surprises. If there are concerns or particular issues regarding an individual's development, work performance or application of their knowledge and skills, these should be addressed by reviewers before gateway reviews. The foundation gateway review takes place after the individual has been in the pay band for a year and during the foundation period all staff who have newly joined the pay band should have at least two discussions with a reviewer. This is to support and develop the individual and help them make a success of their new job. It also confirms that the individual is applying the basic knowledge and skills needed for the post. The second gateway takes place near the top of the pay band and confirms that the individual is applying all knowledge and skills as described within the KSF outline for that post.

While the review has the same components each year, as described in the developmental review process, decisions to pass through gateways are more important and within the National Agreement are linked to pay progression. NHS Trusts and individuals should assume progress through pay gateways but reviewers should alert human resource and payroll departments if this is not the case.

For both the foundation and second gateways, managers and individuals need to select an appropriate range and level of dimensions for that particular post. The Amicus/Family of Psychology working party Table of KSF levels is designed to inform this process but should be seen as a generic guideline for each level of post. It is recognized that different applied psychology qualifications could mean different clusters and levels of knowledge and skills and that applying these within different specialties could mean a more selective choice of dimensions and levels or a choice of specific dimensions and levels that are outside those that are recommended. This cluster of specific dimensions plus the 6 core dimensions will form the key foundations for the developmental review process. They do not limit that developmental review process but their use is mandatory under the National Agreement. Therefore, having chosen dimensions and levels for a particular post managers and staff should consult the detailed dimension descriptors complete with indicators and examples of application that are contained within the Family of Psychology guidance. These are based upon and abstracted from the full Department of Health KSF Handbook and further guidance can be obtained from there and the Society/Division's CPD literature.

Recording the KSF Developmental Review Process

At the back of the DoH KSF manual (DoH, 2004), there are a number of examples and forms. Form 1 is used within the Family of Psychology guidance and is mandatory. This records the 6 core and specific relevant dimensions and specifies areas for development and evidence of achievement. Form 2, which is optional incorporates the relevant dimensions into a personal development plan where development needs/interests and actions are recorded with support needs and planned completion dates. This second form is very much in consort with current BPS and Divisional CPD formats, which will probably have to be amended for use within the NHS to accommodate the structure of the Knowledge and Skills Framework.

Implementing the NHS KSF

Like other aspects of AfC the KSF will present individuals, organizations and professional bodies/trade unions with many challenges. For individuals, particularly those just embarking upon or not used to a developmental review/CPD process, a new nomenclature and language will need to be understood and mastered. There are significant training needs irrespective of profession but as the KSF is both logical and systematic the concepts once grasped can be generalized and developed across professions and grades of staff.

For NHS organizations there is a significant amount of work to be undertaken. This includes, reviewing HR policies, particularly appraisal systems which will need to focus more on competencies than a time-served based approach. Some NHS organizations will be well developed in this area, while others have yet to leave the starting blocks.

Full implementation of the KSF is a requirement for the National Agreement and must be achieved. This will require organizations to further review job descriptions and person specifications and how jobs are portrayed. NHS job vacancies must now include a full KSF post outline for the second gateway so that individuals applying for jobs not only see the requirements of the job from the job description, the requirements of the person from the person specification but also anticipated developmental range and levels of the job for which they will be applying. Developing staff within the review process will again be a significant challenge in terms of both protected time and resources available. The BPS's CPD guidelines (BPS, 2004) portray a wide and varied content to CPD activity and thinking must extend beyond courses and conferences. While the KSF does not determine pay scales at both foundation and second gateways, there could be pay progression consequences for individuals who do not meet their expected development and KSF profiles. This will require further discussions both locally and nationally.

For professional bodies and trade unions, providing membership support will be crucial. The joint Amicus/Family of Psychology Working Group has provided guidelines for the development of KSF profiles for psychologists and these need to be used flexibly and in partnership with staff members. Inevitably there will be some variation but at least within departments the same KSF outlines should apply to the same levels of job as the process needs to be fair and transparent. This will require partnership arrangements within services to facilitate implementation and application of the KSF process.

Implications of KSF on Career Paths

It is difficult at this time to do anything more but speculate on where the KSF will lead or enable psychologists to attain. Applied psychologists within the NHS have relied on time served as a crude indicator of professional competence, e.g., at least 6 years qualified to achieve B/Consultant status. In the world of KSF this simply will not do. We must get used to posts being validated on the basis of the competencies they require of post holders and for post holders to demonstrate these competencies before they can be seen as progressing in their careers. There is no automatic development from one pay band to the next but the process of regrading posts (rather than an individual) and applying for other posts will continue. It may be that progress between bands will be slower than the profession has hitherto experienced and as a result there may be increased migration between services. In the future B/Consultant status will be KSF competency based with applicants having to demonstrate validation of their competencies in order to enter the B/Consultant bands. The role of National Assessors is unclear, though the profession has recommended to the Department of Health that an external quality check and validation by National Assessors should continue in the interests of patient safety and public confidence. The NHS KSF will form the foundation of future mandatory CPD processes whether organized, developed and run by the Society or by the Health Professions Council (HPC). At the time of writing, the outcome of the consultation on registration of applied psychologists (DoH, 2005) is not complete but, whatever the result, it is clear that as an included profession within the AfC National Agreement, the NHS KSF will provide structure for CPD integral with National Occupational Standards. In this sense complete freedom to specify developmental needs has ceased with individuals, departments and organizations needing to demonstrate the linkages between CPD outcomes and job performance within a much tighter and transparent framework than has hitherto been the case. Future evaluation of the KSF will yield necessary information on whether or not it has been successful in achieving its ends.

REFERENCES

British Psychological Society (2001). *Guidelines for Continuing Professional Development for Clinical Psychologists.* The British Psychological Society, Leicester.

British Psychological Society (2004). *Continuing Professional Development.* The British Psychological Society, Leicester.

British Psychological Society (2005). *Lifelong Learning and the KSF for Applied Psychology.* Amicus/Family of Psychology Working Group. The British Psychological Society, Leicester.

Department of Health (March 2003). *Agenda for Change: Proposed Agreement.* Department of Health, London.

Department of Health (October 2004). *The NHS Knowledge and Skills Framework (NHS KSF) and the Development Review Process (October 2004).* Department of Health, London.

Department of Health (March 2005). *Enhancing Public Protection: Proposals for the Statutory Regulation of Applied Psychologists.* Department of Health, London.

Chapter 12
Conclusions and Future Directions

Laura Golding and Ian Gray

We began this book by highlighting how the process of identifying CPD needs, pursuing CPD activities and evaluating the outcomes of these on clinical practice has changed significantly for clinical psychologists and other healthcare professionals over the past few years. Now, in line with Department of Health policy, and NHS developments, we select CPD activities to meet areas of need identified through a process of systematic appraisal linked to our line management structures. Statutory regulation of applied psychologists will require us to record our CPD activity and reflect on whether, and how, it has met its aims. The changes in the policy context, the impact of imminent statutory regulation possibly through the Health Professions Council (HPC) and the wide reaching implications of Agenda for Change (AfC) and the NHS Knowledge and Skills Framework (NHS KSF), combine, with other developments to make this an exciting time for applied psychologists, and other professional groups, working in healthcare. It is also, inevitably, a time of uncertainty and great change and this brings with it a number of potential challenges. One of the many areas where these changes will impact is on CPD which has been granted much more importance as a result of these recent developments.

The chapters that followed our introduction, explored different aspects of the CPD context and process – to provide readers with an accessible and practical account of CPD developments in response to the changes outlined above. The book has explored the relevant literature, discussed a range of concepts and theories pertinent to CPD and drawn on existing examples of good practice within the NHS. We begin here by briefly summarizing these chapters and the main conclusions of each. This is followed by a synthesis of the main themes of the book, identification of the challenges that lie ahead and our reflections about the future direction for CPD and clinical psychology.

Chapter 2

Chapter 2 began by challenging the assumption that CPD is, *per se*, a 'good thing'. It unpicked some of the central components of CPD and critically evaluated the evidence base taking account of the fundamental need to demonstrate efficacy against the yardstick of improvement in the quality of patient care. The chapter discussed self-appraisal, a central element of CPD, and revealed worrying research evidence that suggests that not only are we not very good at appraising our CPD needs but those professionals most in need of CPD are most likely to be weaker at self-appraisal.

The chapter examined the usefulness of the British Psychological Society's (BPS) decision to make CPD mandatory in the context of evidence of ill-fated mandatory CPD initiatives in other professions and countries. This chapter asks the difficult, but necessary, question of whether our CPD activities are likely to be incorporated into our routine practice and, more importantly, whether they lead to better patient care. The chapter ended with a discussion about the important relationship between CPD, malpractice and protection of the public. Notwithstanding the caveats entered by Green regarding the limited evidence of effectiveness of CPD, he concluded that a commitment to CPD and its contribution to reducing professional isolation is not only likely to offer some reassurance to the public but exposes the practitioner to the influence of colleagues and professional developments in what is a rapidly changing profession.

Chapter 3

This chapter set the policy context for CPD within the NHS. *The New NHS: Modern, Dependable* (DoH, October 1997) set out a ten-year vision for the modernization of the healthcare system. One of its main aims was to focus on quality in the NHS. The modernization of the NHS set the context for government policy on lifelong learning and CPD. This led to the explicit statement that, by April 2000, employers should have had in place training and development plans for the majority of health professionals.

The NHS Plan (DoH, July 2000) articulated the government's strategic direction for the NHS and its subsequent implementation policies and guidance. Chapter 3 discussed specific policies focusing on lifelong learning, CPD and the role of Workforce Development Confederations

(WDC) and Strategic Health Authorities (SHA). It described the impact of the DoH publication, *Working Together, Learning Together: A Framework for Lifelong Learning in the NHS* (DoH, November 2001) in developing the CPD and lifelong learning agenda and the organizational infrastructure. Finally, this chapter brought the policy context right up to date with an examination of current developments and their impact on CPD for the profession. These included consideration of AfC, the development and implementation of the NHS KSF, statutory regulation and the possible future role of the HPC.

Chapter 4

With a practical focus, this chapter introduced a cyclical process of identifying and reflecting on individual CPD needs and linking this to the BPS's requirements and the profession's guidance on the appraisal process. This was further developed in relation to practical workshops carried out in the North West of England where a 'SWOT' analysis was used to facilitate identification of CPD needs in groups of clinical psychologists. Other techniques for identifying CPD needs, such as critical incident analysis, critical reflection and reflective practice, were also introduced.

The problematic area of funding for CPD was discussed including a very practical exploration of meeting CPD needs at low or no cost. It made the important point that CPD does not need to be directly equated with financial allocation of funding and struck a cautionary note about not seeing CPD as only being about attending expensive conferences.

Looking to the future Gundi Kiemle introduced the NHS University, (NHSU 2003), and the government's e-learning strategy and their potential contributions to CPD and lifelong learning. This chapter ended with detailed guidance on the process of organizing a CPD event including examples of pro formas for financial arrangements and evaluating the outcome of such events.

Chapter 5

Chapter 5 examined the relationship between newly qualified clinical psychologists and CPD. Written by two recently qualified clinical psychologists, it drew on both the authors' personal experience and the available literature exploring why the period immediately following qualification is a particularly important phase with regard to CPD needs.

The chapter explored the transition from trainee to qualified status and the extent to which pre-qualification training prepares newly qualified clinical psychologists for their future careers. The authors illustrated this chapter with examples of good practice in CPD for newly qualified clinical psychologists in the UK. The chapter ended with a summary to guide employers and employees and a checklist to aid in the monitoring and development of CPD practices for newly qualified staff.

Chapter 6

Chapter 6 explored the role of CPD mid-career for clinical psychologists. In particular, it reviewed the pertinent issues in relation to CPD and the transition to the position of a B/Consultant Grade Clinical Psychologist. The authors looked at the differences between 'A' grade and B/Consultant roles with reference to AfC. They focused on the particular CPD issues which arise mid-career including, individual versus service needs; the development of managerial versus clinical skills and resource issues. The chapter described in detail, as an example of good practice, the aspiring B grade course run in the North West of England for clinical psychologists working with children and their families.

Chapter 7

Chapter 7 focused on the not inconsiderable implications for psychology service managers of mandatory CPD and also the emergence of a strong CPD agenda in the context of major service and policy changes in the NHS. The authors reviewed some of these policy initiatives with specific discussion of recent developments such as *Organising and Delivering Psychological Therapies* (DoH, 2004) linking them to managerial responsibilities and leadership issues. The impact of change in general and its implications for CPD was discussed with reference to the expansion of the profession and the incorporation of other applied psychologists into services. The chapter included discussion of psychology service managers' CPD needs as managers.

The authors went on to consider the role and implications of the many NICE guidelines and the role managers need to play in the

Department of Health's work on equality and diversity within the NHS. The importance placed on greater user participation in service design and delivery was discussed with a concluding section providing a summary action plan which is daunting to say the least. Support and development opportunities for psychology service managers are of paramount importance.

Chapter 8

This chapter by Milne, James and Sheikh presented a research framework of how CPD might be evaluated with specific reference to supervision, a key component of CPD and lifelong learning. They began by addressing systematically five key questions.

The first question, 'What is the right thing to do?' was addressed by describing and analysing a supervision cycle developed from the teaching cycle (Goldstein, 1993). The evidence underpinning the efficacy of this cycle was reviewed. This was followed by the question, 'Has the right thing been done?' which described a methodology for evaluating training and supervision, 'PETS' (Process Evaluation of Training and Supervision, Milne and James, 2002).

The third question, 'Has it been done right?' addressed the key issue of evaluating supervision or CPD to determine whether it is delivered in a competent manner. The authors described a scale which they are developing to evaluate and guide competent practice in supervision.

The fourth question, 'Did it result in the right outcomes?' was discussed in relation to Kirkpatrick's (1967) taxonomy addressing four levels of outcome. This taxonomy was applied to supervision with a review of relevant research findings demonstrating its usefulness.

The final question, 'Was the CPD context right?' looked at the role played by organizational climate, people and other factors in fostering the right environment for delivery of effective CPD. This section concluded with a discussion and review of approaches to managing the CPD environment.

Chapter 9

This chapter addressed the role of the BPS and its subsystems in developing and implementing the CPD agenda. It started by outlining the role of the Society regarding CPD and set this in the context of government policies with specific reference to the HPC. This was followed by a section on the move to mandatory CPD and an outline of the responsibilities of members of the society especially those who hold practising certificates. The role and responsibilities of the Society Standing Committee for CPD was then described.

The Society's policy statement on mandatory CPD was developed with a more detailed review of the implementation process, for example the use of online logging of CPD activity and the evidence framework for developing a CPD log. The contribution of the Division of Clinical Psychology through its CPD sub-committee and guidelines was explained with examples of key areas of professional competence to be addressed by CPD and an outline of a four-step CPD learning model.

Chapter 10

Chapter 10 placed the rest of this book in the all-important multiprofessional context. As with most other professional groups, it is easy for clinical psychologists, and other applied psychologists, to take a somewhat parochial view of their CPD needs and ways of meeting them. This chapter described and explored the multiprofessional context to CPD and thereby placed the rest of the book in a wider context. Here, Claire Grout explored the nature of multiprofessional learning, the pros and cons of this and the available evidence base. She described how learning together supports improved patient care within the NHS and enhances the working lives of healthcare professionals. This was followed by a discussion of the effectiveness of multiprofessional CPD which included an overview of the evidence, demonstrating in which situations the outcomes are likely to be most positive.

Towards the end of this chapter, Claire Grout discussed the inevitable tensions in uniprofessional and multiprofessional CPD and identified why this may happen and how potential difficulties can be addressed. The last section of the chapter placed the CPD requirements of clinical psychologists in context by comparing them with the requirements of other key professional groups within the NHS.

Chapter 11

This chapter described the NHS Knowledge and Skills Framework (KSF) and its position within the overall AfC process. It explained the structure of the KSF, including the core dimensions and the profession specific dimensions, described post outlines and how these will be directly linked to progression through the pay scale and the developmental review process. Throughout, the chapter linked the KSF process to the wider NHS CPD context and made explicit where these are interwoven. This chapter brought the book right up to date, at the time of writing, ending with a development within the NHS that is playing a crucial role in terms of CPD and developing the workforce.

Key Themes and Final Reflections

Every chapter of this book has explored, in some detail, an important aspect of CPD for clinical psychologists and other applied psychologists working in healthcare. Many of the issues discussed are not unique to clinical psychologists and the need to consider our CPD requirements within the broader multiprofessional context has been highlighted. Throughout the book several themes have recurred.

The Likely Impact of Statutory Regulation and the Mandatory CPD Requirements

At the time of writing, with the Society's rejection of the current proposals for statutory regulation by the Health Professions Council (HPC), there is uncertainty regarding the timing and process for statutory regulation. The HPC completed its consultation on CPD at the end of 2004. It plans to analyse and report on the findings of the consultation and will then publish its final proposals on CPD and seek parliamentary approval for the process. At the time of writing, the HPC's proposals for its registrants' mandatory CPD differ from those of the BPS and currently lack sufficient detail on how they might map on to the Society's CPD procedures. Once the HPC's CPD process has been given approval, and should statutory regulation of applied psychologists within the HPC take place, all applied psychologists will have to adhere to the HPC's CPD process in order to register and remain registered for the duration of their careers. This would bring into question the status of the BPS's CPD process for its applied members. At the time of writing, these issues relating to CPD have yet to be clarified and resolved. Interesting and challenging times lie ahead.

There is some doubt whether statutory regulation of applied psychologists, through the HPC, will occur. Were statutory regulation to occur, for the first time this would link the ability of applied psychologists to work with the general public to proof of ongoing competence. It would place a new and immediate emphasis on CPD for the profession and highlight a range of issues. These include questions such as how will CPD activity be funded, how will it be recorded and how will we demonstrate whether CPD activity has had an impact on our competence?

CPD and 'Returners' to the Profession

An issue related to statutory regulation, which will gain increasing importance over the next few years, is the CPD implications for clinical psychologists returning to clinical practice after a break (e.g., due to extended maternity leave, long-term sick leave, a purely academic career, a career break etc.). Unlike some of the larger healthcare professions, the issue of 'returners' to our profession has never been adequately addressed. Yet, as we expand as a profession, and as other potential non-clinical roles develop, this will become a greater issue. Likewise, a related need arises when clinical psychologists are required to change clinical specialty by their employer – a rare but not unknown scenario. What mechanisms exist to ensure that 'returners' to the profession are competent? How would they, or their employers, know if they were competent to practise autonomously? What role will CPD have in this? To date, this has not been a significant issue for us due to the small size of the profession and the flexibility of the NHS to accommodate part-time workers, but what will the future hold?

A Need for Management and Leadership Training

Recent developments within the NHS, the organization of psychology services into larger departments and the expansion of the profession has meant that managers are facing new challenges. At the time of writing, much time and energy is being spent on the NHS's 'New Ways of Working' initiative (see www.modern.nhs.uk). Applied psychologists are doing their part to meet this challenge through collaboration between the New Ways of Working team and the BPS. A probable future development will be a new Associate Psychologists career grade. These developments will lead to newly configured services and new ways of service delivery all of which have an impact on the organization, delivery and management of psychology services within the NHS. This in turn will add to the demand for leadership and management training to enable managers to meet these challenges effectively and creatively. Coupled with the modernization of the NHS and the emphasis within the NHS on leadership development, a recurring theme in this book has been the need for clinical psychologists at different stages of their careers to access leadership and management training. This is a key area of need and development for the future. We have highlighted existing examples of good practice and provided addresses and website links to relevant training courses. Many leadership and management courses exist within the NHS. The range of courses available is bewildering. More needs to be done to ascertain the leadership and management skills needs of applied psychologists within the NHS so that we can be guided towards existing courses that will meet these needs and be involved in the development of new courses where unmet ends exist.

The CPD Bridge between Pre- and Post-qualification Learning

The QAA's emphasis on NHS university training programmes producing staff who are not only fit for award but fit for purpose and fit for practice (The Quality Assurance Agency for Higher Education, 2003), highlights the close relationship between pre- and post-qualification training. We began this book by considering what a difference a day makes when moving from being unqualified to qualified. It is increasingly recognized that preparation for CPD needs to begin pre-qualification and that lifelong learning starts as soon as clinical training ends. This theme has been highlighted through this book.

The Importance of Multiprofessional Learning

The case has been made for clinical psychologists to engage in multiprofessional CPD activities. Many of us do this routinely, but the direction of travel within the NHS is such that there is a need for this to continue while also preserving some CPD activities that are uniprofessional. The arguments for and against this have been made. A key document that makes the case for shared learning in mental health, with an underpinning shared values base, is the *Ten Essential Shared Capabilities for the Mental Health Workforce* (DoH, August 2004). This important document includes as one of the ten essential capabilities 'Personal Development and Learning'. This capability is described as including 'keeping up to date with changes in practice and participating in lifelong learning, personal; and professional development for one's self and colleagues through supervision, appraisal and reflective practice' (DoH, August 2004). This highlights the importance not only of lifelong learning in delivering high quality mental health services, but also the importance of a shared values base and learning opportunities.

CPD and NHS Modernization

The substantial amount of change that has occurred in the NHS over the past six or seven years has been a constant theme. While generally being viewed as beneficial, these changes have led to major changes in the organization and delivery of services across the NHS. This in turn has led to many changes in the roles of clinical and other applied psychologists in healthcare which, in turn, raises CPD needs. The proposed reforms to the Mental Heath Act, the increased emphasis on meaningful service user involvement, NSF's, NICE guidelines, Agenda for Change, the NHS KSF and many other changes, past, present and future, all raise new CPD needs.

Keeping Up to Date

The CPD agenda is very firmly established for clinical and applied psychologists as well as the wider NHS workforce. This book has explored the many different facets of CPD for applied psychologists and other healthcare professionals. While writing it, we have been struck by the speed with which the wider CPD and professional context keeps changing. The information contained within this book is correct and up to date at the time of writing. For readers to gain maximum benefit, however, we strongly recommend that you ensure that you remain completely up to date by regularly checking some of the websites cited in this book. In particular, we encourage readers to track the developments with the move to statutory regulation for applied psychologists, and the development of the NHS KSF, via the HPC, Department of Health and BPS websites. Readers can also ensure that they are up to date with mandatory CPD requirements and record-keeping processes by regularly visiting the HPC and BPS websites. Readers can track wider NHS developments, relevant to CPD, via the Department of Health's website. Keeping abreast of such developments does of course count towards your own CPD activity!

Conclusion

This book provides a framework for greater understanding of the CPD agenda. It also provides the basis for action planning by individual clinicians and service managers to develop effective CPD systems. Such systems go some way to ensuring that we maintain and improve our professional competence and are, therefore, safe to practice. Our service users deserve nothing less. What a difference CPD should make!

REFERENCES

Department of Health (October 1997). *The New NHS: Modern, Dependable*. HSC 1998/167. Department of Health, London.

Department of Health. (July 2000). *The NHS Plan: A Plan for Investment; A Plan for Reform*. Department of Health, London.

Department of Health (November 2001). *Working Together, Learning Together: A Framework for Lifelong Learning in the NHS*. Department of Health, London.

Department of Health (July 2004). *Organising and Delivering Psychological Therapies*. Department of Health, London.

Department of Health (August 2004). *The Ten Essential Shared Capabilities: A Framework for the Whole of the Mental Health Workforce*. Department of Health, London.

Goldstein, I. L. (1993). *Training in Organisations*. Pacific Grove: Brooks/Cole.

Kirkpatrick, D. L. (1967). Evaluation of training. In R. L. Craig and L. R. Bettel (eds.), *Training and Development Handbook*, New York: McGraw-Hill.

Milne, D. L. and James, I. (2002). The observed impact of training on competence in clinical supervision. *British Journal of Clinical Psychology*, 41, 55–72.

NHSU (2003). *Towards delivery: Draft Strategic Plan* 2003–2008. NHS, London.

The Quality Assurance Agency for Higher Education (2003). *Handbook for Major Review of Healthcare Programmes*. QAA.

Index